Facing the Glass Booth

Facing the Glass Booth

The Jerusalem Trial of Adolf Eichmann

Haim Gouri

Translated by Michael Swirsky
With a Foreword by Alan Mintz

Wayne State University Press
Detroit

Published by Wayne State University Press,
Detroit, Michigan 48201.
Manufactured in the United States of America.
08 07 06 5 4 3 2

Library of Congress Cataloging-in-Publication Data

Gouri, Haim, 1923–
[Mul ta ha-zekhukhit. English]
Facing the glass booth : the Jerusalem trial of Adolf Eichmann / Haim Gouri ; translated by Michael Swirsky ; with a foreword by Alan Mintz.
p. cm.
Includes bibliographical references and index.
ISBN 0-8143-3087-8 (pbk. : alk. paper)
1. Eichmann, Adolf, 1906–1962—Trials, litigation, etc. 2. War crime trials—Jerusalem. I. Title.
KMK44.E33G68 2004
345.5694'420238—dc22 2004006483

This work was first published in Hebrew as *Mul ta hazekhukhit* by Hakibbutz Hame'uhad, Tel Aviv, 1962. A revised edition was published by Hakibbutz Hame'uhad, Tel Aviv, 2001.

∞ The paper used in this publication meets the minimum requirements of the American National Standard for Information Sciences—Permanence of Paper for Printed Library Materials, ANSI Z39.48-1984.

Published with the assistance of the Lucius N. Littauer Foundation and the Memorial Foundation for Jewish Culture

Contents

Foreword

It is difficult to exaggerate the importance of the trial of Adolf Eichmann, the SS Obersturmbannfuhrer (Lt. Colonel) who headed the RSHA Section IV B4, the Race and Resettlement Office of the Nazi government, which administered the extermination of European Jewry. Historians of modern culture have yet to unravel the tangled skein of factors that helped move the Holocaust from being a topic barely spoken of in public discourse to one of the dominant subjects of our time. Yet in any reckoning the Eichmann Trial is likely to be considered a pivotal event, especially in the United States and Israel, the two countries with the largest concentration of Jews and Holocaust survivors. Fifteen years after the end of World War II and long after the recollection of the war crimes tribunals had faded, the Eichmann Trial pried open world memory. During the intervening time, Europe had thrown itself into the enterprise of reconstruction, Israel had fought a war of independence, absorbed waves of immigrants, and built a state, and America enjoyed the prosperity brought by victory while American Jews moved vigorously into the mainstream of American life as bars to their full participation in it were lifted. The trial returned the world's attention to the unfinished business of the war. Reported around the world and displayed on American TV sets on special nightly broadcasts—in an era before satellite transmission, the footage was rushed daily from Jerusalem, where the trial was held, to Tel Aviv whence it was flown to New York—the trial marked one of the first great turning points in the march of the Holocaust from the margins to the center of public awareness.

The resonance of the Holocaust in Israel had been decisively shaped by the Zionist ideology that brought the Jewish state into existence. Zionism arose in the nineteenth century not only as a political solution to the persecution of European Jewry but also as a far-reaching critique of internal Jewish culture and society.

Zionism was put forward as a movement of body and spirit that would liberate Jews from the debilities of hyperintellectuality and political innocence by returning them to a productive relationship with the land, *their* land, and putting them in charge of their own historical destiny. As part of the rejection of the diaspora, Zionism ridiculed the images of both the assimilated Western Jew and the traditional shtetl Jew. The rejection was also a prediction. Zionist thinkers at the turn of the twentieth century foretold the eventual disappearance of European Jewry. Its destruction would come from either without or within: from seductions of assimilation in the West or from the violent eruptions of anti-Semitism in the East.

When the Nazis seized power in Germany, the Yishuv, the Zionist settlement in Palestine, was already well established and growing daily. During World War II, the Yishuv itself was vulnerable before the onward march of Rommel's Afrika Korps; although the leaders of the Yishuv knew about the mass murder of European Jewry, there was little they could do beyond participating in the Allied war effort. After the Liberation, efforts focused on locating the survivors, smuggling them illegally into Palestine, and rehabilitating the war orphans in educational youth villages. All the while, the energies of the Yishuv were engaged in preparing for the eventual dissolution of the British Mandate and conflict with the Arab countries that resulted in the War of Independence of 1948.

The Holocaust receded into the background in the 1950s as Israeli society mobilized to deal with mass immigration, external threats to its security, and the challenges of building a modern state. A special day of remembrance of the Holocaust was set aside in the spring on the anniversary of the Warsaw Ghetto Uprising, but the observance of the occasion emphasized the scattered instances of heroic resistance rather than taking into account the true breadth of the catastrophe. It was in the spirit of this heroic norm that Israel's prime minister at the time, David Ben-Gurion, ordered the state intelligence service to track Eichmann down in hiding; he was discovered in Argentina, captured, and whisked to Israel to stand trial for crimes against the Jewish people and humanity. By this daring operation, Ben- Gurion sought to demonstrate to the world that it was Israel that was now prepared to act forthrightly on the international stage to pursue and defend the interest of world Jewry. It is one of the great ironies surrounding the Eichmann Trial that what began as an effort to display heroic leadership led to a long-deferred immersion in the tragic past.

The trial was held in the largest public hall in Jerusalem, the nation's capital, and the proceedings were broadcast on national radio and closely covered by the daily press. Poet and journalist Haim Gouri reported the trial for *Lamerhav*, the newspaper of the left-labor Ahdut Ha'avodah Party, and it is his daily dispatches for a full year beginning in April 1961 that make up the present volume. In *Facing the Glass Booth: The Jerusalem Trial of Adolf Eichmann*, Gouri shows us aspects of the trial that cannot be gotten from reading either the court transcript or historical studies of the period. In his vivid and direct reportage we discern the timbre of the witnesses' voices and the nuances of gesture and grimace as they struggle to maintain control of their testimony. In Gouri's writing we experience the courtroom as a charged field in which the impassive man in the glass booth is confronted by his accusers amidst the rational legal exchanges among the prosecutor, defense counsel, and judges. Each witness disturbs this atmosphere in a different way and affects the mood of a highly reactive audience in the gallery. The gruff patter of Gouri's fellow newspapermen as they move back and forth between the courtroom and the press room becomes a kind of Greek chorus that frames the procession of witnesses and documents in evidence. Significant as well are Gouri's own reflections as he moves between the outside world, in which a new state is living its life and celebrating its holidays and the aerial world inside the courtroom, in which inexpressible horrors are explicated daily.

Yet as important as is the light shed by this book on the Eichmann trial itself, more important still is the light reflected back upon the identity of the observer. The significance of Gouri's authorship of these observations lies not only in his gifts as a poet and a journalist but also in his exemplariness in relation to his generation. Born in Tel Aviv in 1923, Gouri was part of the first generation of Jews to grow up within the culture of the new Zionist settlement in the Land of Israel. This was a generation, moreover, whose coming of age coincided with the struggles for the establishment of the state and with the bloody sacrifices made on its behalf. The greatest influence on the formation of Gouri and his contemporaries was the socialist Zionist youth movements with their emphasis on honesty, directness, hard work, this-worldliness, and group solidarity. In the context of the youth movements which were wholly committed to Hebrew as the language of national revival, the principled rejection of Jewish life in the diaspora that had been developed in classical Zionist thought became something more: an antipathy, verging on a loathing, for the image of the enfeebled, passive, God-ridden, Yiddish-speaking Jew of Eastern Europe. These young people had little firsthand knowledge of the world. Although their parents made the move to Palestine, their grandparents remained behind, and what they knew of Jewish life there was drawn from literature and caricature.

The news about the murder of European Jewry came to these young men and women in the midst of their clandestine struggles against the British in anticipation of their departure and the attack by Arab armies. The Jews of Europe were thought to have passively submitted to their fate like "sheep to the slaughter," in the biblical phrase. This perception of impotent victimization stood in the most powerful contrast imaginable to the heroic images of the New Jew in charge of his destiny that had been projected in Zionist thinking. The natural reflex in the face of such horror was shame and avoidance. In the aftermath of the 1948 war, in which thousands lost their lives in active defense of their nation and homeland, and then in the frantic projects of absorption and nation-building in the years following, the encounter with the Holocaust was largely put aside.

It is a stunning experience to see the question of the Holocaust suddenly return to consciousness in the pages of Gouri's dispatches from the Eichmann trial. In his reporting of this protracted spectacle, we sense the progressive dismantling of a comprehensive array of pre-judgments about the way in which European Jewry perished and also, and more importantly, about the way in which they lived before they perished. Much of the information that was presented at the trial had in truth already long been available and published in Israel. Gouri's reports document the electric immediacy of the trial, in which latent information was transformed into public knowledge. This awakening is given further credence by the authority of Gouri's voice. Despite his special gifts and his heightened moral sensitivity, Gouri speaks in these dispatches as a typical Israeli, that is as a representative of the Ashkenazic, native, secular Zionist intellectual and political leadership of the country at the time. Because he is so deeply connected to his audience, he, in a sense, brings them with him as, together, they undergo the ordeal of facing the horror and letting go of old assumptions.

Many assumptions are altered during the course of the trial. Gouri's readers are led to rediscover the rich complexity and variety of Jewish life in the diaspora after having long been indifferent to the subject. In Gouri's descriptions of the testimony offered by the witnesses at the trial, one can trace a marked shift in attitudes toward Holocaust survivors in Israeli society. Survivors had generally been perceived as shirkers tainted by moral suspicion. The trial, moreover, afforded Israeli Holocaust survivors their first opportunity to relate their experiences to the nation as a whole. The encounter with the reality rather than the perception, the pathos and painful eloquence of their accounts, and the new role of being bearers of valuable testimony were all factors that contributed to a decisive change in the status of survivors in Israel.

Perhaps the greatest change concerns the perception of passivity. At the outset of the trial Gouri shares the reaction of many of his generation in Israel: a sense of "shame at belonging to a vanquished people who had not lifted up a finger." Listening early on to the testimony of Moritz Fleischmann, a former leader of Viennese Jewry, Gouri does not conceal from his readers his visceral response to the description of a series of demeaning humiliations Fleischmann and others were subjected to. "I did not want to listen to or see this short broken man who went on and on about his suffering, his ills, the insults and the jeers. I wanted to get out and go to the stadium to watch the army parade and see ranks of strong men," Gouri admits. "But Fleischmann held me with unexpected power, forcing me to listen till he had finished." Gouri does not flee. He stays and listens and learns as each survivor and historian explores a new strand in the knot of "choiceless choices" faced by the victims. By the end of the trial, Gouri's awareness has been enlarged.

> We were ashamed of martyrdom as of some obvious blemish of the body; we made much of the heroism believing that it gave us the right to hold our heads high. I have not reached a point where I make no distinction between those who died passively and those who rose up against their murderers or tried to do so. . . . But we who were outside that circle of death have forgiveness to ask of the numberless dead whom we have judged in our hearts without asking ourselves what right we have.

What is impressive about Gouri's position is its authenticity. He does not vitiate who he is and the truth of his experience as a soldier in Israel's struggle for independence. Yet the experience of the trial and the complex knowledge it has conferred on him have neutralized the judgment directed against fellow Jews caught within a "circle of death" whose full horror can never be known.

Since the Eichmann trial, Israeli society has been reopening the unfinished business of the Holocaust in many different ways and on many different levels. Gouri's encounter with the survivors, which had actually begun long before the trial when he was dispatched to Europe in 1947 to aid the victims of the war, did not end with the trial. In 1965 he published his stunning novella *The Chocolate Deal*, which traces the lives of two survivors who meet unexpectedly in a European city (*The Chocolate Deal*, translated by Seymour Simkes with an introduction by Geoffrey Hartman, is also published by Wayne State University Press). In the 1970s and 1980s Gouri wrote and produced *The Eighty-First Blow*, *The Last Sea*, and *Flames in the Ashes*, a trilogy of films on the Holocaust, the "illegal" immigration of Jewish refugees to British Mandatory Palestine, and the Jewish resistance to the Nazis. Yet it is only in the reflexive light cast by his daily reporting of the Eichmann trial that we glimpse how the connection was made between this extraordinary citizen- poet and one of the most terrible events of our times.

ALAN MINTZ

Translator's Note

The present English edition of this book was prepared in close consultation with the author. Any errors, however, are entirely my responsibility.

As the author indicates in his original afterword, the date following each chapter of this book indicates when that chapter originally appeared as an article in the daily newspaper *Lamerhav* and not necessarily when the events described occurred. Usually these events happened on the previous day.

I have not translated or italicized a number of official German terms—such as Sonderkommando, Einsatzgruppen, and so forth—that are widely used in English-language literature on the Holocaust and, thus, I assume, are well known. I have italicized but not untranslated such generic terms such as *referent* and *musselmann*.

I have generally rendered the German letters ä, ö, and ü as "ae," "oe," and "ue," respectively.

In transliterating Hebrew names and terms, I have used an apostrophe for the letter *ayin*, "tz" for *tzadi*, "h" for *het*, and "kh" for *khaf* and omitted final *he*. Occasional exceptions were made in cases where the individuals' preferred Latin spelling of their names was known to be otherwise—for example, "Chaim" rather than "Hayim" Weizmann. For persons who were/are known by their Hebrew first names, I have not rendered these names into English equivalents (e.g., Ya'akov for Jacob or Moshe for Moses).

I have based the spellings and transliterations of proper names on a variety of authoritative encyclopedias and historical works, but my main source was the official, published English transcript of the Eichmann Trial, found at the Yad Vashem library in Jerusalem.

The author and other Hebrew speakers quoted in the book always refer to the Jewish homeland by the traditional Hebrew term *Eretz Yisrael* (the Land of Israel) or simply *ha-aretz* (the Land).

This usage has been retained in the translation of their words, even where the reference is to the period (1922–48) when the country's official English name was Palestine. Where the term "Palestine" is part of a name or title, or when it was clearly used in the original language by another speaker being quoted, it has been retained

Certain errors in the latest edition of the Hebrew text—in the spelling and transliteration of proper names, the dating and arrangement of chapters, and the wording of quotations—have been corrected in this translation.

MICHAEL SWIRSKY

Acknowledgments

The Eichmann trial in Jerusalem was a seminal event in the life of Israel, coming as it did only sixteen years after the end of World War II and thirteen years after the founding of the state of Israel. It was not only a journalist's assignment but also a personal contribution to the culture of memory. I was a witness to the trial's proceedings, writing daily accounts of it for the Hebrew-language daily *LaMerhav*. Eventually, my account of the trial in book form saw several editions in Hebrew as well as in French. Now, forty-two years after the trial, the first ever edition in the English language sees light.

Many were instrumental in bringing this project to fruition. I wish to express my profound thanks to all who had a hand in it, but in particular to three whose impact on the publication of this edition I should like to single out. Arthur Evans, who until his retirement in 2002 was the director of Wayne State University Press, offered me a warm and embracing welcome to the family of authors at the press; Alan Mintz, of the Jewish Theological Seminary, and an eminent scholar of Hebrew literature, offered much-needed encouragement and has written a kind and profound analysis on my works, and contributed a poignant essay for this edition; and Hayim Goldgraber, my friend of many years, first introduced me to Wayne State University Press. He has been instrumental in bringing my poetry, fiction, and history to the English-language readership, and it is he who introduced me to the superb translator of this volume, Michael Swirsky. I am immensely grateful to Mike for his excellent work of translation and for his patient and careful attention to editorial details.

A special thank-you goes to my friend Michael Gil'ad née Mickey Goldman. He figures prominently in these pages both as the young survivor of the European hell and throughout the trial as the police inspector, sitting next to the glass booth, a member of the special police unit 06, charged with the investigation and research into Nazi war crimes. He has always been generous with his time and knowledge in matters related to the Holocaust, the interrogation of Adolf Eichmannn, and the details of the trial.

This edition has benefited from several sources of financial support. I want to express my gratitude for the generosity and friendship of attorney Yair Green of Jerusalem. Additional support came from the Memorial Foundation for Jewish Culture and the Lucius N. Littauer Foundation. I am most grateful to Dr. Jerry Hochbaum and Mr. William L. Frost and to the trustees of these two foundations which made this edition possible.

Finally, very special thanks go to Jennifer Gariepy, Nancy Dziedzic, and Kristin Harpster Lawrence, my editors at Wayne State University Press. Their enthusiasm and appreciation of this volume was heartening to me. Their meticulous reading of the manuscript and their insightful comments were reassuring at every stage of the work. I am grateful to them and to all at the press who had a hand in bringing out *Facing the Glass Booth: The Jerusalem Trial of Adolf Eichmann.*

THE FIRST DAY

He entered the glass booth at 8:55 a.m. with no warning. He just went in and sat down. Tall, thin, dressed in a dark suit, a well-pressed white shirt, and a tie. A tight-lipped policeman at either side. That was all.

A silence fell over the packed hall. No one called out. No one shouted. All eyes were fixed on him. People got up, took out notebooks, started to write without looking at what they were writing.

He sat still as a statue. What do we have here, an iron will to remain silent or the obtuseness of a man who does not realize who he is?

All stared at him, as if bewitched: Israelis and Europeans and Americans and Asians and Africans. Among them, many of his own people, Germans.

The silence lasted a full five minutes.

Suspense? No. Astonishment? No. Anguish? No. It seemed to me I was part of a silent chaos that had yet to sort itself out.

Averting my gaze from him for a moment, I spotted seven black gowns, their backs to me. They were the five prosecutors—*ours*—and two defense attorneys—*his*.

The silence persisted, broken by the bee-like buzz of hundreds of people trying to keep their feelings under control.

"All rise!" roared the bailiff.

The crowd rose to its feet in unison. He sprang to attention. A well-trained soldier. He did not move.

Everyone sat down.

Then came the quiet, confident voice of the presiding judge, Judge Moshe Landau, speaking in measured tones: "Adolf Eichmann, rise!"

Again, he sprang to attention.

"Are you Adolf, son of Adolf Karl Eichmann?"

"Yes," the man answered in German.

He was instructed to face the judges. And that is how he would stand for a full hour, unflinching, his head turned to the left.

The statue stood at attention.

Judge Landau read the indictment, count by count.

The hall was filled with people listening, taking notes, hurrying to the cable room. The hall was devoid of blood, of fear, of pleading.

The hall was filled with words.

On the sides of the hall, tape recorders were registering the words spoken, and teleprinters were converting them into letters. But people were trying to do something else, to give the words . . . meaning.

"First count," Judge Landau read. "Statement of offense: crime against the Jewish people, violation of section 1(a)(1) of the Law for the Prosecution of Nazis and Their Collaborators, 5710/1950, and section 23 of the Criminal Code, Ordinance of 1936.

"Details of the offense: (1) The accused, during the period 1939–45, together with others, caused the deaths of millions of Jews, in his capacity as the person responsible for the implementation of the Nazis' plan for the physical annihilation of the Jews, a plan known as the Final Solution of the Jewish Question. . . ."

It took a full hour to read the charge sheet, in Hebrew and German translation.

"Auschwitz, Chelmno, Belzec, Sobibor, Treblinka, Maidanek," the judge's quiet voice intoned, alternating with that of the Israeli interpreter with the Viennese accent. "Between 1939 and 1945 . . . gassing, burning, shooting, hanging. . . ."

The statue remained motionless.

Judge Landau read count after count, charge after charge, his words falling into the sea of silence. The German invasion of Poland. The displacement of the population. The Einsatzgruppen, the "special action squads" which followed like a plague in the conquerors' wake. The slaughter in Poland, in the Baltics, in Byelorussia, the Ukraine. Transports from the Reich, from the west, from the south, from the north.

What count were we up to? Where exactly were we in the proceedings?

Landau continued: expulsions, starvation, epidemics, sterilization, abortion, plunder, confiscation, race laws, forced labor, humiliation, oppression, torture. And then, a phrase that sticks in my throat like a bitter laugh: "Mass transport under inhuman conditions."

The statue remained motionless.

Some time later, awakened as if from a dream, I heard the seventh count: the plundering of the property of millions of Jews, the setting up of the Reichszentrale, the opening of account W. Aktion Reinhardt.

"Within the space of two years," Landau read, "property was confiscated having the nominal value of 200,000,000 marks but, in fact, worth much more in real terms."

This accounting, the indictment stressed, did not include hair, gold teeth, prostheses . . .

The statue did not move.

Where were we? Count nine: "The extermination of Poles, expulsions, forced labor, theft of property. . . ." Count ten: "The murder of Slovenes. . . ." Count eleven: "The extermination of Gypsies. . . ." Count twelve: "The murder of one hundred Czech children . . . expulsion from the village of Lidice. . . ."

On top of all this, he had been an officer in the S.S., the S.D., the Gestapo. . . .

Enough.

The statue remained still.

Dr. Servatius rose. The ruddy, heavyset defense attorney for the man in the glass booth began his argument. Being Jews, he said, the judges were likely to be prejudiced. The Law for the Prosecution of Nazis did not apply ex post facto. Eichmann would not be able to summon witnesses for his defense. He should not be held guilty for acts committed by his country, which, it was clearly hinted, had taken full responsibility by agreeing to pay reparations to the victims. Eichmann was not a leader; the leaders had already been tried, at Nuremberg. The proceeding was illegal, because the defendant had been abducted and forced to stand trial. The defendant had already been convicted by the press. Eichmann was being unfairly accused. Etc., etc.

Though anticipated, it was hard to take the lengthy and tiresome procedural wrangling which the first day of the trial had turned into.

Prosecutor Gideon Hausner rose to the challenge and, hour after hour, all through the morning and afternoon sessions, countered the claims of the defense. Using dozens of examples drawn from the sea of international law, he showed that the circumstances under which the defendant had been brought to trial were not relevant to the question of whether the court was competent to try him, that there was no such thing as impartial judgment in cases of genocide, that such a trial could nonetheless be fair if the judges were instructed to disregard their personal and patriotic feelings, that a judge could not be disqualified because of his nationality, that unless laws could be applied retroactively atrocities would go unpunished and the world would descend into anarchy, and on and on.

He cited hundreds of rulings by foreign courts, punctuating stretches of dry detail with statements like, "The sources of this law go all the way back to the Prophet Amos—'For the three transgressions of Edom. . . .'" He refuted the claim that Israel's violation of Argentine sovereignty had any relevance to the trial, citing the subsequent joint statement of the Israeli and Argentine governments that they "regard[ed] the matter as closed." Raising his voice at one point, he said, "The defendant is here according to law, he has been charged according to law, and the crimes of which he is accused are violations of the laws of this country. He can argue his case and plead his innocence, if he has anything to say."

He was still citing the Nuremberg Trials and international treaties as the hands of the clock approached 6:30.

The first day was coming to a close. Downstairs in the press room, I saw the news industry furiously at work. Hundreds of reporters were pounding at their typewriters and talking on the phone. There were beer bottles, full and empty, all over the tables. And in the heavy air of a Jerusalem heat wave, filled with tobacco smoke of every description, in the foreign languages and foreign faces, I sensed something of what has been called "the climate of great moments."

One friend, a police officer, said to me, "There are more journalists here right now than anywhere else in the world, more, even, than there were at the U.N. when Khrushchev gave his speech."

APRIL 12, 1961

A SPEECH OF ACCUSATION AND LAMENT

I NOW REALIZED I would remember this day for the rest of my life. I wrote in my notebook: "April 17, 1961."

The bailiff shouted as usual, "All rise!"

We stood up.

The presiding judge said, "I declare the sixth session of this trial open. The court has made the following ruling, which will be recorded as Ruling Number 3."

This time, the judges rose to deliver their decision. The question: whether or not they were competent to try the case.

Judge Landau took up the two preliminary points raised by the defense: (1) the disqualification of the judges; and (2) the incompetence of the court to adjudicate the particular charges set forth in the indictment.

The presiding judge spoke firmly. "Will the memory of the Holocaust prevent the judges from carrying out their considered intention to conduct a fair trial?

"No," he went on, "we shall have no difficulty adhering to the guarantees given all defendants under our criminal code, to be considered innocent until proven guilty and to be judged solely according to evidence presented before the court.

"The judge, in his capacity as adjudicator, does not cease to be a creature of flesh and blood, with feelings and urges"—as we shall see—"but he is required by law to control them. We shall abide by this requirement.

"After considering all the claims of the learned counsel for the defense, the court and all its members view themselves as competent to try this case."

A profound silence filled the courtroom.

Judge Landau went on to deal with the intricacies of Dr. Servatius's argument concerning the competence of the court. Though what he had to say appeared to be a mere prolongation of the tedious procedural preliminaries, already in progress for three days, his words did not pertain to that part of the trial alone. Falling ponderously into the reigning silence, they marked the start of a new day, a day almost without precedent, in which the trial was actually to begin.

The presiding judge: "Do you plead innocent or guilty of the first charge?"

The defendant: "Within the meaning of the charge, not guilty."

The judge went on to enumerate each of the charges, asking each time, "Do you plead innocent or guilty?" And fifteen times, the defendant answered, "Within the meaning of the charge, not guilty."

It was the first time his voice had been heard at length.

This familiar formality, common to all courtrooms and all trials, sounded, on this occasion, new and incomprehensible.

And if the first day of the trial had been marked by bewilderment at something not yet grasped, this time the proceedings took on an unparalleled solemnity.

Now all was understood, clear, quiet, and harsh. There was nothing to add or take away.

The defendant having pleaded innocent on all counts, prosecutor Gideon Hausner arose to make his opening statement.

This man, who for two days had dunned the court with citations, precedents, and proofs, who had seemed to be given over entirely to the law and its dusty books and appurtenances, articles and clauses, stood before the court on the third day as a great figure of lamentation. I might almost say of accusation. A former lawyer, he was now the attorney general.

I was afraid he might not make it through the day.

Never had a man born of woman said to another man born of

woman the things Gideon Hausner said to Adolf Eichmann that day.

What transpired then in Jerusalem was the miracle I had not believed could ever happen.

"Standing before you, judges of Israel, to prosecute Adolf Eichmann, I do not stand alone. Standing with me now are six million prosecutors. But they cannot rise to their feet to point an accusing finger at the glass booth and shout at the one who sits there, '*J'accuse!*' So I shall serve as their voice."

A French reporter sitting next to me said, "Ha! He's a strong one, he is!"

In delivering his opening statement, Hausner managed not to succumb to the strain of his task. Later on, however, he, along with many of us and many of the foreign reporters, would find himself at the point of tears.

Up above, the balcony was filled with spectators, some of whom I could see from my seat in the first row. There were those who got up to leave, who could not bear it.

I had never associated the figure of a prosecutor with the kinds of things Hausner was saying then and would go on saying the following day.

I now knew why the esteemed defense attorney from Cologne had been apprehensive.

And Eichmann himself? He listened and took notes. From time to time, there was a twitch in his face. Otherwise, he was impassive as stone.

The indictment was forty-thousand-words long. What part of it would interest the reader of this book? The document purported to cover the twelve years from 1933 to 1945, but it began earlier. In the scope of what it sought to present to the court, which extended far beyond the scope of normal jurisprudence, it was unprecedented in human history.

The indictment could be divided into three principal parts: the rise of Nazism in Germany, the scope and method of its actions, and the losses sustained by the Jewish people.

The defendant fit into this triangle like a piece in a jigsaw puzzle, which the prosecutor assembled in the hours that followed. All expectations that the defendant would break down were disappointed. He sat uncannily silent.

"*Within the meaning of the charge, not guilty.*"

Even those who saw this as a sick joke had to bear hearing it.

"We shall prove to the court . . . ," "we shall show . . ."—the prosecutor said over and over—that the man sitting in the glass booth was the resourceful, efficient, untiring agent of the campaign of hatred launched at the Wannsee Conference, the Final Solution.

The prosecutor erected a brilliant, towering structure. With almost superhuman power, he reconstructed the recent past before the court. He forced the foreign reporters to go down to the basement, to their typewriters and Teletype machines, and tell their far-off readers, listeners, and viewers the story as if it were being told for the first time.

It seemed, for a moment, as if this man, who until then had been reclusive and little known, was animated by a kind of frenzy. But how could we have expected less from a man who began by saying, "I shall be your voice"?

And yet, he, too, had his limitations.

Hausner emerged from his marvelous narrative structure, the *full* account of the Third Reich; emerged from the hundreds of documents, each of which was world-shattering in its potential impact; emerged in full control of this history of hate-mongering, propaganda, humiliation, and death. He revealed its secrets, showing how the wondrous German machine had functioned. Then, suddenly, he pulled back and said, "In all this slaughter there is no chapter more shocking or horrifying than that of the more than one million Jewish children, forcibly separated from the mothers who tried to hide them, whose blood was spilled like water throughout the length and breadth of Europe.

"We shall," he went on, "present to you the orders issued by Eichmann and his staff for the deportation of children."

I looked around and saw foreign reporters as well as our own people close to tears. "Their tears fell inward."[1]

I looked up at the three judges.

It was not my task to turn this incident into a part of the verdict but rather simply to observe.

I went downstairs to look at the television monitor, which was showing the audience in the balcony. The panning camera captured in a few brief moments something no literary text could describe: hundreds of faces, amazingly similar in their expression, as if the prosecutor's narrative had fused them into a single person.

He was reading from a prepared text the testimony of an S.S. man: "Those who got out of the trucks, men, women, and children of all ages, were ordered to strip. . . . They did so without crying out or weeping, then kissed one another. . . . A family of eight went by, a man and woman, both about fifty, with their children. An old woman was cradling a year-old infant in her arms, singing to it. The infant's face was radiant with happiness. The father was holding his ten-year-old son by the hand, speaking to him tenderly as he pointed to the sky. . . . A teenage girl went by and said, 'I am twenty-three,' . . . and people lay pressed together, bleeding."

I remembered some lines from the chronicles of Jewish martyrdom in medieval Germany and France: "And the lad Aharon, seeing his brother being slaughtered, cried, 'Mother, Mother, do not slay me!' And he ran to hide under a crate. She took her two daughters and sacrificed them to the Lord of Hosts. And when this pious woman had offered up three of her sons to the Creator as well, she lifted her voice and called out to her remaining son, 'Aharon, where are you?'"

Except that, in this case, those who were to be shot could not save themselves by converting to another faith.

It was 5:30 P.M, Jerusalem time. The prosecutor said, "I beg the court's indulgence if I abbreviate this portion of my presentation."

1. Line from a poem by Nathan Alterman.—Trans.

And he read lyrics of the song, "Hush, hush, let us be quiet. / Graves are growing here."[2]

The presiding judge said, "We shall recess at this point."

The afternoon session ended a half hour early.

April 18, 1961

2. Yiddish ballad written by Shmerke Kaczerginski in the Vilna ghetto, April 1943.—Trans.

DAY AND NIGHT AND DAY

A DAY HAD passed, and night fell. The night passed, and another day dawned. And when I arrived at the courtroom in the morning I found the prosecutor still speaking, as if the flow of his words had never let up.

I thought he had said everything he had to say the day before, that he had run out of words then.

But there he stood, undaunted. "In this opening statement," he said, "I shall concentrate in some detail on a single chapter in this story, the catastrophe of Dutch Jewry. When the German army turned westward in May 1940, it overran Holland as well."

He mentioned the name of Eichmann. I could anticipate everything that was to follow.

Here, I knew, the familiar story would repeat itself: the Nuremberg Laws, the ban on travel, the expulsion of children from the schools, the restrictions, the curfews. And Hausner said, "Even the use of bicycles, that well-known Dutch form of transportation, was forbidden to Jews, and they were ordered to turn in all the bicycles in their possession."

He went on to describe the time of fearful silence, the calm before the storm. But suddenly, like a candle lit in the dark, he said, "Here the Nazis encountered resistance from the local, non-Jewish population for the first time. . . . After the Jews of Amsterdam were hunted down, in February 1941, a general strike was declared, and it spread to Utrecht, Hilversum, and other places. The gas and electric works were shut down by the strike, and passengers had to be taken off the trains. A revolt had broken out. Quickly, the Nazis summoned S.S. 'Death's Head' units from Germany. Orders were given to shoot. The leaders of the revolt were arrested. Others were executed. Still others were imprisoned and tortured to death. The strike was broken. The extermination process went on."

After a short while, Dutch reporters in the audience went down to file accounts of these things to their home offices.

Twenty years later, the Dutch people were being honored in Jerusalem.

Hausner's analysis of the "process" continued: suspension of rights, confiscation of property, deportation to forced-labor camps (for maximum exploitation before death), gold teeth, wedding rings (after death). "Twenty-nine thousand four hundred thirty-six box-cars, 735 trainloads, of goods confiscated from Jews in the West were sent to cities in Germany."

Eichmann, Eichmann—again and again, the name was mentioned.

"By the end, there were only a few isolated groups of Jews left in Holland.

"This is a brief summary of the extermination process carried out in a single country in which Eichmann was active. The story repeated itself in all the other countries, with slight variations, variations on the theme of horror, murder, and destruction."

Another candle was lit: Denmark.

"The operation was finally carried out on the first two days of October 1943. But here, something happened that astonished the murderers. Most of the Jews' houses were found empty, because the Danish people, who had been forewarned that mass murder was being plotted, had, courageously and at great risk, secretly organized an amazing rescue operation, under the code name 'Little Dunkirk.' In the ports, fishing boats, excursion boats, and sailing equipment had been assembled. Secretly, the Jews had been taken across to Sweden by scouts, students, and other volunteers. In this way, some six thousand of Denmark's Jews were saved."

"Eichmann was furious."

The memorable case of Denmark.

He went on to Belgium, to France. I paused for a moment and wrote, "Ah yes, in France, too, we shall hear the tale of tribulation." He mentioned those in the Maquis, the French underground, who tried to help.

I knew that what was being said then, here in Jerusalem, would find a prominent place in books the world over. I could not imagine otherwise.

A badge of shame or a medal of honor. Yet for every hundred badges of shame, the prosecutor bestowed but one medal of honor for nobility of spirit and love of humanity.

The story of Drancy took us back to André Schwarz-Bart's novel *The Last of the Just*, a tale of the deportation of children that touched the hearts of even the toughest gendarmes.

One of the hardest things to grasp was the devotion of the man in the glass booth to the execution of his plans down to the last detail, the last individual victim. Here, Hausner told the story of Taubert, the Italian Jew Eichmann pursued to the bitter end.

Italy, Serbia, Croatia, Slovenia. . . .

Eichmann even circumvented Hitler, Himmler, and Horthy. He fended off several isolated, pathetic attempts by the German Foreign Ministry to interfere with his plans.

Romania, Bulgaria, Greece, Slovakia, Bohemia, and Moravia. . . .

Theresienstadt, that German Potemkin village set up to fool the outside world.

Enough! No, there was more: the story of Hungary.

Hungary hung in the air, awaiting its turn, like a splendid finale, a final chord.

The story of Hungary was the climax of the saga of deportation from all the four winds. Perhaps, then, I should stop here.

But there remained one concluding chapter: who were all those many dead?

Last week, on Holocaust Memorial Day, three French

reporters happened upon a Jewish school in Jerusalem where the day was being marked. They quickly cabled back the following story. The teacher, they reported, had written the words "Memorial Day" on the blackboard and then told the children in his own words what the prosecutor had been saying at the trial the preceding two days. One pupil, a thirteen-year-old with braids down to her shoulders, stood up and asked, "So why didn't our army go to help them?"

I shall stop now. It is evening. In the streets of Jerusalem there are flags and torches and soldiers, celebrating the start of Independence Day.

April 19, 1961

A MINOR LOGISTICAL OFFICER

THEN I CAUGHT sight of Telford Taylor. Once the prosecutor at the Nuremberg Trials, he now represented a chain of newspapers. The tall American had squeezed into the surging throng, which danced and sang and hugged and lifted children into the air, bathed by colored lights and brushed by flags and streamers.

I spotted him near the Generali Building. The blaring of the music from the loudspeakers, coming after a mad phantasmagoria of fireworks, made conversation impossible.

Wasn't it too much?

No, for the space of those twenty-four hours, from Wednesday to Thursday, I couldn't help agreeing with those who, caught between the glass booth and the nation dancing in the streets, were saying, "This is it! This is what it's all about!"

I had not expected that the trial would take over my life to such an extent, that I would be so absorbed by it that any time off for other pursuits would seem like a stolen vacation.

Soon the witnesses would be called. What would we do then?

For the third day running, we were hearing a tape recording: the voice of Chief Inspector Avner Less asking questions, and that of Eichmann responding.

Thirty-six thousand typewritten pages! A hundred hours! How could Less have endured it? Now things were becoming clearer. Until this point we had been trying in vain to solve the riddle of the man in the glass booth, but now he was doing it for us. Psychiatrists and scholars of German history would find buried treasure in this dialogue.

"It wasn't me," he said over and over, and, to the extent that it *had* been him, "What, after all, was I?" "Having thoroughly examined my own actions, I must state that I am not a mass murderer."

What, then, had he been? "A minor underling." Above him, there had been Heydrich, Mueller, Himmler, Hitler.

He was "a sensitive man," he testified. The mere sight of an open wound horrified him. "'Adolf, you will never be a doctor.'" "I couldn't sleep at night. I told Mueller, 'This is dreadful, hellish, I can't go on.' Yes, I did go to Auschwitz to make various arrangements, but I never looked inside. What could I have done!?"

Solemnly and at great length, he explained the meaning of his "zombie-like obedience." "I had been accustomed to obeying orders my whole life, from the nursery to May 8, 1945. . . . What would disobedience have accomplished? Whom would it have benefitted? The planning of crucial matters of policy was not in my authority. . . . My rank was too low for that."

"I was insignificant," "I was of low rank," "I was a cog"—and on and on, for a hundred hours.

My God, I asked myself, who did give the orders to the Ministry for the Eastern Territories, or to the Oberregierungs people, or to the Amtsgerichtsrat, or to Dr. Wetzel to do something about the gas machines?

"I don't remember." "I've forgotten." "Yes, but what did happen there exactly?" "That is, . . ." And so on.

Finally, the unavoidable question that landed like a hammer blow: "Did you not see it as a matter of life and death for the German people that the entire Jewish people, all the Jews of Europe, be annihilated?"

And to this question he replied, "Sir, had they told me then that my father was a traitor and that it was up to me to execute him, I would have done that too."

As if in a judo match, he turned his submissiveness into a source of strength and pride. "To be an officer means to do one's duty in accordance with the oath of allegiance." "It was a war for the destiny of the German people." "I derived satisfaction from fulfilling my orders." "That was my solace." "I was a loyal S.S. man, diligent and precise."

Then there was more of the "who was I? what was I?"—until Chief Inspector Less, growing weary of it, began referring to him, with bitter irony, as "Little Adolf." "Again and again," he told him, "you try to hide, to back out. You say, 'That wasn't my area of responsibility, that wasn't my concern, those were the orders I received.'"

But Eichmann was undeterred. "I did not have authority over everything. The scope of my task was relatively narrow and limited."

He presented himself as a minor, almost pitiable logistical officer.

But from time to time he had to admit that his department did not deal only with matters "of a logistical character."

Here, and throughout this exchange, the listener was struck by the special vocabulary being used: "logistical character," "appropriate treatment." The latter, Eichmann explained, meant "killing, killing, of course."

There emerged from this dialogue, unprecedented in human history, the following expression: "It would be necessary, as a precondition, to clarify the legal situation in that area of sovereignty."

At issue was the legal cloak the treasonous Vichy government had employed to hand over the Jews, to deport Jewish children from Drancy.

The story of the weeping.

"Legal situation," "area of sovereignty."

One would have thought the dialogue had reached its climax, but then came the description of the Wannsee Conference, held in a garden suburb of Berlin, the conference which decided on the Final Solution. How fondly he remembered that occasion: the high- ranking participants, the hushed conversations, the orderliness, the politeness, the cognac that was served.

To this day, he admired Heinrich Mueller, speaking of him as a father figure. The mysterious, tight-lipped Mueller, head of the Gestapo.

He would blame his superiors, all of them now dead, or his subordinates, who "acted on their own."

An explosion seemed inevitable. It was time for a declaration.

When it came, it actually sent shivers down my spine. It seemed to me that from somewhere off in the distance, across a wasteland of meaningless verbiage, there began to be heard for the first time some actual human words. "In my heart, I am even prepared to atone myself for these terrible events. . . . I do not deserve mercy. . . . I am ready to hang myself in public."

But this statement, which could have been a turning point in this man's life, beyond atonement or the miraculous revival of his soul, turned into a document of obtuseness, of mendacity, of callousness, only deepening the corruption. It was merely a continuation of his agonizingly drawn-out attempt to evade, to get by, to escape; merely an addition to that mass of verbiage that had brought the listener to the point of helpless rage described by Bialik: "Grit your teeth, and bear it silently."[3]

"A minor logistical officer." "Problems of transport." And on and on.

A Hungarian Jew sitting next to me said, "Had Eichmann only carried out orders, my mother and father would still be alive."

But now the turn of the living witnesses was approaching. Could we be without ammunition, with the battle hardly begun?

April 23, 1961

3. A reference to Psalm 112:10.—Trans.

PROBLEMS OF COMMUNICATION

SUNDAY. THE CHRISTIAN Sabbath. I want to say a few words about problems of communication that have arisen at this trial.

This will be by way of apology.

Do not ask me, dear reader, to do the impossible.

They say, rightly, that the opening statement of the prosecutor, Attorney General Gideon Hausner, was an unforgettable event. I can vouch for it; I was there. Had I simply read about the things he described in any of the many books about that era, I'm afraid I would have understood them only at some remove, rather than from within. These things are well known, but his having spoken about them in a courtroom, in Jerusalem, gave the bare facts a wondrous and unexpected power.

We can assume, therefore, that the occasion was in his favor. The mute audience, the cameras, the furious scribbling of the pencils, the people hurrying in and out, the policemen, the frozen expression on the faces of the three judges, the bailiff standing to one side—all transformed what he said into something quite different.

But here a strange thing happened.

Hausner's description of the murder of an entire Jewish family gave one the feeling that some powerful reaction by the outside world, proportional to the enormity of what was being described, was imminent: mountains would split in two, rivers would overflow, animals would flee in panic, the city would go up in flames. The sounds and events of an apocalypse were on their way.

But the thunder and lightning were still far off.

What could we do but sit and listen?

We have been following the dialogue between Less and Eichmann. Here are a few more lines:

Less: "Your plan was for annihilation, the annihilation of all the Jews."

Eichmann: "Not my plan, sir, because I had no connection with this plan."

Less: "Yes, you certainly did have a connection with the plan."

Eichmann: "Yes, I . . . in view of my ancillary work, I am definitely guilty . . . from a juridical point of view."

Less: "We are not talking here about a juridical point of view. We are talking here about naked facts."

I regret attaching any subjective description or evaluation to such lines, lines lost and forgotten among the hundreds of thousands of words that were said.

It was Thursday, 2:27 P.M. And two people were sitting opposite each other, saying these things.

What, then, is the task of the journalist?

"O wayfarer, when you reach the Lacedaemonians, tell them you saw us fall fulfilling the law of our homeland." Thus Herodotus, describing the war of Sparta against the Persians.

Why has this line survived over the centuries?

"When I passed by you and saw you wallowing in your blood, I said to you, 'Live in spite of your blood.' Yea, I said to you, 'Live in spite of your blood.'"[4]

Strolling outside on a sunny late-spring Sunday, I think about the gifted individuals who were able to string these words together, one by one, according to a logic unknown to me, until they produced a miracle of power and beauty. As we stand here, bent over, speechless, these lines, in the magical freshness of their youth, float past.

I went to the books and to the poems, and here is something that happened: When I arrived on Memorial Day at the school

4. Ezekiel 16:6.

where I teach once a week, my pupils asked me, "Teacher, we've heard that you're covering the Eichmann Trial as a reporter. Could you tell us about it? We're having trouble studying today."

I described to them as best I could the things I had seen and heard. Then I got some books from the school library and read them a few poems.

The poems, written long before the trial, gave me a shorthand way of communicating with them. I had to be brief.

The country carries on as usual, day and night, and this trial accompanies it. The one goes on, the other alongside. Away from the courtroom, there is no outward sign of it. But it is in the air and the water, it is like dust on the trees, and when people try to push it away, it comes back without warning as a reflection in their eyes.

So it happened that, instead of the expected earthquake, everything went on as before, an ongoing marvel.

This is not to excuse the inadequacies of those of us who are covering the trial, but it may help explain the difficulties we face.

April 24, 1961

"THAT WHICH WAS . . ."

"If I may mention a personal experience, I visited Tarnov, my home town, in 1937 and again in 1958. In 1937, there had been a flourishing community of twenty thousand Jews there, with a six-hundred-year-old synagogue and other institutions. In 1958, there were twenty Jews left."

Hour after hour, Professor Salo Baron, of Columbia University, stood discussing "European Jewry," which I know more about now than I did when it was still alive.

A Jew, now an American, around sixty, balding, dressed in a dark suit. He spoke softly, in professorial tones, as if lecturing his students. In measured tones, he painted a broad picture of the life that was, from the beginning of the Common Era to the time of Eichmann.

In his methodical way, the professor developed a historical, demographic, and cultural picture, and it made me dizzy.

"Even in the pagan empire of ancient Rome, the law held anyone who damaged a synagogue guilty of desecration. And even when Constantine made Christianity the state religion, the synagogues continued to be protected with the full force of the law." (He would eventually come to *Kristallnacht*.)

Describing the history of the Jews on European soil, he spoke of communities, synagogues, religious academies, schools, welfare institutions, museums and libraries. There had been a great flowering, despite persecution, restriction, and massacre; a life rich in spirit and deed, a life of commerce and labor. They had flourished for their own sake and for the glory of their God and their faith, but they had also contributed greatly to the cultures of the surrounding peoples, among whom they maintained their remarkable way of life. They had been separate and different but also integral to the social fabric of the bigger peoples who owned the land and the water, who ruled and conquered.

In measured tones. A very long lecture, so full of facts and figures that I felt I was drowning.

One set of figures after another. At last, the methodical lecturer disclosed the following: there had been 2,000 Jewish communities in Poland, comprising 3,300,000 people; 30 Jewish daily newspapers in Yiddish and 5 in Polish, as well as 132 weekly magazines, including 4 in Hebrew; theaters and publishing houses; political parties and youth movements.

One set of figures after another. "Even the Jewish community in France," he said, "supported no fewer than 96 newspapers; in Holland, 21; in Austria, 16; in Hungary, 21; in Romania, 54; in Germany, 113." And so on.

And then there were Bialik and Tchernichowsky, Sholom Aleichem and Sholom Asch, Wasserman and Feuchtwanger, Kafka and Bergson and Einstein and Freud, and all the other luminaries.

There were the doctors and chemists, the poets and revolutionaries (of whom Heine wrote that they had "spilled their blood on all the barricades of freedom"), the statesmen and philosophers.

Eichmann took notes throughout the lecture, dealing as it did with his particular subject, the subject that had concerned the Jewish Section of the Gestapo. He had always taken a close interest in it. He took notes and listened. It fascinated him. He learned from Professor Baron that, had he not done what he had done, there would now be twelve million Jews living in Europe.

"Worst of all, perhaps," Baron went on, "was that so few children were left, so few. In Bohemia, Moravia, and Silesia, the 1930 census showed 117,551, while in October 1945, it was down to 14,489."

Eichmann went on writing, with the seriousness of a well-organized professional. This, after all, was statistics, his field of expertise. Had he not, by his own testimony, been concerned primarily with transport timetables?

The morning session was devoted to the marvelous panorama of European Jewish life as it had been.

The afternoon session was devoted to the ashes.

Professor Baron finished.

Any questions?

Yes, Dr. Servatius had a few. "Herr Professor"—I am not quoting him word for word—"you have told us at some length about antisemitism. How do you explain the fact that Jews were so universally hated?"

The hall fell silent.

The quiet, scientifically rigorous professor clearly would have preferred not to take up the German's challenge, this attempt, in the finest tradition, to raise the discussion to a lofty, spiritual plane.

Baron began by explaining that xenophobia—"disliking the unlike"—was an underlying motif. He also described the religious background. But he did not give the answer that was expected, and the questioner might well have regretted evoking this reply and the academic debate that followed.

The two then fell into a philosophical argument—Eichmann was still listening and taking notes—about Hegel and Spengler and the "spirit of history" and determinism and freedom. The court was elevated to the heights of intellectual and legal discourse.

Baron, in his quietly persuasive, professorial manner, juxtaposed man's responsibility for his own actions, good and evil, with the "spirit of history." We were still up in the clouds, but the hems of those clouds were red with the great conflagration that had taken place. It was an argument ex post facto, when everything was over and done with. And Eichmann was still taking notes.

April 25, 1961

SHMUEL GRYNSZPAN AND BENNO COHEN

"I SOLEMNLY SWEAR that my testimony in this trial shall be the truth, the whole truth, and nothing but the truth."

"What is your full name?" asked the presiding judge.

"Zindel Grynszpan," the witness answered.

"And in Hebrew?"

"Shmuel."

"Zindel Shmuel Grynszpan," the presiding judge said.

In the witness box stood a short, gray-haired Jew, about seventy-five (he was born in Radomsk, Poland, in 1886), with a pointed beard. He wore a shabby brown suit and a yarmulke. He was speaking Yiddish.

He had married in 1910. The following year, he and his wife emigrated to Hanover, Germany, where they lived for the next twenty-eight years. On October 27, 1938, they were deported, along with 120,000 other Polish Jews.

"How many children did you have in Hanover?" asked deputy prosecutor Ya'akov Bar-Or.

"Eight."

"How many sons?"

"Four."

"How many of your children were still living in 1938?"

"Two sons and one daughter. One of my sons lives here in Israel. The other was killed by the Germans."

The elder son, Mordekhai Eliezer, had been born in Hanover in 1919, the other in 1921, also in Hanover.

"What was his name?"

"Hirsh Feivel Grynszpan. In Germany, they called him Hermann."

Here on the witness stand stood the elderly father of Hershel Grynszpan, the Jewish lad from Germany who, at the beginning of November, 1938, had shot the third secretary of the German consulate in Paris, Baron Ernst vom Rath.

He stood erect in the box and told his life story and that of his family. I had not known he and his surviving son Mordekhai Eliezer had been living for years in Kiryat Shmuel, near Haifa.

It was as if this old man had come from another world. At first he had difficulty adjusting to courtroom procedure, the administration of the oath, the translations. But then he told his story in a clear, strong voice. It was to become one of the signal accounts of the cruelty and violence that marked that dark time.

"If it is hard for you to stand, you may sit," said the presiding judge.

"In deference to the court, I can stand," the patriarch replied.

"What happened on October 27, 1938?"

The witness told the story of the deportation of the Polish Jews from Germany: how they, including him and his family, were summoned by the police; how, weeping and wailing, they were ordered to sign the expulsion order; how they were left there for twenty-four hours, until Friday night; and how, the next day, they were taken to the Polish border, to which trains had come from all over Germany: from Berlin, Cologne, Hamburg, Duesseldorf. Yes, it had been on the Sabbath day, October 27. Each person was allowed to bring ten marks. "You brought no more in; you will take no more out." He described the expulsion across the border. "The S.S. men beat us over the head. I was struck and fell down. My son helped me up, saying, 'Run, Papa, or we will die.' We came to a small town. It was raining. A number of people collapsed. Others had strokes. We were hungry. Afterward, trucks came with bread."

He then wrote a letter to his son Hershel in France, telling him about the expulsion. "Do not write to us in Germany any more. We are now in Poland."

Dr. Servatius had no questions.

"Thank you very much, Mr. Grynszpan. You may step down."

Here, the story of the father ended. We know the sequel. The boy got the letter, obtained a pistol and shot vom Rath, in revenge "for the suffering and indignity inflicted on my family and my people," he declared.

The story of the father ended. As in a relay race, the baton was to be taken by Benno Cohen, who had been the chairman of the Zionist Organization in Berlin. He would tell of the pogroms of November 9–10, 1938; of the famous *Kristallnacht*, the night of the broken windows and smashed crystal; of the synagogues being set alight in the streets of Germany; of the beatings, the arrests, the murders. The beginning of the end.

Zindel Shmuel Grynszpan, the old Jew from Haifa Bay, had not known then, on October 27, what was about to happen. He never saw his son Hershel again.

As we have said, of his eight sons and daughters, only the one son, Mordekhai Eliezer, was left.

Benno Cohen, too, belonged to the first group of witnesses, who testified concerning the period preceding the Destruction. His testimony tells of a different, earlier Eichmann, the Eichmann who came as a Gestapo detective to a Zionist meeting, the Eichmann who summoned the heads of the community and the Zionist leaders to Gestapo headquarters and, in language filled with curses and obscenities, harangued them about emigration. Jewish newspapers were still being published, the Zionists were still running their training farms, and the transfer of Jewish assets was still allowed.

Cohen spoke about 1933–39. (In March 1939, he had immigrated to the Land of Israel.) That period, which for the Jews of Germany was a hell of disillusionment and despair, of degradation and suicide, of synagogues going up in smoke, of bonfires of books surrounded by cheering crowds, of bans, expropriations and evictions—that time had been a paradise in comparison with what was to follow at Maidanek.

The pre-Holocaust period, filled with the portents of apocalypse.

Robert Weltsch could still write in the *Judische Rundschau*, "Wear the yellow badge with pride!"

But even then, even then, it had already begun. "Many Germans," Cohen said, "informed on their competitors, in order to be rid of them. They were taken to concentration camps and returned broken human beings. Women came to us who had received the ashes of their husbands, who had died in the camps, in the mail, accompanied by a brief note: 'Your husband died of a heart attack. We hereby enclose his ashes. Postage due: M 3.50.'

"The burning of the Reichstag. The annulment of civil rights. It was the beginning of the new era.

"In shop windows and on billboards appeared such slogans as 'Jew: die!,' 'Caution: mortal danger!,' and 'Watch out, Itzik!'

"From cities all over the country, we received the bleak news of a rash of suicides, Attorney So-and-So or Dr. So-and-So putting himself to death, unable to bear the loss of his position and dignity."

But proud voices were still heard. The witness read from the pages of the *Judische Rundschau*: "'The fact that the Boycott Office has ordered signs showing the yellow patch on a black background placed in the windows of boycotted shops is freighted with symbolism. This order is meant to shame us. *We accept it, but we intend to make it a mark of honor.*'"

But the great self-delusion did not stop there: "'This is a time of excessive emotion. . . . Let us hope for calmer times. Let us hope that the movement that prides itself in having raised the nation up will not be interested in putting others down, though it believes it has a quarrel with them.'"

But it turned out that this "movement," whose representative was now sitting in the glass booth in Jerusalem, was indeed interested in "putting others down."

Cohen's testimony continued. Along with passages from the special Yom Kippur prayer composed by Rabbi Leo Baeck, I heard, for the first time, details of the Nuremberg Laws.

"The laws for the protection of German blood and German honor," "German blood: a guarantee of the existence of the German people," "the ban on mixed marriages," "A Jew is one who had three grandparents who were Jewish by race," etc.

"At this hour," Baeck's prayer affirms, "the whole House of Israel stands before its God. We stand strong before Him, strong in confessing to Him our sins, as individuals and as a people. With the same strength, we express our abhorrence of the lie being fomented about us, the calumny against our faith. . . . Ours is a history of spiritual greatness, spiritual genius and glory. On them we lean, now that adversaries have come to defame us. . . . Our hearts are filled with sorrow and grief."

The presiding judge assigns exhibit number T/69 to this prayer, composed in 1935, the very year the Nuremberg Laws were instituted.

April 26, 1961

THE STORY OF GOD'S SERVANTS

"THEY GAVE ME a pail of boiling water and a rag and told me to scrub the sidewalk outside the Metropole Hotel. There was caustic soda in the water, and my hands quickly swelled up. Then they brought out our Rabbi, Dr. Taglicht, a man of seventy, and he, too, was ordered to wash the sidewalk. He did it wrapped in a prayer shawl. As he crouched there on the ground, the guard standing over him asked, 'How do you like it?' The rabbi answered, 'If this is God's will, I am His servant.'"

I recorded these words as they were spoken by Morris Fleischmann, who had been one of the leaders of the Jewish community in Vienna.

I did not want to listen to this broken little man go on and on about his sufferings, his ills and indignities, the way the mob jeered at him and his fellow Jews.

"We were beaten. We were hungry. We were like the wet walls of a urinal."

I did not want to see him, and I did not want to hear him. I would have preferred to go today to the military parade at the stadium, to see Jews at their strongest and most beautiful. But with an uncanny force, this Morris Fleischmann grabbed hold of us by the scruff of our necks, as if to say, "Sit still and hear me out."

"The shortest of the guards was nearly six feet tall," he said, making me aware of how short he himself was.

These, too, are your own flesh and blood, I said to myself. They are in a position to demand that you sit through this, that you not run away. No, you will not run off to watch the parade.

And what would the coming weeks bring?

There would be other witnesses, telling at length what they had endured, and the trial would go on and on.

"An off day," they told me in the corridors.

The prosecutor quoted at length from the memoirs of Rudolf Hoess, the commandant of Auschwitz. What did *he* have to say about Eichmann? "Eichmann was tireless," he had written. "He was totally devoted to the Final Solution of the Jewish Question." And again, "Eichmann was full of energy, always hatching new plans and looking for ways to improve and streamline things, taking pleasure in a job well done—that is, the destruction of the Jews."

The evidence provided by Hoess and S.S. Captain Dieter Wisliceny about the man in the glass booth, together with the things he said about himself and the testimony of two or three other witnesses, would have been enough to wind up the trial.

In fact, the trial was over before it even began. The tape recordings did it. But the prosecution had decided to call forty witnesses, so that we would go on hearing about these things day and night.

How were we going to endure this recitation *in memoriam*? And what, then, would we make of it?

One of the witnesses was Fleischmann, who was forcing me to listen to his presentation.

He was telling the story of the humiliated chief rabbi, who had replied, "If this is God's will, I am His servant."

I do not know what God thought of that answer, given by His servant on that Viennese sidewalk.

They say the rabbi's answer went to the heart of theology and belief, evoking Job, God's faithful servant.

But Fleischmann would also tell of bribes paid to survive and escape, of the hiding of money, of the sound of jackboots in the streets, of the expulsion of the Viennese community.

He had sworn "to tell the whole truth and nothing but the truth," sworn by the God of that same rabbi who had scrubbed the pavement, and he was, in the end, telling the tale of his own helplessness, with a frankness and explicitness that made me hang my head in shame.

That story got to me, it did.

He was followed by Franz Eliezer Meyer, a Jew from Berlin, very precise and proper in his manner, as the German Jews are. He said, "At that time, Eichmann's treatment of me was correct. He let me sit down, and he addressed me as 'Mr.' But by 1939 he was behaving brazenly and rudely, like a tyrant with power over life and death. Then the Jewish leaders had to remain standing in his presence."

These witnesses, too, were dealing with the "before." A later period was described by Wisliceny and Hoess, who had been hanged. And now we were into a third period.

Benno Cohen, Morris Fleischmann, Franz Eliezer Meyer—all belong to the first period, according to Wisliceny's breakdown of the history. The fact is, they are still alive.

The trial ended before it began.

But we shall have to listen to all the witnesses, every last one, in the days and weeks and months to come. There will be no escape and no reprieve.

We wanted a trial, and we got one.

April 27, 1961

THE DISCIPLES OF THE ANGEL OF DEATH

For several days I was absent from the courtroom. Yesterday, I returned to hear the stories of Tzvi Pechter, Ya'akov Gorfein, Noah Zabludowicz, and Moshe Bejsky. This time I sat up in the balcony.

The hall was full. Eichmann took his place in the booth. Pardon me, not Adolf Eichmann but the ghost that had gone on sitting there.

The first witness was Tzvi Pechter.

But rather than proceed chronologically, hadn't we better begin with the last witness, Dr. Bejsky? And what about the others? Who had put them in this order?

In the corridors, they said rightly that Bejsky's story would be the high point of the trial, that this man would raise it to the highest possible level. Why? Because of his personality, his learning, his polished Hebrew?

I do not know by what measures of magnitude or system of classification horrors are ranked.

Dr. Bejsky himself said of the deportation of the Jews of Hungary in 1944 that "it was the most sorrowful transport operation [he] had ever seen." It seemed strange and incomprehensible, because I had thought that in telling his own story he had exhausted the subject. But it may have been the witness Gorfein, who went on and on, until someone two rows ahead of me in the balcony got up, raised his hands, and shouted toward the glass booth, "Bloody dog! They killed my whole family! My whole family! Let me have him! Let me have him! Kill him!" And like an overgrown child, his voice fading into the distance, he was carried away by the police, who had come quickly to subdue him and remove him from the hall.

Once again, there was talk of measures of magnitude. "This is the worst day so far," people said.

But I left the courtroom with two subjects I wanted to write about.

The first was dates and names. The second was the question, Why didn't you resist?

Tzvi Pechter told of the forced march from Hrubieszow to Chelm on December 2, 1939. The old Jew described his personal odyssey, which about ten thousand people had shared. But he remembered names and dates, and this enabled him to lift the tale out of the night and fog of legend that enshrouds those days and thus pay last respects to those who did not make it back.

He took us out of the realm of statistics and into that of *names*, where life begins anew. It was a desperate and wondrous revolt against the Germans, who had turned names into numbers. "First they took two Jews, one, with a yellowish beard, named Shmuel-Hersh Kobrashok, and another, with a long beard, named Binyamin Rosenberg. Then they took a third, named Loewenberg. It was when they took Loewenberg," Pechter said, "that the great tragedy occurred. His son lunged forward, shouting, 'Let my father go! I will go in his place.' 'You come too,' they replied. And they shot all four of them. The bullets passed through their foreheads.

"And there was a fellow there by the name of Noah Wertman, whose head was smashed with the butt of a rifle."

And this was in December 1939, according to the Gregorian calendar.

Ya'akov Gorfein spoke Hebrew fluently. He was younger and stood straighter than Pechter.

"And you believed it?" the prosecutor asked.

"We did, because each time the Gestapo would come and announce that the Fuehrer had given orders not to deport any more Jews, that they needed workers, that there would be no more expulsions, no more killing or shooting."

"Tell me, when they loaded you onto the trains bound for Belzec, why didn't you resist?"

"We no longer had the strength. We just wanted it to be over with. We wanted to die quickly."

"Why did you jump from the window?"

"I had an impulse nevertheless. A spark of something. But I would not have jumped if my mother had not physically pushed me."

Judge Raveh: "Do you have any idea how many people from your town survived?"

"Five or six."

"Out of thirteen thousand?"

"Yes."

I suppose I should also tell about Noah Zabludowicz, whom the newsmen called Noah Pandre,[5] about that violent man who at nineteen was, in his words, "the fastest runner in the neighborhood," about the beating he took while under interrogation by the Gestapo.

He preceded Moshe Bejsky, to complete the cast of characters.

Among Zabludowicz's tales of beatings, interrogations, and evictions, he told of the S.S. men who burst into a house in which a number of families were crowded, then ordered the parents to exchange spouses and have sex in front of their children.

I didn't understand why Judge Halevi was skeptical about this story.

"Did you yourself see any such instance, in which husbands and wives were separated?"

"I did."

"Where they forced men to lie with women who were not their wives?"

"Yes, I saw it."

"With your own eyes?"

5. Eponymous, roughneck hero of a novel by Zalman Shneur.—Trans.

"They made the men lie with women. . . ."

"And you were in the room?"

"Yes."

"And what about the baby?"

But this story I cannot tell. I shall now go on to the testimony of Dr. Bejsky.

Suddenly I realized that today I had not once looked into the glass booth. The events being described were larger than he was, although he had been one of those who had made them loom so large.

I return to the subject of "Why didn't you resist?"

"I don't think it can be explained. A person who wasn't there wouldn't understand. It was the third year of the war. We had been through a lot, but we still had some hope. We were working. They needed us. It was clear that with the slightest pretext they could easily finish us off. There were so many of them. Eighteen years later, one cannot describe the *fear*. It was a kind of terror, after all. Facing a machine gun. Watching a boy being hung. Losing the capacity to react. The belief that the war would end. There was a camp housing a thousand Poles in a similar situation. Their homes were just a hundred meters away, but they never tried to escape. Where could the Jews have gone? We were wearing concentration camp uniforms. Our heads were shaved. In 1943, we still didn't know what was in store for the deportees. Later we did. What happened then cannot be described today." And so on and so forth.

The witness said all these things sitting down. At times his voice faded and became inaudible. Then, abruptly, he would speak up, as if trying to justify himself, to explain—to the judges, to his people, to the whole world.

May 2, 1961

THE MIRACLES

Yesterday was the day of the miracles.

Quite a few days had gone by since we heard the man shouting from the balcony. The time had passed quickly. I will begin with the odd language that was used, a language without adjectives.

Dr. Leon Wells was in the middle of his testimony. Oh yes, I forgot to mention that, before Wells began, Dr. Servatius had objected to calling him to the stand. "His testimony could be highly significant in terms of the historical process," he said, "but it would not be relevant from a juridical point of view, because it would not touch on the responsibility of the defendant."

Nonetheless, Wells had been called, and now he was speaking. He was the strangest man I had ever seen. He spoke English, his adopted tongue, with a Polish accent. His speech was monotonous and unadorned, as if he were creating an abstraction of himself, as if he were actually somewhere else and the person speaking only a stand-in. It was this person, not he, who had belonged to Death Brigade 1005, the unit that burned the bodies, ground up the bones, and erased all trace of what had been done.

When he mounted the witness stand, his face froze into a mask. "And my grandfather said, 'Yes, my son, we are the last ones left here.'" Or, "At the end of September, my father, my uncle Ya'akov, and his wife and two children were liquidated. The Friday before Yom Kippur, they took my grandmother, my two aunts, and eight of my cousins." Or, "I saw my father weep for the first time. I asked him what to do. 'I don't know,' he said. 'We're living through a time when a father doesn't know what to tell his son.'"

And he, the last survivor in his family, was telling about the unit responsible for erasing the evidence of the killing.

The presiding judge: "What is a 'grinding machine'?"

The witness: "It was like a big concrete mixer with large steel balls inside. The bones would be thrown into the machine and ground up. First, the bodies were burned. Whatever ash remained we would put through a big sieve, like a flour sifter.

"For a long time, I looked for body number 182. That was my body."

"I did not understand your last remark, Dr. Wells," said the presiding judge.

"Thirteen months later, I was part of a group that reopened the mass grave of some people who had been shot, of which I was one. As I told you, I had escaped. . . ."

During the morning recess, a colleague said to me, "The foreign reporters are arguing. They're quite critical of this witness. They say he's lying, making things up, and that it's not good for the trial."

I, too, found myself arguing with one of the English-speaking reporters, a man named Frank Linder. It turned out he was a special correspondent for *Bildzeitung*, a paper published in Hamburg and Berlin with a circulation of 3.8 million. "This fellow is combining one story with another. He couldn't have been in all those places himself. He couldn't remember all those details."

I left him and went back upstairs, where I listened to more of Wells's plodding, drawn-out testimony. "There was someone there named Brill who found among the still-warm bodies those of his two daughters, and he burned them." He went on to tell of the graves in which bodies of men in black uniforms were found. "These were Ukrainians who had carried out the action against the Jews and were themselves shot in turn." In the same monotonous tone, he told of the Jewish girls who pleasured the S.S. men at night but then refused to continue and began running away. "They were taken at once to the trucks and brought to us for burning. The back door would be opened and, one by one, they would be thrown into the fire, after having been shot in the back of the neck."

Living corpse number 182 went on speaking. The man is a genius. Recently, he received an international prize for his work in optics or cinematography; I can't remember which. I looked at his face, his black hair, his terribly Jewish eyes, as he responded to the prosecutor's question, "Why didn't they resist? Why did they go quietly to their deaths?"

And in a prolonged, frozen hush, the man explained why it had been impossible to resist, why death had been seen as a way out. He told of the mother who spit in the face of an S.S. man. "They took her child away from her and smashed its head against a tree, then hung her by her feet as the other prisoners looked on."

His voice was uninflected, his face expressionless.

What was the matter with the witnesses today? Why did all of them choose to talk at length about children? Here, for example, was Henryk Ross, the enigmatic photographer from Lodz, who took many, many pictures and hid the negatives, then came back from the dead, developed the pictures, and brought them to the court. He talked about the children who had been thrown from high floors down onto the platforms.

Dr. Ya'akov Buzhminsky told of a woman in the Przemysl ghetto who begged a soldier to take pity on her little boy and kill her instead. "The Poles on the other side of the fence reached out and asked for the child, so that he would be spared. The German shot her and then tore the child to pieces like a rag."

What was the matter with these witnesses? We had thought there was nothing more to say about the children. We had finished with that subject! The attorney general had already covered it. Why did they keep coming back to it? Had any children survived? What year were we up to? When was it that 120,000 died of starvation in Lodz? What was Servatius doing here? Yes, he would have liked to summon Krumey, Six, von Thadden, Merten. But their testimony for this trial was to be taken there, in Germany, not here.

Buzhminsky went on. He had been rescued by a lonely Polish woman who later married him. Thus had he managed to stay alive long enough to see the day of deliverance.

We had yet to hear about the part-Jews who were taken to the Lodz ghetto, or the unfortunate Hitler Youth members who went on beating the Jews until it turned out that they, too, were Jewish. A few days later their parents told them that they were Jews. After that they got nothing to eat. They understood.

Back to Buzhminsky.

"I saw the commandant of the ghetto give a Jewish boy eighty lashes," he said. Being a doctor, he was able to state definitively that no child could survive more than fifty. Yet this boy survived.

"Is that boy present in the courtroom?" asked the attorney general, as if pulling a rabbit from a hat.

"Yes, he is," answered the Polish witness.

"Would you point him out to us?"

Everyone turned toward the balcony, waiting for someone there to stand up.

"There he is!" the man said, pointing at Police Inspector Micky Goldman, who was sitting next to the attorney general on the dais.

"That's the boy!" Hausner said, turning to the judges.

Goldman, quiet and trim, ever the Section 06 man,[6] did not look up. There was a buzz of excitement in the hall. The circle was closed. The boy who had been whipped was now a man, sitting three paces away from the glass booth.

May 3, 1961

6. Unit of the Israel Police charged with interrogating Eichmann before the trial.—Trans.

WHY FEAR DEATH?

> Why should we fear death,
> With its angel riding on our shoulders?
> Hayyim Nahman Bialik, "Davar"

DAY, THEN NIGHT, then day again. They mounted the witness stand, one by one. The last remnants of the *revolt*.

Two or three I knew personally, as friends.

Now, in giving their testimony, they would be entering another realm. We saw them life-size from a distance of, at most, twenty yards, but they did not belong to us, were not our friends. They were strangers. Not from here but from there.

From beyond the lost time, the expanses of alien land, the rivers and forests and cities of the shadow of death, they had come here to testify.

They were part of the endless, uninterrupted procession that was laying out for us the map of Jewish torment, a map that corresponded precisely to the map of the Third Reich at the height of its power.

We knew they would come, and each day we awaited them. But they came late. Others had preceded them: Grynszpan, Cohen, Meyer, Fleischmann, Pechter, Gorfein, Bejsky, Wells, Ross, Buzhminsky, and the rest.

And when they got to the witness stand, they tried to explain to the whole surviving Jewish people, to everyone in the world who was willing to listen, the secret and meaning of the revolt and why it had come so late.

Before them, we heard the others' stories, and after them, too.

Like a rough tour guide, the trial had taken us through the streets and cities and times, the camps and ghettoes and ovens, until we reached the Jewish Fighting Organization and its marching song "Do Not Say We Are Coming to the End." But we only reached them after passing the mass graves of two thirds of the Jewish population of Europe.

From time to time, we felt like asking Hausner, "When are we going to get to the revolt?" Had those witnesses intentionally been held in abeyance until after the testimony of Leon Wells?

(After Wells, the burner of bodies and grinder of bones, had finished testifying, we saw him standing near the cafeteria, smiling and erect. A Jewish reporter from Poland, a correspondent for one of the news agencies, went over to him and said, "Are you Dr. Wells? I have regards for you from Poland." And for a moment it seemed to me as if a sleepwalker was bearing regards to a dead man.)

Had Leon Wells, the grave opener, been preparing the ground in his testimony for the appearance of these rebels, who had come to restore us to the real, human world, after the mass procession into the jaws of death that belonged, in our eyes, to a world that was unreal?

Today the *rebels* will be speaking, people all over the country said. The *Voice of Israel*, which had stopped broadcasting the testimony, announced that the next morning at 8:55 the live broadcast from the courtroom would resume. Tomorrow would be a special day, people said.

And we waited for them to appear. Was it the disgrace of belonging to a people that had been defeated so effortlessly, at the mere wave of a hand, that made us want to see them so badly?

I do not think it was a disgrace, for disgrace is something measurable.

Did the victims of the earthquakes in Agadir or Chile feel disgraced by the crumbling mountains or the rivers that suddenly changed their course?

And, as we now know, this was how all the others, too, allowed themselves to be ground up: the Poles, the Russians of military age, and all the rest, denizens of a defeated Europe who had been selected for death.

What happened is beyond honor or reproach. I think we wanted to see the eyewitnesses of the revolts again in the courtroom now because they had brought us back to reality, which had been lost in the thick, dreamlike fog of lies; because they had shattered the ingenious, unending conspiracy of deception; because they had murdered the illusions of those who hid behind their pink and yellow and blue cards[7] (think of the still-fresh testimony of Dr. Dworzecki).

Writing this now, far from the courtroom, I do not have with me a transcript of Abba Kovner's exact words, but he related that, in the summer of 1942, the Vilna underground, which he led, realized that "Ponar mean[t] death"[8] and that death would not end at Ponar, because "Hitler ha[d] decided to destroy all the Jews."

But Kovner, who had taken a solemn vow to tell nothing but the truth, had to admit now that the apprehension that a "final solution" was at hand was, at the time, still in the realm of speculation.

Another piece of the puzzle: Yitzhak Zuckerman said he learned the truth from two people, the Polish scout Henjek Grabowski, who had been sent to Vilna, and the Jewish gravedigger from Chelmno.

At that point, Zuckerman nearly broke down. He had met the Pole at night. "I listened to him. I am from Vilna; I was born in Vilna. In Vilna, I had left behind my parents and the rest of my family. And here he was, bringing me news from Vilna. As a child I had played with acorns in Ponar. This same Ponar! The Jews of my

---

7. Multicolored cards used as deception by the Nazis, handed out to intended victims as though indicating a meaningful work destination.—Trans.
8. A forest near Vilna where the Jews of that city were killed.— Trans.

beloved Vilna were being murdered in Ponar! The very place of my childhood memories."

Five times the word "Vilna" had to be repeated before he could grasp it. The next day, Kovner testified about how things looked from the other side, from inside the city. The Einsatzgruppen had begun their work there. The city that had seemed to the Warsaw Jews a gate of hope—some had sought refuge there—the city the Polish scout had been sent to check out, turned out to be the gate of hell.

"That night, I didn't know what to do," Zuckerman, known as Antek, continued. "The gravedigger from Chelmno, who had fled, told me about the gas vans." The beginning of the Final Solution.

"There was fire to the east and fire to the west. We were in the middle. Could we imagine that the fire would not get to us as well? What set us apart? We were Warsaw Jews."

He put it as a question, one that later would no longer be asked. But Antek, felt compelled to add, "We didn't believe such a thing was possible, that they would attack the whole Jewish people and murder us all."

The smoke of the ovens was already rising into the skies over Poland.

But how was an entire city to be convinced that the next day it would die?

Vilna, struck down with a single blow, cried, "Ponar means death!" In 1942, it foreshadowed the Final Solution.

Kovner told how alone these prophets were, how forlorn they felt amid the pervasive self-delusion, which continued until the very end, to the climax of the orgy of destruction, when the commander of the Jewish Fighting Organization in the ghetto, Yitzhak Wittenberg, was turned over to the Gestapo.

Dr. Dworzecki explained, as a physician, what it meant to be a *musselman*. (I wrote down his words.) It was someone close to death, a symbol of helplessness, who could barely lift a spoon, and when you asked him a question it took him five minutes to answer.

He moved slowly, flickering and fading like a candle.

Hadn't these last, dwindling, vanquished remnants of European Jewry in the East been like a *musselman* when the call to arms came, at various times and in various remote places?

Yes, this people, about to be murdered, had something of the *musselman* about it, yet at the same time, in heartrending contrast, it also had a will to live—another month, another year, perhaps, just possibly. There was an attempt to survive. In the grip of a delusion that robbed it, step by step, of its chances for survival, it demonstrated a blind, passionate vitality.

Meanwhile, those who saw and knew and fought perished in their loneliness.

Until all illusions were shattered, but then it was too late.

I mentioned the call to arms. Now here was Tzivia, whom many had given up for dead, telling about the pistols that could be counted on the fingers of one hand, about the single rifle, about the handful of grenades and Molotov cocktails. About the dynamite that had a price in gold and in human lives.

At last, she came to the story that has no parallel in the annals of war, that of the battle of January and the final battle of April, the effects of which were still being felt when the autumn rains fell upon the ashes of the ghetto. Tzivia's story was linked to that of Rivka Cooper, of the Krakow ghetto, the story of that Christmas Eve when the Tsiginaris Tavern, full of celebrating German officers, was blown up; of the heroic death of her young husband; of the unknown revolt in the death camp; of the tens of thousands of proud, nameless fighters; of Vilna being extinguished; of the forests and the bunkers; of Bialystok and Kovno. The picture painted for the court was of a war waged by the most wretched rebels the world has ever known.

"When the Jews of Warsaw were murdered there was not a ray of light in the world. El-Alamein and Stalingrad came only when Warsaw's Jews were no more," Antek cried.

Kovner, having seen the long, empty street filled with the

remaining belongings of the dead, spoke of the four walls that separated the ghetto from salvation: the hate-filled Lithuanian rabble, the Lithuanian police, the German S.S. and the wall of stone.

This rebel poet did not know that one day another wall would stand between the Jews and their mortal enemies: their brethren who remained would refuse to recognize that they had been doomed. Broken, choked up with tears, he told the story of the handing over of Yitzhak Wittenberg, the commandant, to the Gestapo. After it had been decreed that failure to do so would lead to the ghetto's liquidation, thousands of Jews, brandishing hatchets and live firearms, had besieged the ghetto command and, weeping and screaming, demanded that he be turned over so that they might be spared. They believed they would.

Yitzhak tried to commit suicide. Then he turned himself in. Kovner said, "We ourselves, his comrades in the command, did not want to know where he was. The alternative was to open fire against the future victims, our own people. In the face of what was happening, everything we had built up and planned over the years was collapsing, because things happened this way and because the desire for another hour of life could bring the victims to the point of such madness. How human it was, and yet how dreadful."

There was a connection here to what Tzivia Lubetkin had said about the joy, the terrible happiness of her comrades at the sight of the Germans being gunned down by the last of the fighters.

There was a connection, too, to the powerful words of Antek and other fighters who tried, each in his own way, to answer the question, "Why didn't you resist?" Kovner, in his testimony yesterday, was trying to get at the root of it. "A fighting organization can be created by the order of a national authority or by a grassroots movement. There was no authority that could mobilize the European Jews, nor could there be. Organizing at the grass roots, under conditions of terror, paralysis, and isolation, when *we* were in the glass booth, could be done only by the strongest-willed individuals, and such are not to be found among the downtrodden and despairing."

We have not mentioned the candles that were lit in Auschwitz; the "diary of Justina"; the Aryan-looking girls, living and dead, who ran despatches and whose story remains untold; the woman who strapped explosives to her body, walked dozens of miles to blow up a German train, and then returned to the ghetto.

Nor have we mentioned Dr. Berman's story about Janusz Korczak marching with his young charges to their death, that glorious tale that serves as a beacon of courage and compassion. And we have not yet said anything about the Zionist youth movements that instigated the revolts, a burning bridge between the Land of Israel and the dying multitudes of the House of Israel—a story that is only beginning to be touched upon now in front of the glass booth.

Servatius had no questions.

But it had not yet been determined what, at a trial for genocide, was to be considered "relevant."

May 5, 1961

MARTA'S SABBATH DRESS

What was it that brought the Viennese Jew Leona Neumann to Riga? Who gave her a place to live "in the abandoned homes of the Latvian Jews, of blessed memory"?

Who brought her to the disinfection squad, where one of the fathers recognized his daughter's frock, her coat of many colors?

Who took her from Riga to Stutthof, where, she recalled, they doused the Jews with water, so that they turned into pillars of ice? (It was winter, a northern European winter.)

Who took her by boat to the eastern sea, the Baltic, giving her half a pound of bread for the nine-day voyage, while on the mast there flew the yellow flag signifying contagion?

How is it that she did not die in Riga? How is it that she did not die en route?

How did she finally end her odyssey in Kiel?

From Kiel, the trial jumped to Kolomiya, Ukraine, to Shmuel Horwitz, the superb tailor who had made suits for the S.S. and Gestapo officers.

He was one of the last thirty survivors, out of twenty thousand Jews in the town. As his story began to take on a legendary quality, Halevi interrupted. "Which members of your family survived?" (One had the strange impression that this tailor had purchased his life from the devil.) And lest there be any mistake, Horwitz answered, "No one did."

"Now sit down and speak quietly, if you can," the presiding judge advised Rivka Joselewska.

Yes, it was Joselewska. There was a murmur in the hall when she appeared. So she had made it after all. Her doctors thought she was up to testifying.

But I am getting ahead of myself.

Obviously, the reports of the Einsatzgruppen were sent routinely to Berlin, to Section IV-B4.

It was 1941–42.

We studied the map: Vitebsk, Smolensk, Mogilev, Shklov, Kherson, Nikolayev, Minsk, Kiev, Kamenetz-Podolsk, Dniepropetrovsk, Chernigov, Dubno, Rovno, Odessa.

Like picking a number out of a hat. I drew by chance a piece of paper, all folded up, on which was written September 29, 1941, the day the 30,000 Jews of Kiev lost their lives. On October 13 of that year the same happened in Dniepropetrovsk.

The total for 1941: 400,000.

But 1942 was not such a bad year either. Between September 1 and December 1 of that year, the harvest totaled 363,211.

And this was conveyed to the Fuehrer by means of a special typewriter. For his information.

The rapid pace of the killing drove one German crazy, the one responsible for production, and he declared it "utter swinishness that should be reported to the Fuehrer at once."

Joselewska was called to tell the story of a woman who had been one of these statistics.

She had had a heart attack, but here she was, before our very eyes.

Had it not been for her, I would not know what happened one Sabbath in a town called Povost-Zagordski, near Pinsk, where she was born and where her father had been a respected leather merchant. I would not know that she had two sisters, Haya and Feige, and a brother named Moshe, that she had married in 1934 or that by that marriage she had had a daughter named Marta.

Had it not been for Rivka Joselewska, I would not know what happened on the Sabbath of the New Moon of Elul in 1942, when the Jews were ordered to assemble, leaving all their possessions behind, taking neither food nor drink but only their children.

She ran after the truck filled with friends and neighbors, with Marta in her arms, until at last they got to the spot. "There was a kind of hill there, a raised area, at the base of which was a pit. They lined us up on the hill, and four men, four angels of death, shot people one by one."

"What unit did they belong to?"

They were from the S.S.

At this point the witness recalled that, before they left the ghetto, her daughter had asked her, "Mama, why did you make me put on my Sabbath clothes? They're taking us to be shot!" And when they reached the pit, little Marta, that clever child who had foreseen everything, said, "Why are we just standing here? Let's run away!"

But they could not run away.

The paterfamilias, her father, a proud man, refused to strip. His clothes were torn off him. He was the first to be shot. Then the mother. Then the grandmother. Then Feige and Haya, who wanted so much to live and, stripped naked, pleaded for her life.

People started to get up and leave. The faces of those who remained became indistinguishable.

"Who should we shoot first, you or your daughter?" the German asked.

Here, I stopped taking notes. I later learned from the transcript that her turn had come after her daughter's, that she had survived and, some time later, crawled out. "People were dragging me down, biting and scratching and pulling, while I made my way up."

The Germans were gone.

Suffering from a head wound, she wandered in the fields. Shepherds passing by with their flocks thought she was mad and threw stones at her. Then she went back to the mass grave, where she lay for three days and three nights.

"I called out to my parents, 'Why have I been left alive? What did I do to deserve this? What should I do now? I have no one.'"

"And now you are married and have two children?"

"Yes," the witness answered.

"Thank you, Mrs. Joselewska."

Rivka Joselewska was no figment of my imagination. When we filed out of the courtroom into the daylight, the sky was overcast and the wind was blowing. A young lawyer said to me, "It's crazy to call such witnesses. Hausner's going to turn us all to stone. He doesn't realize he mustn't do this."

In the afternoon, we left Povost-Zagordski and went on to Paris, to France and the West. We left Marta and turned to Abetz and Dannecker, to other regions of the IV-B4 empire, to the documents, the hundreds and hundreds of documents.

The man in the glass booth, who had listened impassively to Joselewska, began now to sway back and forth: the documents were coming!

While I was down in the press room writing these things out, I saw Gavriel Bach on the television monitor, presenting this dreadful ammunition before the court: documents and more documents!

Joselewska has left. She went to Ramat-Gan to be with her dear departed Marta's stepbrothers.

"Now do you understand the verse, 'By your blood shall you live'?"[9] a friend asks me, adding, "We're all pigs, don't you think?"

"Why?"

"Clinging to life the way we do."

May 9, 1961

9. Ezekiel 16:6.

DOCUMENTS, AMSTERDAM, COPENHAGEN

Hour after hour, the prosecution went on presenting documents.

"What's happening upstairs?" a reporter friend asked me.

"Documents!"

"Let's go have a drink," he said.

But the documents continued to pile up. There were nearly six hundred so far.

What do those documents do at night, in the cartons, in the cabinets, within the four walls?

The documents do not remain silent. If you listen, you can hear them shouting hoarsely.

He was afraid of them.

They were all different, but each had an amazing power of recall. Time had not altered them. Many were cited only by their names and numbers. But not one of them was willing to keep silent.

Before your eyes, the papers became burning cities, people cast on heaps with their limbs dangling, trains rushing eastward, children ascending to heaven.

This is a trial of documents. The documents have a strange, incomprehensible power. Every one of them speaks with ten thousand voices.

Who can keep track of all these documents?

What's this? Exhibit number T/519. "On the night of the 3rd and 4th of September 1943," I read, "a major operation will get underway for the first time, under orders from Reich Security headquarters, to round up the Belgian Jews and take them to employment in the east."

It didn't take much imagination to visualize that night.

Exhibit number T/520.

I read: "In Breendonck, 450 were shot dead, and 12 were hanged. During the executions, those still alive were made to sing, 'We'll never forget Breendonck, the Jews' paradise.'

"One hundred forty-five people were packed into a steel boxcar sent from Antwerp to Malines," exhibit T/520 continued. "When it arrived, a dreadful heap of bodies spilled out of the car." Here, an exact eyewitness description of the sight was supplied. "Ninety of the passengers did not reach Malines alive."

Exhibit T/520 went on to the subject of Maidanek and then Auschwitz. Exhibit T/520 was full of figures.

These documents. We weren't familiar with most of them. At this rate, three thousand would accumulate by the end of the trial. The three judges would have to read them, every last one, and then pass reasoned judgment on the man who had something in common with these papers and pictures. The common denominator had a name: the life and death of the European Jewry.

Dr. Josef Melkman took the witness stand. In 1953, I happened to be in Amsterdam giving a lecture at a Jewish youth seminar, and I stayed in his home. Little did I know that eight years later he would be standing here telling his own story.

There in the west, near the dikes and the land stolen from sea, on the very edge of Europe, a new story began that fit in with the others that had been told.

Ah yes, people said, we forgot about Holland.

The places of the foreign reporters had been taken by our own people. The hall was full. We had not yet gotten to Greece or Slovakia or Hungary or the camps.

Holland.

He told his tale wearily. I remember in particular what he said about the strike.

Question: "Dr. Melkman, when the 400 Jews were arrested in February 1941, what was the reaction of the Dutch population?"

Answer: "In Amsterdam, a general strike was declared. It began with the streetcars and spread to the factories. Then it spread to other cities. But the strikes were suppressed."

At gunpoint, the Dutch watched this ancient, noble Jewish community being wiped out, like a limb being torn from the living body of their country.

Jewish Amsterdam was taken to Bergen-Belsen, Mauthausen, Theresienstadt, Sobibor and Auschwitz.

Out of 140,000, 104,000 never returned to the Netherlands, to the old synagogues and to the fields of flowers.

What can I add to his story? The words hunger, cold, beatings, hangings, death, transports, plunder, and fear recurred again and again, to the point where I no longer grasped their meaning. Why had the crisis come on this particular day, when the death of the Dutch Jews was being related?

In my notebook I wrote: "The members of this glorious community, which, more than any other in Europe, had known extended periods of tranquility and prosperity, were to meet up with *eaters of human flesh* in Bergen-Belsen."

"Mr. Weiss, who now lives in Jerusalem, was the senior official of the community, and as such he felt obliged to record all the details of life in the camp. He mentions fourteen instances of cannibalism there," Melkman said.

This afternoon, something strange happened in the court. Werner David Melchior, a tall, blond, blue-eyed man who had lived in Denmark and whose father had been the acting chief rabbi there at the time of the German conquest, took the witness stand.

A representative of Danish Jewry.

Here, as I have said, something peculiar happened. Hours later, as I look back on his testimony, it seems to me I must have been dreaming. It was as if the events Melchior was talking about had taken place on another planet, and this man had come from there to tell us of the strange people and strange goings-on there. He took his listeners back in time, to a distant, lost world where, by some miracle, people still acted as they do in fairy tales.

Such an odd people. He told his story, but he seemed to be making it up. People listened and smiled. I could have gone on listening to him all night. It was like artificial respiration.

"The Torah scrolls from the synagogue were hidden safely in the cellar of a church," he said.

At the entrance of the university, two students had approached him. He did not really know them and merely said hello, but they replied, "If you need us, here is where to find us. We will help you."

"The ministers and bishops helped us," he said.

"Working people and housewives warned us," he said.

He talked about the "Little Dunkirk" operation, in which thousands of Danes hid Jews, then took them to the coast.

"The Danish police surrounded the embarkation area, protecting us," he said. "Many of us were brought there by police ambulances."

"That night two fishermen took us, me and two other Jews, to Sweden."

"How did you know the fishermen?"

"A relative of ours, a businessman, had a secretary who was engaged to be married to one of them," he said.

He went on with his fabrication: "The courts defended us against slander and abuse," he said. "The entire population took part in the rescue effort. Never had the Danish people been so united in support of the underground as they were during those nights of rescue work," he said, citing a Danish historian who had written about the period of the occupation.

"King Christian did everything he could to protect the Jews. Out of a population of 7500, only 472 were caught and sent to Theresienstadt, and there, too, Denmark continued to extend its protection to them, and they survived."

As he told his story I felt myself returning to a more human world, where people met in peaceful streets, smiled and shook hands—from a night filled with monsters that seemed as though it would never end.

One woman was weeping. "Why are you crying now?"

"I cry whenever someone is kind to me," she said.

May 11, 1961

"THE MARCH TO THE STAR"[10]

> Quite often, love fades to a gloomy end. Sometimes it is killed, and then its death is one of blood and mutilation. Such was the love of Othello, assailed by the terrible blows of jealousy. Ah, blind scorn: to blame Desdemona! The heart clenches in revulsion.
>
> Who is to be blamed for what happened to Thomas, for murdering his love and his life, for sending him to an early death with a broken heart? . . . It bring tears to my eyes—not of pity but of rage.
>
> Julien Vercors, La Marche à l'Étoile

I HAVE OPENED Vercors's book a second time.

I wanted to reread it after hearing Dr. Georges Wellers's testimony about Drancy and Auschwitz.

Vercors weeps as he relates the tale of the "murdered love" and death of Thomas Muritz, the novel's hero.

I, in turn, wanted to weep when I heard Wellers speak about the children of Drancy.

Drancy figures in the book as a last stop. Ernie Levi, in The *Last of the Just*, is also taken there, and it is there that he finds Golda. They and the children then go on together to meet their end in Auschwitz. The story told by the physician Wellers merged with those of Vercors and Schwarz-Bart. As Wellers spoke, the eyes of his listeners were red from weeping over the children of Drancy.

(A friend who is a colonel in the Israel Defense Forces, who has seen his share of fear, hardship, and bloodshed, once heard a little boy crying. The apartment was dark. The parents had gone out without leaving a babysitter. Through the shutters, he tried to comfort

10. From the French *Etoile*, suggesting also the Place d'Etoile.— Trans.

the lad, but he only cried more loudly. Breaking down the door, he switched on the light and saw the boy, in the next room, standing on his bed, weeping his last, exhausted tears. He took the two-and-a-half-year-old in his arms and hugged him. Then he sang sweetly to him until, at last, after midnight, the parents returned home.)

But I really wanted to begin with Thomas Muritz, Vercors's hero. As an old man, he is turned over to the Germans by the Vichy police. When Wellers spoke of Drancy, I thought of him.

I do not think Thomas Muritz is typical of the French Jews. In his life he was not a Jew, because he wanted to be a Frenchman—his life's dream—and a Frenchman he was.

His Uncle Bela (whose family lives in Pressburg) recalls laughingly how little Thomas, who devoured Dumas, Balzac, and Eugène Sue, once asked him, "Uncle Bela, I'm a little bit French, am I not?"

Little Thomas knows that one day he will get to France. The death of his cousin Latzi hastens the day.

Latzi is a cadet in a Budapest military academy. His father holds a high position and is well respected. Insulted by a friend, Latzi demands an apology. The friend spits at his feet. Latzi is furious and throws down a glove, challenging him to a duel. The other doesn't bother to pick it up. Latzi goes looking for seconds, but no one is willing to oblige. He feels that people are laughing at him. At last, another friend decides to reveal to him a secret that his father, out of foolish pride, has kept from him—that his mother is a Jew.

"This man, who despised Jews even more than the worst stray dogs, had a Jewish mother! The next morning, they found his body hanging in his room."

Thomas packs his bags and heads for France, for Paris.

"From the outset," Vercors writes, "he was reconciled to the dust of the highways, the mountain fog, the awful weariness of the long days of travel, the rain, the wind, the sun, the frigid nights, the sweat and the thirst." His goal, after all, is to reach France.

"Love," Vercors says, "does not make me smile. Even less the love of a child. Childhood is a terribly serious thing."

At last, his wearisome trek brings the young pilgrim to the French border. He crosses the frontier at Delle. It is St. Jean's Day. He reaches an inn. Enchanted by the place, he squanders all his money on a fine meal, then falls asleep in a bed laid with clean, white sheets. He is in *France*.

Before Thomas goes on his way, the innkeeper tells him, "You are one of us." And he feels excitement rising within him and filling his eyes with tears.

That same day, he gets to Paris and heads straight for a bridge he once saw in a dream, the Pont des Arts. "He stood there gazing at the last rays of the setting sun as they turned red over Passy and bathed the towers of Notre Dame in gold."

Thomas Muritz belongs to France, and he settles there. In his passionate love for French literature, he founds the Muritz publishing house.

Eventually, he binds himself inextricably to France by marrying a Frenchwoman. She comes from a provincial town, "a child of the ancient soil of France. She was beautiful, modest, innocent, sentimental, refined. Her name was Chambord."

Vercors skips to the second part of the story. On its opening page, I read the dedication:

"To André, who died for France. To his brother Georges, who was badly wounded. To Max, who died for France. To Lucien, who died for France. . . . To all those who are no longer with us, my brothers, my old friends."

Yes, Thomas Muritz's eldest son André fell fighting for France in World War I.

The years pass. Vercors comes to the saddest part of the story. World War II. France is conquered. A time of loneliness and exile. When he returns to Paris, whom should he meet but the elderly Thomas, wearing the yellow star on his coat. Vercors is crushed. Thomas tries to console him, energetically defending the honor of his beloved France. The love of his life.

Thomas's mother is a Jew. All the men in his family are Protestants.

The French turn him in to the Germans (Laval, Vichy, the police). "Joseph was sold by his brothers." "With a trembling hand, this country handed over its adopted son."

"I am choked up with pain," the author says. It is here that he mourns his beloved Thomas Muritz and his "murdered love," saying, among other things, "God, why didn't You blind him completely? Why, in his last split second, did You want him to see the worst side of us all, all men, all nations?"

I leave Vercors now and return to the courtroom in Jerusalem.

In Drancy, too, I found Thomases. Georges Wellers, the Jewish physician, told us about them as well as about the children.

The Western Jews, the poor Western Jews.

There, in Drancy, they collected all those who were truly *French*. Aside from the authentic Jews, who fooled no one and were not fooled themselves, there were those who were brought back to this lonely people only on the threshold of death, after an exhausting journey that had taken generations, a long journey with a single aim in mind: to be erased and forgotten, to become part of the dense forests, the rich soil, the smoke-filled cities, the cathedrals, the theaters, the Seine, the Loire—the powerful and delightful beauty of France.

Alongside the open, utterly exposed Jews, who upheld their traditions with pride, persisting in their beliefs and their daily prayers, or who at least did not deny these traditions, you would find those who came back abruptly, running under the whip and looking frantically about, as if trying to awaken from a bad dream, all those Thomases, of blessed memory, whose blood and whose children's blood had been spilled in war after war on the soil of their adopted homeland, until, at last, they were torn away from it in order to be reunited, packed together, with all those other Jews—all of them.

Seeing the names of Dutch, Belgian, and French cities on the map of calamity that was tacked up on the courtroom wall, I felt as though I were dreaming.

Wellers brought us back to Drancy. His story was connected with the confession of Rivka Joselewska, from Povost-Zagordski. The voice of the wounded Marta now rose to join the piled-up cries of the children of Drancy, those tortured Pierres and Annettes, while Rivka's father stood next to the murdered René Blum, the tall, sensitive man who had stooped to pat the heads of these doomed angels until his heart broke. Here were Ernie Levi and Golda and the aged Thomas Muritz, the hero of the story we have just told. Here was the elite of French Jewry, those who had come from Spain at the time of Ferdinand and Isabella as well as those who had come from the East and, at the end of their journey of hoped-for salvation, kissed the soil of France, only to be transported in freight cars back East, where they would meet up, briefly, with the Jews of Salonica, Budapest, and Warsaw, and the fire would forge them into a single people, a chosen people.

Now Wellers would be returning to the faculty of medicine in Paris, the city that belonged to him, still alive, and to Thomas Muritz, long dead.

Wellers would leave behind, in front of the glass booth in Beit Ha'am, the story of the children of Drancy.

I believe those children will be with humanity forever, accompanying it on its journey like a shining planet circling a star. I believe humanity can never free itself of their tortured souls, and even when we do not think of them, we shall have to live with the knowledge of what was done to them.

May 12, 1961

THE NARROWING BOOTH

This time, the witness stand was occupied not by one of the victims, but by one of the victors.

This time, the witness did not tell us about the liquidation that took place on such and such a day, in such and such a place.

This time, the stand was taken by a man who had marched with the American army through the smoking ruins of Germany, one of those whom the victors had appointed to mete out judgment and punishment.

It had not been easy to get him to the stand.

Dr. Servatius had fought a desperate battle to prevent him from appearing. The defense attorney knew how dangerous, how "relevant," this man was, how harmful he could be to his client.

The battle between the two attorneys had gone on for some time. After a recess, the presiding judge announced, "We shall permit testimony about things the witness learned from persons now deceased, insofar as they concern the matter of this trial. The same will apply to evidence related to disobeying orders from higher up." (This point will be significant later on.) "As for things the witness learned from persons now alive, we shall consider each case individually, according to the circumstances."

"Judge Musmanno!" the bailiff called out.

A thin, silver-haired man in his sixties, wearing a dark suit, took the stand.

He put his hand on the Bible and took the oath.

It was Judge Michael A. Musmanno, a member of the Pennsylvania Supreme Court, a retired rear admiral and formerly one of the judges of the international military tribunal at Nuremberg. He had tried those responsible for running the concentration camps and was later the presiding judge in the case of the Einsatzgruppen criminals.

But this was not all he had done, and here we came to an interesting point. The judge, when he was a commander in the United States Navy, had been ordered to investigate the fate of Adolf Hitler.

"What did you do in this regard?"

"I visited prisoner-of-war camps, displaced-person camps, and various military bases, and I sought out those who had been close to him."

"Who were they?"

"Admirals, generals, adjutants, secretaries, bodyguards, his barber, his cook, his wine steward."

Here we came to our proper business.

Had these confidants of Hitler spoken about Eichmann or his activities?

He mentioned names: Goering, Ribbentrop, Frank, Kaltenbrunner, Schellenberg. Every one of them had described the same group as having been responsible for the destruction of the Jews: Hitler, Bormann, Himmler, Heydrich, and Eichmann.

We knew very well that we were dealing with a gang of criminals every one of whom had been hanged, a bunch of liars who would sell each other out when faced with death or try to drag those close to them into the grave with them.

But each of them had referred to the man sitting in the glass booth as one of the five main protagonists, although he had been inferior to the others in rank.

And when you put that testimony together with what Dieter Wisliceny and Rudolf Hoess had said about Eichmann as the killer of the Jews, you have to wonder about those journalists, both Israeli and foreign, who have decided that what we have before us is merely a "minor bureaucrat," "a colorless clerk," disciplined, precise, and efficient.

It would not be difficult for Dr. Servatius to prove that Goering, Ribbentrop, Frank, and Kaltenbrunner had been liars. Judge Musmanno did not deny it, nor did he doubt they had been guilty of the crimes for which they were hanged; but he was prepared to agree with them that Eichmann had been the main perpetrator of the annihilation.

The witness spoke with an uncommon severity, his words sharp and carefully chosen. This man, who had sent dozens of Einsatzgruppen commanders to the gallows, was still filled with hatred for them.

He was dredging up ghosts from another time. He had stood facing those he interrogated, on the grave of a defeated Germany, just before they were led to the gallows. It was a time of reckoning and vengeance.

I did not know what importance the Jerusalem court attached to this testimony, which was hearsay repeated long after the fact.

Presumably, it provided information on two important points: (1) Eichmann's status, and (2) the problem of "only carrying out orders."

It was clear as day: the learned defense attorney would try to prove (a) that his client had been a small cog in the machine, and (b) that he could not refuse to carry out the orders given him.

Musmanno's sharp, vigorous testimony further delineated the emerging portrait of the man. He had not been a minor figure but a specialist who became a mighty ruler with the fate of millions of human beings in his hands.

"The staff of the Einsatzgruppen was mostly appointed by Himmler according to Eichmann's recommendations." Eichmann's friends commanded all these units, which Musmanno called "slaughterhouses on wheels."

And it was in connection with these units that we came to the most significant point in the American judge's testimony, the problem of orders.

"I was carrying out orders." "What else could I do?" Etc.

We came to the Schultz document, Exhibit T/686. Schultz asks Heydrich to release him from his responsibilities in the Einsatzgruppen. "For service-related reasons," he replies, "I hereby release you from your command and transfer you to another assignment."

Musmanno added: "Anyone who did not wish to kill Jews did not have to do so." If one could prove he was not up to killing in cold blood, he was excused, because he would only get in the way of those who were willing and able to do so. "The Nazi leaders were efficient" and thus eager to get rid of those who were "soft."

Schulz, Nosske, others.

But Eichmann, it turned out, did not ask to be excused from his job. Apparently those were the best years of his life. He even got to that 102-year-old Italian Jewish woman and that paralytic old man in his wheelchair. He pursued his mission with a frenzy. How had Rudolf Hoess put it? "He was indefatigable."

The glass booth got narrower by the day. The man in it grew larger before our very eyes. He was approaching his true dimensions.

And watching his power grow, we experienced a choking disgust, the feeling that "his fight for his life was getting uglier and uglier," as one friend put it to me.

May 16, 1961

Heinrich-Karl-Ernst Grueber

An Eichmann, a Grueber, and Germany somewhere in between—here in Jerusalem, yesterday, before our very eyes.

Had this man taken the witness stand to exemplify the difference between good and evil, which sometimes choose people as their symbols?

And Germany in between? Apparently not. Germany had been closer to the pole of Eichmann. But who could say, in numerical terms?

Alongside the murderers with their various ranks and responsibilities, alongside those who hated and those who kept quiet, who were indifferent or who rejoiced at the calamity of others, were those rare individuals, those lonely candles in the darkness, ambassadors of kindness and compassion: the Gruebers. They must never be forgotten.

Who are you? Heinrich-Karl-Ernst Grueber.

On the stand we saw a big man with wrinkled features, his smooth, gray hair carefully combed back, wearing a black suit.

"You are now serving as Protestant bishop of Berlin, are you not?"

"Yes, since 1945. Before the war, in 1939, I was a minister in Karlsdorf, an eastern suburb of Berlin."

Here began the unique story of a noble, courageous soul, a German, who had taken the side of the persecuted and abused, doing his best to help them. He had paid a heavy price for being different, for refusing to submit to the dark, insane Eichmannism of that time, when mendacity, callousness, and violent hatred held sway.

He was a lonely man. Heartbreakingly lonely. Evidently he, his family, and his assistants in all the branches of the organization he established throughout the Third Reich were never more numerous than the pages of the New Testament. Or perhaps they were a few thousand in all.

A lonely man, an exception, the righteous man in Sodom.

We knew he had helped the Jews because he was their friend, because he respected them. We know he was a human being. That noun, unmodified, was now the highest superlative.

As early as 1938 or 1939, he knew that "the Jews had been turned into second-class citizens." He went to see Rolf Guenther with three Jews. There was only one free chair in the room. "If they have to stand, I shall do so as well," he said.

He had gone to see people, tried everything, used his connections to help and to warn. He had taken care of "both communal and individual matters," as he put it.

He brought up the holiday of Passover.

"Do you have any knowledge of the Jewish holy days and festivals? If so, where from?"

He knew from his theological studies. Later, he would be able to recognize the Jewish holidays by the troubles with which they coincided.

"We trembled with our Jewish friends, and we asked ourselves, 'What is going to happen next?'"

He had met with Eichmann.

"How were you treated by Adolf Eichmann?"

"Well, the impression he gave me—and I hope the defendant will not take this amiss, because I have not come here full of hatred or vengefulness—but I must say he impressed us"—how moving was his use here of the first person plural—"as a block of ice, or of marble."

Grueber had not known at the time how powerful that block of marble was. He only remembered that it never said yes. It was always either "no" or "we'll let you know."

We'll let you know what we decide to do with them, with those you have chosen to help.

Eventually, Grueber was to add two new expressions to the vocabulary of the trial: "the bicycle rider, whose head was bowed to those above but who ran over those below" and "the mercenary, who forgot his conscience as soon as he put on his uniform."

One makes choices. This man had chosen his fate. This fact shocked us, for we knew he had chosen to help those who had been robbed of all possibility of choosing. He chose, and this earned him happiness and peace of mind, an exalted sense of integrity, even though he also endured much suffering. "But there is no suffering greater than that of one who looks upon the distress of others," Grueber said.

"I had confidants all over Germany who would keep me informed of what was going on." He knew what was going to happen to the Jews of Stettin in February 1940, and he went to plead for them. "I went to all the offices, all that were open to me." To a general in Stettin he said, "If I were a general, sir, not a single boxcar laden with Jews would ever leave for Poland."

But the generals were lacking in "civic courage."

He was summoned to Gestapo headquarters in the Alexanderplatz, where the higher-ups warned him that if he did not put a stop to his activities they would do so for him.

The path he chose eventually landed him in Sachsenhausen.

He tried to join the deported Jews of Alsace-Lorraine and on December 19, 1940, he got to Sachsenhausen. It was inevitable.

In October 1941, he was transferred to Dachau, where he found some seven hundred other clergymen interned. Here the witness painted a picture of fear and torture. In this hall more terrible things had been heard, but the thought that this man had chosen his fate stuck in our minds.

"While you were in the camp at Dachau, did you hear about Maidanek or Auschwitz?"

"At Dachau we were sent the clothing of those who had been gassed. Something happened that affected me particularly deeply. It was when children's shoes arrived for the first time," the man said, his voice breaking, his glasses shining, his face hinting that he might break down at any moment.

But he was a strong man who had been through hell. After a heart attack, he had lain as if dead and, after roll call, was thrown onto a pile of corpses. "My friends saw that I was still alive and took me secretly to the infirmary." He persuaded the doctor-murderer in charge, a Dr. Rascher, the grandson of a minister, to spare him by telling him that "his late grandfather was observing his grandson's behavior from beyond the grave, and it allowed him no rest."

But it was June 1943. He attributed his release to his courageous wife as well and to the fear that had begun to seize Himmler, which led him to make a gesture to placate the United States.

He returned to Berlin. The path of suffering and the dedication of this man, who had chosen to be with the persecuted, continued. Neither Sachsenhausen nor Dachau had "reformed" him. He returned physically broken—"I could not even climb stairs unaided"—but undefeated in spirit.

Servatius was obliged to ask some questions. This witness was more than relevant. His very existence and the very choice he had made were a living accusation against the defendant.

Here, an abyss opened before us.

Servatius wanted to prove that, on the whole, the church had identified with the regime and that, as a result, his client, as a member of the regime, had been faithful both to the church and to the German people. Grueber confirmed that many churchmen had betrayed their calling and collaborated enthusiastically, but he spoke of those who resisted.

The excerpts read by the defense attorney from official Christian periodicals sent a shudder through the hall. Meant to be ammunition against this noble individual and in defense of the man in the booth, they were a frightening mixture of crude antisemitism and smug Christian hypocrisy. Now the attorney for the defense was ready to raise his voice. "Was Eichmann obliged to think his actions wrong when such things were being published? This was after the rise of the Nazis to power, remember, and torch-lit processions were shouting 'Germany, awake!' and 'Jew, die!' It followed that there was clear Christian endorsement of the actions of the defendant, who saw the death of the Jews as an inseparable part of the awakening."

But Grueber answered softly, "It was not I who edited those articles. I was then a discharged school principal, unemployed for many months."

What could he say to such a proposition, which tried to exculpate Eichmann by showing that representatives of the religion of love had betrayed their own faith?

What could he say, other than to speak of his lonely decision to swim against the tide? Grueber was undaunted, and now he, too, raised his voice. Many were blinded and went astray, he said, but it was a long way from the ecstatic roar of "Heil Hitler!" to what happened afterward.

Servatius held his ground. He would have to base his client's defense on the church, the intelligentsia, the academy, the medical establishment, and so on.

Eichmann sat in his booth like a little boy whose big, strong father had taken up the cudgels for him. He did not rise to his feet. He did not pound the table. This sort of defense, which made him out to be a nobody, a poor little man who had made a mistake, was easier for him.

Here the noble Dr. Grueber, abused and persecuted, had become the great accuser, a fully human person who, from the heights of his life and suffering, could look down with contempt on Hitler, his party, his murderous henchmen, his Eichmanns, and the faithless "German Christian" church, while the man who, with a single phone call, had been able to seal the fate of untold multitudes, sat silently, approving his defense counsel's clever ploy.

I don't know if Servatius's reasoning will save his client from the gallows, but his defense was a terrifying indictment of the entire German people.

What was going on in that hall?

May 17, 1961

AFTER A MONTH

This week, we marked thirty days since the Eichmann Trial had begun. I shall not try to sum up what happened during that time but only make a few comments.

Let us begin with the defendant. I do not know if he has changed. People who read faces say he has become weaker, older, almost ghostlike. I myself see no outward sign of change. Entering the booth this week, he appeared to me to be exactly the same man who had entered it on the first day of the trial.

An English journalist told me he had heard from the editor of one of the Israeli newspapers that Eichmann had lost twenty-five pounds and that his heartbeat had become irregular.

That may be true, but I would prefer to think otherwise. I would like to go on seeing him as an unsolved riddle, as opaque as always. It seems unlikely that his heart is breaking with remorse. Fear of death, perhaps? That would be even uglier.

I went and asked one of the policemen if there was any truth to it. He did not want to say any more than that "he's strong as an ox."

Is he still getting letters from his wife? Until recently, I know, he did get letters from his family. He was given only photocopies of them. A recurrent line in them was, "We are praying for you daily."

In all likelihood, God hears all prayers. Heaven is a very big place.

I don't see Dieter Wechtenbruch, Servatius's deputy. There has been a rumor that the young man couldn't take it. A Swedish visitor, who at the start of the trial was staying at the Geiger Guest House, where the defense, too, was lodged, told me that after Hausner's opening speech the man had said, "I can never again believe anything Germans of that generation say. I now know the truth."

"How is that secretary?" a cabbie driving me to Beit Ha'am asked. "I don't know," I answered. "I only saw her once, on the first day, and that was the last time she appeared in the courtroom."

"A nice girl," he said. "One evening they came to the downstairs room at Suramello's club. I danced with her. It was nice."

That had been a while ago, at the Journalists' Ball, which was held on the evening of Independence Day. Many German reporters were there. They had come just to see what was going on, and they would introduce themselves by saying, "I am twenty-five," or "I was interned in a concentration camp during the war."

Later, they felt more comfortable and started to enjoy themselves.

Most of the foreign reporters have left. The press room is largely empty. They say the trial is no longer in the headlines in other countries.

The Germans have mostly stayed. An Israeli who has met with them tells me they are still being asked to send in full reports.

Other reporters have gone home or on to Laos or Evian. But press clippings that reach here from other parts of the world show that the trial is still making waves, even if it has been relegated to the inside pages.

The prosecutor's office receives letters every day, from all over Israel and all parts of the world, letters of congratulation and even poems. There is also a steady stream of hate letters, threats, and curses.

Someone wrote: "One man killed six million. Now six million want to kill one man. What's the difference?"

Other letters are written in the same pitch-black ink once used by the young painters to draw swastikas on the shop windows and the synagogues.

The places of the foreign reporters are, as I have said, being taken by Israelis. Looking around at the audience that fills the main floor and the balcony, one sees an exact cross section of the country's population.

At first we thought the spectators would be mostly people whose lives had been directly touched by the defendant. But lately you can see all of Israel there: all ages, all ethnic backgrounds, city people and farmers, people from outlying areas of the country. And many tourists.

In the rainbow of colors, you can also see khaki—army officers and soldiers—scattered throughout the crowd.

It has been a full month.

No, I am not trying to sum up the month. Not now. Things seem to be getting clearer, but I cannot help thinking there is much clarification yet to come.

When Dr. Karl Grueber came to the end of his testimony and added the Christian comment about "love that forgives and wrongs that are forgiven," many in the hall wept. Germans wept. Jews wept.

Had this not taken place in the context of the trial, where it was predictable and reasonable, it would have been dangerous, because what this extraordinary man was doing was leading his listeners to the very edge of catharsis and release.

If the existence of the world depended on words, a cosmic upheaval would undoubtedly have taken place at that moment.

The man's last words now seem strange and unreal to me. "Love that forgives and wrongs that are forgiven." Suddenly, in the face of the hard reality of what had happened, these tattered magic words seem like mere preaching. He spoke them out of the depths, but the facts had proven too strong for them.

I asked my friend what had happened today. I had not been in the courtroom. There were a lot of documents, he told me. Nothing particularly important. After a moment, he added: Oh yes, they talked about eight thousand Yugoslav Jews who couldn't be transferred to "the East," nor could they be sent by boat down the

Danube to Romania, and the man in the glass booth ordered that they be shot on the spot.

Yes, we do forget to mention small details. Like the German-Jewish dignitaries foraging for potato peels in the stinking garbage at Theresienstadt.

How long has it been since we first came into this hall? A month? But none of us will emerge from it unchanged.

May 19, 1961

YITZHAK NEHAMA OF SALONICA

"Yitzhak Nehama!" Shlomo, the bailiff, shouted.

A short man in a gray suit, about fifty, took the stand. He put his hand on the Bible and was sworn in.

Where had I seen him before? On Hashomer Street in Haifa? On Levinsky Street in Tel Aviv? Yitzhak Nehama, a native of Salonica.

After Berlin, Vienna, Krakow, Warsaw, Minsk, Vilna, Paris, Amsterdam, Brussels, Copenhagen, Oslo, Belgrade, and Bratislava, we had come to the respected Jewish community of Salonica.

Before Nehama came up, Bar-Or had been presenting document after document: Merten, Wisliceny, Brunner, Schellenberg, Eichmann. Decrees, confiscation, transports.

Now a living document, Yitzhak Nehama, was being put forward.

"When were you born?" Bar-Or asks.

"In 1910, in Salonica."

"When were you drafted into the Greek army?"

"During the war with Italy. In 1939 I was in Albania serving as a nurse in a military hospital, so I was lucky."

He was discharged in March 1941.

He walked for twenty-eight days. "What can I tell you? It was hard, hard."

He was no scholar or intellectual. His Hebrew was strongly accented and hard to follow.

When he finally got back to Salonica, he found the Germans there. A decree was issued that radios were to be confiscated. "They were so keen on confusing us," he said to the presiding judge. "You have no idea."

Then they took the pianos. And the telephones.

Finally, they got around to the Torah scrolls.

"Three trucks came, and they took scrolls that had been brought from Spain.[11] The rabbis cried, 'Let them take us, but not these scrolls!'"

Bar-Or wanted relevant details.

How were the Germans dressed?

"They were Gestapo," Nehama said. "I don't remember. Brown uniforms. Gestapo. Like soldiers."

He had had a stationery shop. We got to the confiscation of Jewish property. "I tell you, every day they made trouble for the Jews. They would take merchandise and not pay for it." He sighed and continued, "Our life was very hard."

Every so often the presiding judge would ask him to speak more clearly. The Salonicans tended to drop their final consonants.

What happened on July 11, 1942?

"I'll tell you," Nehama said. "There was a notice in the newspaper *Nea Evropi*[12] ordering all the Jews to assemble in Liberation Square. It was the Sabbath. As soon as we came, the Germans started beating us. Right away, without waiting."

"Are you familiar with that place?"

"Sure, sure, sure."

Bar-Or handed him another photograph and said, "That is a picture of someone who had a bucket of water poured over him."

Nehama: "That happened to many people. There was a lot of beating. People passed out. They told us not to move. The sun was so hot. The Germans wanted to have their fun. It was a game to them." Then he studied the photograph. Germans were cheering

11. The ancestors of the Salonica Jews had been expelled from Spain at the end of the fifteenth century.—Trans.

12. Greek-language occupation newspaper.—Trans.

from the windows roundabout. "That's a German soldier, and these are frightened Jews."

As if recalling distant events, he brought everything back to life with a few terse words, holding the photo in front of him. He studied it a little longer, working his jaw silently, then looked up as if he wanted to say something.

"I'm showing you a man being whipped," Bar-Or said.

Then Nehama said, "I'll tell you, here's someone who fell down, and the German soldiers are laughing at him."

That Sabbath, the Germans assembled nine thousand Jews and ordered them to work.

"They didn't let up," he said. "It lasted from 8:30 until 2:30. On the Sabbath. They made us take off our hats."

The prosecutor handed the witness one picture of the beating after another.

"The same thing. The same thing," he mumbled.

"Do you recognize this man?"

At this point something occurred that was to be repeated many times during the trial. The witness put on his glasses and, after a few seconds of silence, said softly, "That's me."

Lifting his right hand and raising his voice, he said again, "That's me!" He kept his hand in the air and, after a moment, added, "If you could only have seen how I looked by 2:30, what a beating I had taken." And then he asked a question which no one could answer: "I didn't owe them anything. Why did they do this to me?"

The question boomed out into the hall, twenty years late. "Why did they do this to me?"

"There were German girls clapping. I lost consciousness. What a beating they gave me. I lost consciousness."

For two weeks he lay in bed sick, only to be ready for the next stage.

Hard labor. He worked in the quarries. A hundred grams of bread. Sour cabbage soup. Mueller, the overseer. "May his name be blotted out, if he is still alive," Nehama cried. There was a laugh in the audience, and the presiding judge pounded the gavel, calling for silence.

The Jewish community ransomed the laborers with bribes.

He returned to Salonica, only to be confined to the ghetto.

Rabbi Gaon, of blessed memory, was shorn of his hair and beard. Children went up to the second floor and saw him. "The rabbi didn't want to go on living," said Nehama.

Bar-Or, a bit impatient, asked, "What happened in April 1943?"

"You want me to tell you what happened to me?" asked the man, pausing in his slow, halting presentation to consider the question.

"Yes, to you," Bar-Or said, interrupting his reverie.

He then told how his home had been struck by typhus, while the Jews were being rounded up at a certain spot in the Baron de Hirsch quarter. They came to get him too. A Greek officer whom he knew tried for a while to persuade the German officer to leave him alone. But at last he said, "Yitzhak, there's nothing I can do."

They changed all their remaining money into Polish zlotys.

The train was bound for Auschwitz. He spent thirty-eight days there. Then he was taken to work in a factory for "anti-aircraft tanks." He accepted the presiding judge's correction: "anti-aircraft cannons." From there he was sent to Mauthausen, then to a camp called Grozen I, near Vienna. When he said them, the names sounded so strange and remote. To this day, he had trouble pronouncing them.

On May 4, 1945, outside Vienna, he was liberated.

The questions led Nehama back to Auschwitz. "How many of you got off the train?" Seventy-eight, he answered. Afterward, he realized they had meant the boxcar, not the train, and he corrected himself: 2,700.

"People had brought a lot of things with them, umbrellas, for example. It rains in Poland." He saw people there in pajamas, speaking French. He asked them, "What's going on here?" And they answered, "You'll see."

"There was a great hue and cry there." He tried to describe what was happening. "Fathers looking for their sons . . ."

"How many of those people are still alive?" the prosecutor asked, interrupting him.

The witness came back from the railway platform at Auschwitz to answer the question. "There were 56,000 Jews in Salonica. One thousand nine hundred fifty returned."

"And of those you knew personally? Of the people on your train? Of the 2,700?

Nehama gestured as if asking for a moment to think. He looked down and counted on the fingers of one hand, mumbling under his breath, "Here four people are still alive, three in America. . . . From the whole train, there are about ten, from the whole train."

There was silence in the hall.

Judge Halevi: "What happened to your wife?"

Nehama: "I had a father and mother and four brothers and sisters and a wife. I am the only one left. The only one."

"Dr. Servatius?" The presiding judge turned to the counsel for the defense.

"I have no questions," he said. "I would merely like to point out that there are no S.S. men in the photographs that have been presented."

But hundreds of documents presented both before and after Nehama's testimony led directly to Eichmann, Merten, and Dieter Wisliceny.

Like a magnet, the defendant drew all these stories to himself.

May 23, 1961

THE GHOST OF THE PAST?

THE IMAGE OF Yitzhak Nehama took its place in our mental gallery of the witnesses.

We had not yet had a chance to ponder the fate of the Greek Jews when we were sent on to Romania.

On the stand now was Dr. Theodor Loewenstein, of the Romanian Department of Yad Vashem.[13]

Short, pudgy, gray, and balding, he was quite different from his predecessor.

I wrote down fragments of his testimony: "Transnistria was our Auschwitz. It was the grave of Romanian Jewry. . . . No one ever returned from across the Bug. . . . Half the Jews of Romania were exterminated during that period."

But enough for now about such witnesses. We shall come back to them when we resume memorializing the dead.

Next we were taken to Slovakia, by the only witness to be called in the afternoon session, Dr. Ernst Abeles.

In my notebook I recorded the following: In September 1941, the Nuremberg Laws were applied in Slovakia. Then the Jews were required to wear the yellow patch. From age four up.

We know now what the Jews then did not know, that the Nuremberg Laws led to Auschwitz.

This was in 1941. But in the course of his testimony, Dr. Abeles would eventually get to 1943. In that year, two people who had escaped from Auschwitz (how, by God?) came to the leaders of

13. Israel's state-sponsored Holocaust memorial authority.— Trans.

the community, the people dealing with welfare, external relations, and rescue, and told them the truth, and the latter passed the message on to Turkey, Switzerland, and England.

At that point, in 1943, we, or our representatives, also knew what they knew.

Geographically, Slovakia borders Hungary. Here in Beit Ha'am, one night separated the two countries, and I began to sense the presence of a ghost in the hall.

Although, as the prosecutor put it, it was the murderer who was on trial here and not the murdered—Abba Kovner said, "We shall not settle our accounts in his presence"—it seemed to me that, hidden in the shadows, another, parallel trial had been underway here the whole time.

You could feel it strongly during this afternoon's session, particularly toward the end, when the witness had finished testifying and was being cross-examined at length by Judges Yehuda Raveh and Binyamin Halevi.

"Did you meet with Wisliceny?" Bar-Or asked the witness.

"I had contact with him on several occasions," he replied.

Interwoven into this trial is a whole other matter that is maddeningly difficult to comprehend, hard as we all are trying.

The witness and his friends, the leaders of the Slovakian community, the party apparatchiks, the people from the Palestine Department (which arranged emigration) and so on—were all, it seems, still behaving as if normalcy had not yet broken down. As representatives of the community, they held meetings with the murderer. He had them in the palm of his hand, even though, at least at the outset, they thought they were conducting ordinary negotiations on their people's behalf.

Wisliceny was "stern but polite." He lectured them about his plans: "The Jews who are taken from the business sector will undergo a process of productivization to further the war effort, and this experience should prove useful to them when they reach their homeland."

This was a ruse, and in the course of the testimony we saw how it was ultimately exposed, revealing the certainty of destruction and death. But for the time being, there were meetings and discussions. We were shown a baffling pattern of relationships: while desperate rescue efforts were being made, the elders and leaders of the community were, at this stage, also unwittingly collaborating with the monster, held captive by it and unable to act otherwise.

By the end of 1941, under the slogan "a Jew-free Bratislava," 40 to 50 percent of the capital's Jews were transported to distant places, where they became the first victims.

Some months before this, Abeles had been summoned to a meeting with Eichmann and Wisliceny in the office of the leader of the Jewish community in Szebeczi.

The dignitary offered Eichmann a cigarette (a pathetic gesture from another world) and only earned a rebuke: "Put the cigarettes away!" They went over financial matters together. Eichmann was angry that Abeles had wasted so much money on welfare payments.

While this discussion was going on, the machine guns of the Einsatzgruppen were already closing in on the Jews of Russia and the Baltic countries.

But these Jews knew nothing about it.

It was a strange relationship. Abeles discussed welfare matters with Eichmann and his deputy, and later he brought up the status of the Palestine Department.

People who had been cast into an inferno went on playing their accustomed roles, conducting business with the murderers of their own people in hopes of being allowed to carry on, somehow, with their lives.

In March 1942, Wisliceny informed them that the "productivization efforts have failed, and it has been decided to deport the Jews by the end of this month."

The transports to the east began. In cattle and horse trains.

Wisliceny was present personally to see them off.

At that time, Abeles was trying to help teenage girls who had been confined to a prison camp, where they suffered from hunger and cold. On Wisliceny's orders, he was arrested. Beaten and afraid, he was made to live in a kennel.

His wife left no stone in Slovakia unturned in her efforts to free him. Finally, there was a bribe, and he was temporarily released.

The theme of bribery recurred throughout his testimony. Ultimately, a staggering sum was offered for all the Jews of Europe.

Upon his release, he was brought before Wisliceny. The latter stripped him of all his responsibilities but added, "I have let you go so that no one will think your arrest was merely a matter of personal vengeance. Go thank your wife."

What was this, the depredations of a sadist, the result of a bribe, or a desire to go on making use of the man?

The train was racing toward perdition. A "shadow government" of the Jews of Slovakia was set up, comprised of "Gisi Fleischmann, Rabbi Weissmandel, Frieder, and Kovacs, all of blessed memory, as well as Winterstein, Neumann, Steiner, and myself."

The similarity between the stories of Slovakia and Hungary was growing clearer. In both cases, it was a picture of heroism, of desperate pleas for help, of insistent approaches to the Catholic clergy.

Again, there was a bribe.

In this second instance, Rabbi Weissmandel, through an intermediary, offered Wisliceny $40,000 to stop the deportations.

Meanwhile, the full scale of the horrors was coming to light, and Weissmandel and Steiner eventually offered Wisliceny "two to three million dollars" to stop the deportations throughout Europe.

This was the third instance of bribery. The Europa Plan.

Wisliceny went to Berlin and returned. A deal was possible, except in the case of Poland, where the fate of the Jews was already sealed. He suggested monthly payments in goods (a preview of the Joel Brand affair?).

The offer made its way to Turkey, England, and Switzerland, but there was no reply, and its trail was lost.

And as for 1944? There was a revolt in Slovakia. Among the rebels in the mountains were Jews. The revolt was put down. The pace of extermination was speeded up, with the end in sight. The Jewish leadership had been disbanded.

The witness hid out in a cellar until January 1, 1945. He was betrayed, arrested.

Alois Brunner, one of Eichmann's deputies, was approached with a fourth bribe—millions of Swiss francs to spare the remaining Jews of Slovakia. "We are tired of Europe," Abeles told him. But it was him alone the hangman was willing to let out, to send to Switzerland, and only if he would act as an informer and hand over certain secrets.

I was losing my way in this dark, confusing story. The name of Kastner[14] kept coming up. The witness's own tale of suffering became intertwined with other half-forgotten stories that have long haunted us and will continue to do so. It was a mixture of heroism, helplessness, and hopeless illusions.

The much-admired Gisi Fleischmann, on her way to die in Auschwitz, waved goodbye to the Jewish children whom she had accompanied there.

The judges were unrelenting in their questioning. The story of the captive Jewish leaders, the lives and deaths of some, the miraculous survival of others, together with the story of Hungary, of the murdered Kastner, filled the hall with a suffocating tension.

"When the two young escapees came from Auschwitz, we learned the truth," the witness said. They had sent word to Turkey and England. We were apparently approaching a minefield.

"In the summer of 1943," asked the judge, "when you reported to Istanbul and Geneva and London about Auschwitz, was no report sent to the United States?"

"That I do not know," the witness replied.

But we did know that the story of Hungary was coming up.

May 24, 1961

14. Dr. Israel Kastner, a Hungarian Zionist leader who negotiated with the Nazis during the war and was later accused of collaboration; though exonerated in an Israeli court, he was murdered in revenge.—Trans.

EXHIBITS T/1091 to T/1099

In connection with the assassination of Heydrich, the prosecutor called our attention to page 3016 in the transcript of Avner Less's interrogation of the defendant.

Less: "What happened to the children from Poland, Czechoslovakia, and the other countries who had been taken from their parents, or whose parents had been killed, and who were termed 'fit for re-germanization'?"

Eichmann: "That I do not know, sir. I have no knowledge of that at all. This episode, which I do not . . . Here I was . . . Could my office have had any authority over this matter?"

Less: "Did you have any connection at all with the Head Office for Race and Resettlement?"

Eichmann: "No, I never had any connection with it. . . . And so, did I . . . I cannot recall."

Less: "Do you know anything about transports of children sent by the B.D.S.[15] from Prague to Lodz, where they were handed over to Krumey?"[16]

Eichmann: "No, no, I have no knowledge of the matter."

Exhibit T/1091: "We hereby inform the Central Authority for Transferees to Litzmannstadt[17] that on June 12, 1942, Czech children

15. District S.D. commander.
16. S.S. Lieutenant Colonel Hermann Alois Krumey was commandant of Lodz.—Trans.
17. The name the German authorities gave to Lodz.—Trans.

who cannot be Germanized will arrive in Litzmannstadt for a temporary stay. . . . S.S. headquarters has been informed of this, and the office in Litzmannstadt has received notice from the Race Office in Berlin."

It was all done in an orderly fashion. The next day, on June 13, Krumey informed the commander of the Security Police and the S.D. in Prague that eighty-six children had arrived, and he asked for clarification from Section IV-B4, Eichmann's office, as to "what should be done with these children."

This query was tagged Exhibit T/1902.

One might well ask what connection there was between the fate of Czech children and Section IV-B4, since the latter was only responsible for finally solving the Jewish problem. The answer is that the prosecution wanted to prove that the defendant's office had improvised solutions to other problems as well, since it had at its disposal the mechanisms of mass killing, the accepted channels, and the appropriate means to carry out "certain operations."

But I am interested in this matter for a different reason, which I shall spell out later on.

So let us continue. The above-mentioned document was shown to the defendant, together with another document, Exhibit T/1093. There, Krumey writes to the Reich Security Head Office, to IV-B4, to S.S. Obersturmbannfuehrer Adolf Eichmann, having first consulted with him. "Subject: the transfer of eighty-six Czech children from the town of Lidice to Lodz." In the letter he points out that "on June 13, eighty-six children arrived from Lidice, and I would like to know what is to be done with these children, for according to a ruling by the Race Office, seven of them can be reclaimed for the German race. As I have not yet received a reply, I urgently request instructions as to what should be done with the children, who have been brought here without any belongings."

Mr. Bach announced that he was now coming to the central document in this affair.

Even I, with my meager knowledge of the law, found this document most interesting.

Krumey explains why he is turning to this particular department for instructions. "I am turning to IV-B4 in this matter on the assumption that these children are to be given special treatment. Meanwhile, seven children whom the Race Office can recover for the German race have been taken out [of the group]."

"This office," Bach explains, "was the address for the killing of children, even non-Jewish ones. Krumey, too, was aware that this was the address for solving, in this way, the problem of children who could not be used for any other purpose."

That was Exhibit T/1094.

After the two documents were read to Eichmann, he answered, "I do not recall this, but since it was connected to my department, I could well imagine that the matter was dealt with from a purely technical, logistical point of view, . . . that they were added to a trainload of Jews."

Meanwhile, things were getting very, very interesting. The Prague office of the Security Police and the S.D. informed Krumey that "on July 7 another twelve children who cannot be reclaimed for the German race will arrive in Litzmannstadt, but six other children, who can be reclaimed for the German race, will be with them."

The presiding judge: "Tag this document Exhibit T/1096."

But we weren't through yet, for yet another document, written by the Race Office of the Reichsfuehrer S.S., dealt with those same twelve children and the same additional six, who arrived along with two lists of names. The twelve are termed "lost."

"Exhibit T/1097," the judge announced.

Twelve children were sent to Krumey in Litzmannstadt for "additional action," in coordination, it turns out, with the Reich Security Head Office.

Had that office not been interested in their receiving "special treatment"? We would soon see.

The die had not yet been cast, because yet another document, Exhibit T/1098, a letter sent to the Reich Security Head Office, to S.S. Obersturmbannfuehrer Adolf Eichmann, dealt with the same twelve children "ages one to fifteen, who cannot be reclaimed for the German race." "Further instructions are requested," it said. (It will be recalled that the first letter spoke of eighty-six children.)

The matter was not allowed to rest. Krumey then received a telegram from Guenther, Eichmann's deputy. "Krumey, in Litzmannstadt, is to transfer the children who cannot be reclaimed for the German race to the State Police office in Lodz. The police have already received further instructions."

Then, pursuant to this policy, there is a confirmation that, in accordance with the directive issued by Eichmann's Section IV- B4, the children have been transferred to the "State Police."

"This will be Exhibit T/1099," Judge Landau declared, in a quiet, official tone.

Yes, afterward we learned from a Czech government publication dealing with those children that from the time they were transferred, on IV-B4 instructions, to the "State Police," they were never seen again. The children disappeared. They no longer existed.

Less shows the defendant the documents.

Eichmann: "I would like to say the following. This did, in any case, originate here. Yes, this did, in any case, originate here. I do not mean to imply that I . . . but the department, I see here quite clearly."

Less: "And in 1942 you were head of the department?"

Eichmann: "Yes, I was head of the department. That is quite clear."

The reader may be wondering why I have chosen to dwell on this long-forgotten episode, a minor, marginal matter compared to the story of the destruction of the Jews of Slovakia and Hungary that was now unfolding before our eyes.

But a close reading of these documents will reveal in a flash how these people operated.

It could have been simpler, couldn't it? Czech patriots shoot Heydrich, the murderer. The assassination takes place near the village of Lidice. The Germans vent their wrath on the village. They level it to the ground and kill all its inhabitants.

What is incredible—though it explains once and for all the nature of the Nazi modus operandi—is this batch of documents, a small sampling from a vast sea.

Whole authorities, offices, and departments were occupied day after day with the important question of what to do with these children, the eighty-six Czech children, seven of whom could become Germans and the rest of whom were "lost," and what to do with the other twelve "lost" children, age one to fifteen, and with the six who were lucky enough to be suitable for "germanization."

Questions were asked, and answers emerged from the letters and telegrams and phone calls. The matter was passed back and forth between Lodz and Prague, between Prague and Berlin, and back to Lodz again. The Office for Race and Resettlement was involved, as was Himmler's bureau. Then the matter was referred to Eichmann, sent back to the Security Police in Prague, and returned to Krumey's office in Lodz. How many secretaries must have been kept busy typing all this correspondence.

The orphans are gone forever. No one has seen them since.

But the correspondence remains. Seeing it laid out in this series of documents, only a few samples from the great pile that accumulated, you wonder if you are not going mad.

May 25, 1961

HUNGARY, HUNGARY

How LONG HAS this trial been going on?

I've lost track.

Minutes represent hours. Hours represent years. And on average each of the living witnesses speaks for a hundred thousand dead.

But time has passed, and we have come to Hungary and the year 1944.

So we should be done soon.

Today, Avraham Gordon and Franz Tibor were to testify, and then, next week, we will hear from Joel Brand and Hansi Brand and other witnesses, and that should take another week. Then the very last witnesses, representing Auschwitz, Treblinka, Maidanek, Chelmno, Sobibor. . . .

The prosecution would rest.

We have come to Hungary, but for me personally, this was a second encounter. I had first gone there two years after the war.

One day, I was at a memorial meeting held by some Budapest Jews for their dead. One speaker, a man named Salomon, if I remember rightly, spoke in Hungarian, but then added in Hebrew, "'I am looking for my brothers!'"[18] And the whole crowd wept bitterly.

A colleague of mine who hailed from there told me, "Not one family in Hungary remained intact. You have no idea what went on there."

Afterward, I did learn what had happened there. Today, I know.

Why had Dr. Bejsky, the Polish Jew, said that "the most

18. A reference to Genesis 37:16, the Joseph story.

wretched transports I saw were those of the Hungarian Jews"?

At the recess, someone in the courtroom, apologizing profusely to avoid misunderstanding, said to me, "In Hungary, after all, more Jews survived, proportionally, than in Poland. What makes the story of the Hungarian Jews any more horrible?"

Today's witnesses supplied the answer.

Q.: "When did the mass deportations from the provincial towns in Hungary begin?"
A.: "On May 15."
Q.: "When did they end?"
A.: "On the 7th of July, or maybe it was the 5th."
Q.: "How many Jews were they able to deport during this time?"
A.: "I believe it was 600,000."
Q.: "In Budapest, did you get any reports as to how the deportation was being done?"
A.: "Yes."
Q.: "What were the reports?"
A.: "That it was being done cruelly."

The witness, the elderly Dr. Pinhas Freudiger, formerly of the Jewish Central Council of Budapest, put his face in his hands and began to weep.

Wisliceny had suggested that the deportation proceed at the rate of two trains per week. Eichmann demanded a faster pace, four trains per *day*. And he had his way. Each train carried three thousand people. If you multiply twelve thousand by the fifty-two days, you get the witness's figure.

May 15 to July 7. But in what year? In 1944.

"In 1942," Antek had cried from the witness stand, "there was not a single ray of light anywhere."

But now it was 1944. The Soviets had reached the Carpathian Mountains. The Allies were in Italy. The invasion from the west was imminent. Germany was being bombed. Its fate was sealed.

It is the timing of the destruction of Hungarian Jewry and the pace at which these unfortunate people were killed, supplying the ovens with a final course, that give the Hungarian episode a special place in the chronicle of destruction.

We are faced with a string of paradoxes.

Up until May 19, 1944, the Jews of Hungary enjoyed unbelievably good conditions. They seemed to be on an island of safety in the ocean of Jewish devastation. With all the restrictions placed upon them by the Hungarian government, the country seemed like paradise in a Europe that was devouring its Jews.

This fact reinforced the all-too-familiar sense of security, the confidence that "it won't happen to us." And when you put this together with the character of the Hungarian Jews, tens of thousands of whom were assimilated and a hundred thousand of whom had renounced Judaism altogether, so that they were an integral part of the Hungarian people, you see why these Jews had no trouble believing that, by some miracle, they would live through it all.

Those who had been furthest from the catastrophe were swept away by it with unprecedented speed when it finally came.

The Jewish paradox is matched by a German one.

The year was 1944. Germany was moving rapidly toward defeat in the war. Faced with military disaster, with their forces retreating and steadily crumbling on the eastern and southern fronts and another front opening, with massive nightly bombing destroying Germany itself—it would have been logical for the Germans to put aside any thought of solving the Jewish problem in Hungary, which should have appeared inconsequential in view of their own impending collapse.

But now something insane and appalling happened, just the opposite of what might have been expected. Because time was short, because all was lost, it was essential to hurry up and finish the job.

On one hand, there was the Hungarian Jews' false sense of security, lit up by the prospect of an imminent Allied victory. On the other, there was the German blood lust, which brooked no delay.

Hausner had referred to these things in his opening statement for the prosecution: Eichmann's department had focused its efforts here after completing its work everywhere else in Europe, and it had had a lot of experience.

The machine was well oiled. Everything ran like clockwork.

The German army conquered Hungary on March 19, 1944, and the machinery began to turn that very day.

The poor Hungarian Jews. They couldn't believe it.

Bach: "Dr. Freudiger, when did you first realize that those transports were headed for Auschwitz?"

"I knew it even before they started sending them there, because I had gotten a letter from Rabbi Weissmandel some days before May 15. He wrote at that time: 'To our great sorrow and distress, the final decree has been issued.'" Here the witness broke down crying. "I read the letter and passed it on to my colleagues on the Central Council, but no one wanted to believe it. They said to me, 'It's impossible. How can Hungarian Jews be sent out of Hungary?'"

No, I won't cover everything now. I won't go into the question that keeps coming up, of how and why they did not know or did not give warning. Nor will I go into all the questions about rescue. We'll come back to these things. We'll have to.

This morning there was an outburst in the court: a man began shouting in Hungarian, continuing even as the police dragged him out: "You fed us tranquillizers! You collaborated with the Nazis and saved your own families! My family perished!"

The foreign reporters rushed after him as if they had come upon buried treasure, then quickly sent their scoop out to the world press.

Ah, the day devoted to Hungary.

What else should I tell about it? There was the postcard thrown from one of the deportation trains by a Jew named Reich that miraculously—"bless the hand that sends this card," he had written—reached his wife, who was now in the stand. "My darlings," the card read, "today, Wednesday, in the afternoon, they packed us up, and we're on our way. May God be with you, my dear family, may God be with you. With hugs and kisses, Your father."

The woman received another wonderful letter from her doomed husband. Bach read the letters aloud "to spare her the emotional stress."

Or perhaps I should dwell on the story of Mrs. Elisheva Szenes, who told of Dr. Mengele pointing his finger to the right and the left.

Or the story of Dr. Foeldi. A few lines. His wife, son, and daughter were all sent to the left.

"But I could see my wife. How did I know it was she? My little girl was wearing a red coat. The patch of red meant that my wife was there too. It got smaller and smaller. I went to the right and never saw them again."

May 26, 1961

THE PSYCHOLOGIST

THE TRIAL GOES on and on, and again I feel the weakness and dizziness that sometimes overcome a person faced with the infinite.

I must apologize. Like most people, I do not grasp the infinite. How, then, can I express it in a way that will be intelligible to others?

Let us begin with the psychologist.

The presiding judge: "What is your full name?"

The witness: "Gustav M. Gilbert."

The attorney general: "Professor Gilbert, what is your present position?"

The witness: "I chair the department of psychology at Long Island University, in Brooklyn, New York."

It turned out that this witness, who had served as a psychologist in the American army and then in espionage and intelligence, had been asked "to examine the defendants [in the principal war-crimes trials], to determine the state of their mental health, to supervise them and to ensure the proper conduct of the trial[s]."

Q.: "Professor Gilbert, did they know you were Jewish?"

A.: "At first I did not tell them I was a Jew. I wanted to see whether there was anything to the Nazis' claim that they could always recognize a Jew. But they didn't identify me as such. When I informed them that I was Jewish they said that Jew-hatred was stupid, that none of them was an antisemite, and that, on the contrary, some of their best friends were Jews."

He had examined them, giving them intelligence and personality tests.

Together with Judge Musmanno, psychiatrists, and clergymen, he had been given access to the defendants' cells.

The attorney general asked that Professor Gilbert be allowed to relate what he had heard at Nuremberg from Goering, Ribbentrop, Keitel, Frank, Pohl, Ohlendorf, Hoess, and Kaltenbrunner.

Servatius objected, referring to similar objections he had made earlier: "In my opinion, that is hearsay."

The presiding judge: "We shall allow it." This was ruling number fifty-eight, based on the precedents of rulings seven and twenty-seven and on paragraph fifteen of the Law for the Prosecution of Nazis and Their Collaborators.

Thanks to the presiding judge's decision, we heard some very interesting things today.

Gilbert had gone with Musmanno to see Hermann Goering in his cell. (Incidentally, Musmanno's testimony, seen by some of the foreign reporters as suspect in part, was greatly reinforced by Gilbert's.) Goering told them that "when Hitler died, he left behind a political testament stating that the Jews had been responsible for the war and should be punished." Goering lied by saying he had had nothing to do with the destruction of the Jews, and he named the familiar names: Himmler "and his boys," Heydrich, Eichmann.

Then the witness went to see Kaltenbrunner. "I remember that day very well, because it was perhaps the only time I lost my composure, my professional detachment. A survivor of Auschwitz had testified in court how in 1944, when the Germans saw that time was short, Jewish children had been thrown alive into the ovens." The witness had asked Kaltenbrunner, "In view of all of this, sir, do you still maintain that you knew nothing?"

"No, no," he had said, "I didn't know anything. It was Heydrich and Eichmann who were responsible for carrying out the extermination program."

This was not the first time the witness was saying these things. He had recorded them at the time in his journal, later published as

Nuremberg Diary. Aside from being an incriminating document, this book still serves as an interesting and important text for study.

He recalled Goering adding, "Wisliceny is just a little weasel who looks big because Eichmann isn't around."

We shall come back to Goering.

Oswald Pohl, head of the main administrative office of the S.S., and Kaltenbrunner had blamed each other, but they were in agreement that "Eichmann was the man involved in the extermination."

Then we came to Rudolf Hoess.

Q.: "What did Hoess have to say about Eichmann?"

A.: "He couldn't talk about the extermination, it seemed, without mentioning the name of Eichmann. . . . It became clearer and clearer to me that Eichmann was the key figure in the whole extermination program."

He had gone to see Hoess because he "wanted to know what motivates such a man to do what he did."

"Hoess wrote out his life story for me, as is customary in psychological examinations."

Q.: "Have you kept it until now and not published it?"

The audience, stunned, then heard the following: "Yes, it has not been published, other than a few excerpts that I included in my second book *The Psychology of Tyranny*. Hoess wrote it before being brought to trial in Poland. He wrote it in the course of two days, April 10–12."

Q.: "Is this Hoess's handwriting?"

A.: "Yes."

The court had been given a pile of loose pages handwritten by the commandant of Auschwitz. From where I was sitting, I could only see a few blurry lines, penned by the man who oversaw the killing of two and a half million men, women, and children.

The presiding judge: "This will be Exhibit T/1169."

Hoess had testified at Nuremberg.

Q.: "How did his testimony affect the other defendants, as far as you recall?"

Some of the defendants had appeared to be shocked by it, and Gilbert had had to determine "to what extent the expression of shock, and of guilt and contrition, was real or feigned."

Frank, he recalled, was one of the ones who had expressed shock, saying, "This will be spoken about for a thousand years."

And Keitel had said, "Those S.S. swine! Had I known about this I would never have allowed my son to join."

But then we came back to Goering and Hoess. Goering's reaction had been that "this is nothing but horror propaganda. Of course those S.S. men were just a gang of thugs, but it's still nothing but horror propaganda."

Gilbert had cautioned Goering: "Do you want to go down in history as a man who dismissed with a laugh the death of two and a half million people?" To the court, Gilbert added, "the only way to approach Goering at that time was to appeal not to his conscience but to his concern for his place in history."

Goering had claimed that "it is impossible, technically and practically, to murder two and half million people in the space of only three and a half years."

So on April 23, 1946, Gilbert addressed the following query to Hoess in writing: "Goering wants to know how it is technically feasible to kill two and a half million people in the course of three and half years."

The next day, Hoess had told him exactly how.

If I may be permitted a brief comment, I have often had the feeling, in this interminable trial, that there is nothing more to be said, that "now I've heard it all," and there's no point in going on. Rudolf Hoess's explanation to Goering, written at Gilbert's request and here marked Exhibit T/1170, was a document to end all documents. Describing the extermination process in detail, including an analysis of pace and capacity, it provided a reliable, professional digest of everything that was done, although Hoess's account differed from Eichmann's in some details.

The court interpreter read Hoess's response to Gilbert's query aloud.

This strangest of audiences sat dumbstruck. "The freight trains of Jews being sent for extermination went by way of specially constructed railway sidings that led to the extermination facilities." It was with these words that the document began.

It ended, "the ash of the incinerated corpses was ground up and taken to distant points along the Vistula River to be dumped."

As I have said, there was some disagreement between him and Eichmann. "Taking the figure 2.5 million, which Eichmann says is the number of people brought to Auschwitz for extermination," Hoess continued, "one would have to assume that each day saw the arrival of two transports, together bearing 4,000 people, of whom 25 percent were found fit for work [and thus not killed outright]. All together, the interruptions between operations lasted some nine months, leaving twenty-seven months. Each month, then, 90,000 people would have to have been killed, totaling 2,430,000."

But Hoess had thought this was exaggerated. "Tallying up the figures from the various mass operations that I recall, and even allowing a certain margin of error, I come up with 1.5 million at the most."

But we learn from his testimony that "all the luggage would remain on the platform," that "Zyklon-B is a crystalline acid that vaporizes instantly on contact with oxygen," that "the arrivals were told to arrange their clothing so that they could easily find it after showering," that "those who could not walk and women with small children were taken [to the gas chamber] in trucks," and so on and so forth.

Sitting in the row in front of me was a thin woman heaving with tears. It was the wife of Shmuel Yosef Agnon,[19] whose writings provide a grand panorama of life in the Jewish diaspora, as it was.

Q.: "What was Rudolf Hoess's state of mind when he wrote these things?"

A.: "He was in his usual state of apathy. He was the kind of person who automatically answered any question put to him."

19. Leading twentieth-century Hebrew writer and Nobel laureate.— Trans.

The prosecutor raised his voice. "How can a human being do such things?" He was trying to find support in Gilbert's testimony, for Gilbert had "come in contact with the greatest of these criminals."

The presiding judge: "Do we need a psychologist to determine whether the defendant is guilty?"

After arguing the matter, the judges decided that the testimony should not be admitted.

The witness then had a lengthy confrontation with the counsel for the defense and stepped down, surrounded by reporters. He told them what he had not been allowed to tell the court. Bending an ear to listen, I learned interesting things about the "schizoid personality" and the type of remorse experienced by such people, who are incapable of empathy with the suffering of others. I learned about their minds and their attitudes toward accepted morality and questions of good and evil. I learned that they were a social-psychological rather than a psychiatric category. And so on.

The reporters listened, made notes, nodded their heads.

May 30, 1961

PART OF THE CRIME

> It begins with firm rationales without end
> Of who is worth saving and whom to expend.
> It begins with the ones who, at judgment time,
> Will be held to account for part of the crime.
>
> Nathan Alterman, "The Archimedean Point"

WE WERE DEALING with the testimony of Joel Brand, who had been sent on the strangest of missions. Had this man been a Christian, he would have been canonized St. Joel for having been forced by the devil to bargain for the lives of a million human beings.

But Joel Brand was a Hungarian Jew, a broken man now, whose hands trembled whenever he lit a cigarette.

Today, the whole world knows about the deal Eichmann offered him: a million Jews for ten thousand trucks.

"It was a terrible, cruel proposition," the witness groaned. "It destroyed my life. I had a million people looking over my shoulder, people who in the end he killed anyway. On the other hand, I, or we, had to grasp at even the slightest possibility of rescue. When he promised to spare 10 percent of the people right away and to blow up the installations at Auschwitz in exchange for the first thousand trucks, it seemed like a way of rescuing our people, or at least beginning to do so."

So he set out on his mission. His family and his people were hostages.

On May 18, 1944, he flew from Vienna to Istanbul.

Q.: "So you made it to Istanbul?"

A.: "Yes."

Q.: "Did you meet with representatives of the Jewish Agency?"

A.: "Yes."

He tried to see the American ambassador, Laurence Steinhardt, in Ankara but was arrested by the Turks.

Q.: "And then you went to Aleppo to see Moshe Sharett?"[20]

A.: "No, I was on my way to Palestine to meet Sharett, because he had been refused a visa to Turkey."

Q.: "En route, you crossed the border from Turkey to Syria and were arrested by the British authorities?"

A.: "Yes, when I got to Aleppo."

Q.: "Did you then meet Moshe Sharett in Aleppo?"

A.: "Yes."

He had met with Sharett and given him his message, but the British did not release him and took him to Cairo, where he was held for four and a half months.

Q.: "And that was the end of your mission?"

A.: "No, for me that was not the end of it."

Q.: "But you passed on the message and never returned to Hungary?"

A.: "That's right. I passed it on and was not permitted to go back to Hungary."

What, then, had happened after Brand was arrested? What?

In fact, we knew, more or less. But today some hitherto-unpublished documents were allowed to tell the story.

"I would like," said the prosecutor, "to submit an authenticated report from the Jewish Agency archives that includes Moshe Sharett's report on his meeting with Joel Brand in Aleppo; then a series of authenticated documents from the Weizmann[21] archives in Rehovot."

20. The Hebrew name taken subsequently by Moshe Shertok, who was to become Israel's first foreign minister and second premier.—Trans.

21. Chaim Weizmann (1874–1952) was a scientist, Zionist leader, and Israel's first president.—Trans.

A hush fell over the courtroom. A moment later, the earthquake struck.

The documents that were then read aloud to us clearly constituted a severe indictment of Great Britain and the Allies, for they essentially blamed them for standing by while the Jews of Europe were slaughtered.

And these things were being said here, now, in Jerusalem, in court—and there was no running away from them.

We shall not at this point call ourselves, too, to account, although some day, heaven help us, we shall have to do so.

The presiding judge: "Can you describe the documents in brief?"

The attorney general: "The documents are reports on Brand's mission that reached London, mostly from Sharett, memoranda prepared in London concerning meetings with senior officials in the British Foreign Office; a report on a meeting with Anthony Eden; the reaction of the British to the proposed deal and why it was never effected; Weizmann's demands on the British; and so on."

The last document was a set of notes prepared for Weizmann dealing with the material he was to testify about at Nuremberg.

The attorney general began with the documents in Exhibit T/1177. He described the message sent by J. H. Cole, of the British Foreign Office, to Weizmann on June 9, 1944, summarizing Brand's communiqué, received in Istanbul on May 5, about the deal Eichmann had proposed. Cole was passing on to Weizmann the message that had been sent by the Jewish Agency. The prosecutor explained that the Agency would send Weizmann, through the Foreign Office, messages that had to go by way of that office in any case. "It was a safer, faster connection." Perhaps we shall have occasion to say more about this.

Weizmann now knew all the details. The Agency had written, from Jerusalem, that "if these Jews are not rescued in time, their fate will be sealed."

The next day Weizmann wrote to Eden, thanking him for passing on the message and saying that he "needed a day to recover from the shock." He asked to meet with Eden immediately and requested his help in getting a Turkish visa for Sharett.

On June 23, A. W. G. Randall[22] wrote Weizmann that it was "inconceivable" that keeping Brand in Cairo meant that His Majesty's Government was "not prepared to give every consideration" to methods of saving Jewish lives—a familiar formula. Randall promised to take up the matter with Sharett when he came to London.

Sharett arrived on June 27 and gave an in-house briefing on what was happening. He spoke about the meeting he and Ben-Gurion had had with High Commissioner MacMichael,[23] where they had demanded that contacts and rescue efforts connected to Brand's mission be initiated at once. The emissaries had reacted angrily to the refusal of the British to allow Brand to return to Hungary. Later on, Sharett also reported on the results of Weizmann's June 2 meeting with G. A. Hall at the Foreign Office. "The matter will be brought before the War Cabinet," Hall had told him.

I did not note down the names of the documents, but only tried to hear the cry that arose from them. Weizmann had told Eden that the catastrophe was imminent, and Eden had expressed his deep sympathy but added that he would have to be very cautious—the feeling was that he had already gone too far—and that the Americans and Soviets would have to be convinced. Etc., etc.

At these meetings, Weizmann had demanded that the Germans be contacted immediately. The Allies, he said, should announce that they were prepared to accept Jewish refugees, and they should recommend that neutral countries do so as well. They should issue a warning that anyone who harms the Jews will be

22. Head of the British Foreign Office Refugee Department.— Trans.
23. Sir Harold MacMichael, the British High Commissioner for Palestine.—Trans.

regarded as a criminal. And they should bomb the railway lines leading to the death camps, as well as the camps themselves.

Sharett met with Randall on July 12. Again, the subject of Brand's mission was raised. Randall told him the suggestion that British and American protection be extended to the Jews in the occupied countries had been under consideration but had been rejected, he said. And on and on, in the same vein.

Later on we read the summary that Permanent Undersecretary Richard Law had written on September 1, 1944, to a stunned Weizmann: "On the 6th of July, you spoke with the Foreign Secretary about the bombing of the Birkenau death camp . . . [and other] steps that might be taken to put an end to this. . . . Mr. Eden immediately brought this to the attention of the Secretary of State for Air. The matter was discussed to the fullest extent by a team of the Air Force, but I regret to inform you that, in view of the great technical difficulties involved, we have no choice but to refrain from using your proposal under the present circumstances."

Judge Halevi: "What were the technical difficulties?"

The attorney general: "The author of the letter may have known, sir, but I do not. I myself do not think there were any."

I have gone on far too long citing passages from these documents without conveying more than a suggestion of the horror they inspired in us. The present writer was in a Palmah[24] camp in Mishmar Ha'emek[25] where hundreds of young Palestinian Jews stood ready to undertake even the most perilous, most hopeless missions of rescue. They were well-trained fighters chosen for the "German" and "Balkan" platoons.[26] Who knows how many European Jews would still be alive today if these volunteers had been air-dropped into the valley of the shadow of death. I knew them. They were lions.

---

24. A pre-independence Jewish defense force.—Trans.
25. A collective settlement in northern Israel.—Trans.
26. Because they could pass as Germans or Slavs.—Trans.

"When the Balkan Plan was cancelled," writes Yehuda Barak, commander of the "German Platoon," in *Sefer hapalmah* (vol. 1, p. 568), "they also cancelled the great plan of Eliahu Golomb" to parachute a squadron of Palestinian Jewish fighters into Poland, a squadron built around the "German Platoon." And when it finally became clear that the British high command was not at all interested in this irregular support, the platoon was disbanded.

Weizmann rose at Nuremberg to relate how the Jewish Agency had offered the British authorities to parachute hundreds of Palestinian Jews into Europe to assist the Allies and prevent the destruction of Hungarian Jewry. "When the plan was approved by all authorized military bodies and arrangements were made to carry out this plan, the Colonial and Foreign offices intervened and, because of political considerations, ordered the military authorities to refrain from applying this program."

What was it Eichmann had said to Hansi Brand? "You see, no one wants your Jews. . . . Cable your husband that I am starting up the mill."

May 31, 1961

THE YOKE OF GUILT

I FLEE THE courtroom, then flee back.

I'm damned if I speak about it and damned if I don't.

I went back to hear Aviva Fleischmann testify about the forced march to Austria.

What brought this strange audience once again to tears?

There were three pregnant women. When the time came to give birth, they squatted on the concrete floor. There, at the farthest end of hell, at the end of the march. It was December. It was snowing. A powerful flashlight was brought. "I want to see how a human being comes into the world," the Lagerfuehrer announced.

"What happened to the children, Mrs. Fleischmann?"

"The children lived for an hour, an hour and a half. The lice attacked them, the typhus, the dysentery, the hunger.

"My friend's husband, who had once been a human being, recognized me. He lay there and spoke a single word, 'Water!' I went to the well to fill a canteen. The Lagerfuehrer stood by watching. He kicked my arm, and the canteen went flying. I couldn't go back to the man without water."

"Out of the eight hundred men, how many survived?"

"Twenty," the witness answered.

The woman's eyes were dry. She was immortal.

So what do you say?

To repeat, I'm damned if I speak about it and damned if I don't.

What to say? Whom to talk about? The Germans, the Ukrainians, the Lithuanians, the Slovaks, the British?

About the British, for example, what would you like me to say? They didn't care.

About the *Jews*? Where? There or here?

When this trial is over, at least people will stop arguing about the behavior of the Jews there, stop judging them. They have told us everything. One day, we, too, shall have to speak.

I am afraid.

Something is homing in on us inexorably, the refrain, "And you? What the hell did you do?" Even a British reporter, listening, pale, to the reading of the Weizmann archival materials with their frightful indictment of Great Britain for not seeing the need to "use the proposal" of Dr. Chaim Weizmann—even he could well pose such a question.

And you?

You accuse us of being cynical, obtuse, apathetic. You say we did not lift a hand to help, that we were indifferent to the sight of the last, doomed survivors going to their deaths.

And what about you?!

We go back to those years.

What do you say, then? I say that there the Jewish people was exterminated, while here—after El-Alamein, after the danger of another Maidanek here had passed—the brethren of the murdered did not do what they should have done when the news came.

We knew long before the episode of Joel Brand.

Unable to bear the yoke of guilt, we are trying to foist it off on our leaders.

"They knew more," we say. "They, our leaders, our guides, were the ones responsible." "They should have given us the word." "There are different degrees of responsibility, aren't there?"

It is hard to argue with the claim that our leaders owe the people an accounting.

No, there is no real comparison. There is a huge, glaring difference—is there not?—between the leaders of a murdered people shouting and pleading and sending memoranda, sitting in the waiting rooms of the MacMichaelses, the Edens, the Moynes, and those who commanded the victorious armies, the bombers and battleships.

But . . . many witnesses have been examined in this trial. Why, I want to ask them, did you not resist? Why didn't you kill Eichmann? Why, oh why, didn't you flee? And other such questions.

These questions fly back in our faces like a boomerang, wounding and shattering. Why didn't you reveal the truth? Why didn't you sound the alarm? Why didn't you demonstrate? Why didn't you fast? Why didn't you drive the world mad? What answer can you give? Can you honestly say you did what you could to help?

I fear, however, what it will mean to raise such questions at this particular juncture, when our people are memorializing their dead and settling accounts in an atmosphere poisoned by scandal and politicking.

There is something about life "going on" nowadays that accounts for life "going on" then. It is something that often keeps people from recognizing those fateful moments that call for extraordinary responses, departures from the norm.

What should we do, then? Hunt down those responsible? Why not? Aren't we entitled to do this? Shouldn't those who are showered with flowers and fame also be subject to stoning? Yet we would still not have answered the question that implicates us all, in the first person plural.

They knew more than we did. True, but we knew too. In May 1943, we knew that Jewish Warsaw was no longer. We heard the broadcasts on the BBC. Even earlier, we knew that the Jewish tribe in Europe was coming closer to extinction with each passing day.

We went off to fight the Nazis. Tens of thousands signed up. We marched into the battlefields. But at the same time, life here went on, while there it was death that went on, as if in a nightmare of helplessness.

How are we to give an accounting today? I do not know. But at the same time, it is clear to me that we cannot avoid doing so.

I do not presume, in these brief lines, to give an answer. There is probably an explanation for everything: the knowing and not knowing, the weary obtuseness, the rapid pace of events, the thought that we *were* doing something, the helplessness and hopelessness of not having a state or an army.

The more I think about all this, the more afraid I am. The questions are too harsh to be avoided, yet too dangerous, today, to face. But they will always hover over us.

"Have you ever tried to put out a great conflagration with a cup of water?" a friend once asked me, shamefacedly. Since then, I have asked myself again and again why we didn't give our lives if only to be that cup of water. But I am asking this question much too late.

JUNE 2, 1961

OUR GLORIOUS BROTHERS

LET US RETURN to the documents and the witnesses. After writing what I did about the "yoke of guilt," I felt ill at ease. I spent several hours yesterday going over things that had been written or said during those years, years that continue to cast a pall over our lives. Now I feel I must come back to the subject—but carefully, for every word that cannot stand up to the harshest scrutiny can do irreparable harm.

Back to the courtroom, to the short Friday session.

Two figures loomed before me. One was S.S. Reichsfuehrer Heinrich Himmler. The other—to be distinguished from him in six million ways—was Israel Gutman,[27] who had been in the Warsaw ghetto and Maidanek and was now a member of Kibbutz Lehavot Habashan.

We had come to Maidanek.

The part of the trial dealing with the events country by country was over.

The part dealing with the extermination camps was beginning.

With all due respect to the other witnesses—all the testimony being given is equally strong—this time I shall allow myself to focus on just one, Gutman.

But first let us speak of Himmler.

If anyone asks which of the documents presented at this endless trial was the most horrifying, tell him it was Exhibit T/1277.

---

27. A leading Holocaust historian.—Trans.

Had it not been read aloud in court, had it not been entered into the transcript, one might have thought it was a mad hoax perpetrated by a sadist.

On March 21, 1945, Himmler writes to his Swedish physician and friend Dr. Kersten: "Over the many years we have known each other, we have discussed many problems, and your approach has always been a purely medical one, detached from political considerations. The well-being of both individuals and humanity as a whole have always been uppermost in your mind. You will be interested to know that, during the last three months, the idea we so often discussed has come to fruition: 2,700 Jewish men, women, and children have been transferred to Switzerland. This is a resumption, in practical terms, of the path my assistant and I consistently pursued until this war and the universal folly that it led to made it impossible to continue." And he went on in a similar vein.

Judge Halevi: "This is one of the most hypocritical documents we have seen."

The attorney general: "The most hypocritical and the most cynical."

What else could they have said?

We were coming to Exhibit T/1288, Himmler's famous speech to the senior S.S. command at Poznan, on October 4, 1943.

It had the tough, man-to-man tone of an internal briefing. "I would now like to say something about the deportation of the Jews, the extermination of the Jewish people. This is one of those things that roll off our lips—the Jewish people shall be exterminated, says every Party member—. . . but then along come all eighty million Germans, and every one of them has his 'good' Jew. 'Clearly, the rest are swine,' they say, 'but this special friend of mine is a wonderful Jew.' . . . None of these people has put himself on the line, none has gone through what you have gone through. Many of you know what it means to deal with a pile of a hundred bodies, or five hundred, or a thousand. To endure this and yet remain decent, aside from the normal human weaknesses—this is what has made us tough. This is a glorious page in our history, a page that has never been written and never will be."

Like a person in need of rescue, in need of artificial respiration, I went looking for Israel Gutman. While the prosecutor was presenting his documents, I found Gutman outside, waiting to be called.

I went up to him. "You are a kibbutz member, aren't you?"

"Yes," Gutman said.

"Where from?"

"Lehavot Habashan."

"And you're the one who's going to testify about Maidanek?"

"Yes," he replied.

He was called to the stand at 12:15. The prosecutor asked that he be heard because he had come a long way, from the Galilee. Despite the lateness of the hour, the court acceded to his request.

"Israel Gutman," the bailiff shouted.

He took the stand and was sworn in. Then, fastening his gaze on the man in the glass booth, he began speaking.

His testimony had to be cut short because of time pressure. It was not his fault.

Here was a man of iron, who had to be restrained and subdued continually by the prosecutor and the court. It really seemed unfair to the witness this time, because he had some very important things to say that would remain unsaid and unheard. But what he did manage to say was enough to fill our hearts with both admiration and anguish.

Having been through Exhibits T/1277 and T/1288, we were led by Gutman, through Maidanek, back to the land of the living, to hope, to human greatness.

He was one of those who had been wounded in the Warsaw ghetto when it was set on fire and defeated. He was hiding in a bunker. The Germans pumped in chlorine gas. "I don't know when or how I got out." He was taken with the others to the Umschlagplatz, the square where the Jews were assembled, and put on a train.

"We thought the train would take us to Treblinka, but it went to Maidanek."

With this witness we came to the subject of the death camps. He had survived Maidanek, Auschwitz, and Mauthausen to tell us things we hadn't known and to introduce us to some names.

As I have said, there is no way of ranking the suffering of one witness over that of another, and I shall not try to do so, especially since this witness did not have a chance to talk about his own.

He did tell us, among other things, about the revolt at Auschwitz, the revolt of the Sonderkommando, about the international underground, about Hadassa Zlotnitska, about Rosa Robota and others.

He didn't have a chance to finish. He could have gone on for hours. He was one of the few who could tell us new things, about unknown episodes of hair-raising courage in the very depths of hell.

We shall have to make do, then, with some fragments of his testimony.

"The revolt of the Sonderkommando was partly successful, and you were at that time a member of the underground organization that carried it out?"

"Yes."

The witness and his friend Yehuda Laufer, who now lives in Haifa, were ordered to smuggle explosives out of the factory where they worked. It could have been done by young women who worked there as well, but they were closely guarded. Their friend Hadassa Zlotnitska tried to persuade the women to do it, but they refused. One of the group was sent to Birkenau, and he approached Rosa Robota, who was in charge there. She, in turn, persuaded the women under her to cooperate, and every day they managed to smuggle explosives out in the false bottom of a food container, to Auschwitz A.

Meanwhile, Robota was also smuggling materiel to the Birkenau Sonderkommando, who were getting ready to revolt. Having incinerated the bodies of all the others, they knew their turn was coming to be killed. They could not postpone their uprising to coincide with that of the underground. They blew up the crematorium, killed several S.S. men, and scattered. They were hunted down and slaughtered, to the last person.

Robota was severely tortured.

Q.: "Weren't you afraid that under torture she would give the underground away?"

A.: "Yes."

Q.: "And then she asked someone to send Noah Zabludowicz to her, and he came?"

A.: "He came to see her at night, in the bunker. She gave him a piece of paper, which ultimately reached us, saying that we had nothing to fear, that we should go on with our preparations, that she knew what she would be dying for and that no one else was in danger."

She was executed by hanging, along with four other young Jewish women. "Rosa Robota's last word," the witness said, choked up, "was heard by the other women, who were lined up in formation. It was 'Vengeance!'"

"She knew what she would be dying for." A nameless heroine.

This abbreviated testimony, of which I have only given a few lines, took us back to our glorious brethren, those who made the world a better place and give us pride as well as pain.

Rosa Robota, juxtaposed with Himmler, with Eichmann.

June 4, 1961

BLAZE FORTH, TEUTONIC FIRE

AMONG THE BILLIONS of people who inhabit the planet that is home to the human race, there is one named Michael Podchlevnik who works in a chocolate-wafer factory and lives in Benei Brak.[28]

This man removed bodies from the gassing vans at Chelmno. Through these vans passed all the people of his home town.

Prosecutor: "And in the third van you saw someone you knew?"

Witness: "Everyone I knew in the town turned up in the vans."

Prosecutor: "Including whom?"

Witness: "My wife and my two children . . ."

The heavyset man was grimacing as people do when they cry.

Q.: "And you saw them as they were taken out of the van?"

A.: "I lay down next to my wife and children in hopes that they would shoot me."

An S.S. man pulled him away. "You still have strength to work. Get going!"

Q.: "And that evening you tried to hang yourself?"

Among the tens of millions of Germans, there was a man named Unterscharfuehrer Paul who had a dog named Beri, "a dog the size of a large calf," as the next witness described it.

Unterscharfuehrer Paul would call the dog, Beri, and say, "Man, get the dog!" "As a rule, those whom this dog attacked did not survive. It was too big for them. The dog would attack them, and they would be powerless to resist."

---

28. Suburb of Tel Aviv.—Trans.

There was, in Europe, a man who ordered another man to crawl on all fours and bark, who filled another man's pockets with mice and ordered him to stand at attention.

If you don't believe this, go ask Dov Freiberg and he will confirm it. He lives today in Ramle,[29] in Housing Project 1B. He works today in an engine factory.

He was in Sobibor.

He was fifteen at the time.

"In Sobibor, there was no selection of those who would be allowed to live for a while and those who would be put to death. Everyone who was brought there was killed."

It turned out that among those who did not realize they were doomed to die was one person who did realize it.

"It was May 1942. I remember. A Jew came to our town and told us that people were being taken, not to Ukraine but to Belzec, where they were put to death. People wanted to do I don't know what to him. They didn't believe him."

The fifteen-year-old Dov Freiberg, one of the disbelievers, was taken to Sobibor.

Q.: "You lay there weeping, and then a Jew came and comforted you?"

A.: "I never imagined what would be going on there. I was in shock. A Jew said to me, 'The way you're acting you won't last a single day. Here, put your head on my shoulder. Sleep.'"

It was a statistical certainty that one day a nameless Jew like this one would meet up with Unterscharfuehrer Paul.

In the middle of the twentieth century there were signs all over the world saying "grocery," "cosmetics," "tobacco," "attorney at law," "physician," "pediatrician," "accountant," "fruits and vegetables," and the like. Among them were signs with arrows on them, like "to the cashier," "to the showers." And next to those signs there was a platform, where Oberscharfuehrer Hermann

29. Town in central Israel.—Trans

Michel, known as "the preacher," would stand greeting the new arrivals at Sobibor. "You are going to Ukraine to set up farms," he would say. "But for now, get undressed. Pile your clothes up neatly. We haven't got much time. First, give your money, gold, and other valuables to the cashier."

From there, men, women, and children would go to the showers, following the signs and the arrows.

Q.: "What did you do while you were at Sobibor?"

A.: "I worked sorting belongings and in construction. I would clean the living quarters of the Ukrainians, and for a short while I had to cut off the women's hair before they went into the gas chambers."

Q.: "What did you do with the hair?'

A.: "We loaded it into freight cars."

Of the 150 people who worked with this witness doing various tasks in the camp, fifty were still alive one month later.

Q.: "What happened to the rest?"

A.: "Some committed suicide. Some were injured in one way or another and then shot by the Germans. Some went crazy."

Q.: "Did you try to kill yourself?"

And the witness, who had been fifteen at the time, answered, "I took a belt. I tried again and again. Yes. No. There were signs. There was hope. I hadn't been killed here, I hadn't been killed there. Maybe . . . There were cases of people who got used to it to some degree. They got used to it. We got into another way of thinking."

When he saw the Western Jews in their suits and fedoras, he said, "We thought the whole world was being destroyed."

Many of those who came to Sobibor were "well dressed, as if they were on their way to visit someone. People from France and Holland."

There was an orchestra there.

Q.: "Who played in the orchestra?"

A.: "Jews. When the transports arrived, they would play. Also when the Germans came and told us to play and dance."

Q.: "Were you also told to sing?"

Among the tens of thousands of murderers was a man named Untersturmfuehrer Weiss. "Yes, once he came after we had finished work. They made us line up on the parade ground. He read us the words and then taught us the tune."

"Can you give us a verse or two from any of those songs?"

The witness searched his memory and then recited to us the following song, written by Weiss. Here it is in translation:

Oh, give us Moses once again.
Before Your faithful, part the sea,
And let it stand like walls of rock,
The waters held back steadily.
Lead them through this narrow strait,
And when the Jews have all gone past,
Close the gate behind their throng
And give the nations rest at last.
Jerusalem. Hallelujah. Amen.

After Goethe and Rilke, the Germans gave the world Untersturmfuehrer Weiss.

"Jerusalem. Hallelujah. Amen."

"Life was cheap, and we used to joke about it. But when someone wasn't feeling well, people would help him, because we knew that once you got sick you would be killed."

It was a statistical certainty that among the multitudes condemned to death there would be some who would try to revolt.

Q.: "When did the uprising take place, and when did you escape?"

A.: "On October 14."

Q.: "Of what year?"

A.: "1943."

But we hadn't yet come to the revolt itself. "I would like to summon another witness to describe the uprising," the prosecutor said.

Yosef Resnik, of 94 Ibn Gabirol Street, Tel Aviv, was called to the stand. He tried three times to put on the skullcap for the swearing in, but each time it fell off. (The audience chuckled.)

Who said Dr. Wells, the gravedigger, was lying?

It was all true.

Q.: "So you began digging. What did you find?"

A.: "I was digging with my spade. After one or two thrusts, it slid easily into the soil. It went past a human head."

Q.: "You were opening a mass grave, weren't you?"

A.: "Yes."

It was 150 meters wide by 170 meters long and held ten thousand bodies.

"They brought a grinding machine," the witness shouted.

"We saw a three-year-old child on top of his mother," the witness shouted.

Revolt in hell.

A policeman in uniform approached the witness stand and saluted.

"What is your full name?"

"Ya'akov Biskowitz."

An officer at national police headquarters. Badge number 8877.

Oh, if only the Palmah paratroopers from the "German" and "Balkan" platoons could have joined forces with the thousands of hardy Biskowitzes. But the British were not in favor of it.

The prosecutor: "One of your comrades, who worked in the clothes-burning operation, brought you some familiar pictures one day."

The witness: "Yes."

The prosecutor: "Pictures of whom?"

The witness: "Of my family. He was from my home town, and he was my age. We had been friends there, and he recognized the photographs."

The prosecutor: "I would like the pictures returned to the witness. They are among the few mementos he has."

"Now tell us about the uprising at Sobibor, but be brief."

We had gone off on a tangent and wound up talking about this amazing revolt. The witness was a man named Sasha, who, as a Soviet prisoner-of-war, had organized it. It broke out on the afternoon of October 14, 1943. "Kill as many Germans as you can, and then run." It was all organized in military fashion, as if by a shadow army. Weapons had been smuggled.

"Neumann, the mounted overseer, went into the carpentry shop shouting and never came out. An S.S. man went into the shoe-repair workshop and was killed. Two were killed in a wagon. The 'cashier' Hermann Michel"—the one who gave speeches about Ukraine—"was at his post. I had a knife, and I stabbed him. Meanwhile, we heard cheering. The revolt was underway."

Eighteen Germans died. Three hundred of those condemned to death escaped.

Possessed now by his memories, he wanted to go on and on.

The presiding judge: "There is much to tell about. But you understand . . ."

He was given a chance to tell about the escape into the forest, about the partisans. He wanted to go on. He had waited nineteen years for this day. He forgot that he was an Israeli policeman. "I saw something else that was shocking, and I'd like to tell about just one more incident," he pleaded.

The presiding judge: "I'm very sorry. Many other people have things to say."

"Blaze forth, Teutonic fire."[30]

Maidanek, Sobibor, Chelmno. "The chimney-gate of heaven," as the Germans nicknamed it.

The Jews who came from Lodz and Bratislava, from Holland and France, all dressed up for a visit.

30. A phrase from Uri Tzvi's Greenberg's poetic cycle "*Rehovot hanahar.*"—Trans.

Of the tens of thousands who died at Chelmno, only three survived, and they were here: Podchlevnik, Zurawski, and Srebnik. Two had already spoken. The third would have his turn.

The nations have not been given any rest, despite the poet Weiss.

The murderers who wanted rest are now in the hands of the murdered, and those who kept silent are as well.

And we reporters come home at night and stand gazing at our children, asleep in their beds.

"Jerusalem. Hallelujah. Amen."

JUNE 6, 1961

A FOREST AND A SMALL RAILWAY STATION

Avraham Lindwasser finishes testifying and steps down. On his way up the aisle, he meets Eliyahu Rosenberg. They speak briefly and sit down next to an elderly man named Ya'akov Wernik.

They shake hands excitedly.

A South American reporter sitting in front of them turns around and sees them together. She turns pale, pulls out a handkerchief, and covers her face with her hands.

The audience waits quietly, looking around at the dais, the judges, the walls, the ceiling. Wernik, Lindwasser, and Rosenberg converse softly. Then they, too, fall silent.

Three veterans of Treblinka Camp 2!

I hadn't realized that such people were still among us. Now I knew. At one time we recruited some of them into Gahal.[31]

The Gahalniks hung out in the army camps in 1948. They couldn't speak our Israeli Hebrew, and in the evenings they would keep to themselves, wandering around in the streets or on the beach for want of a place to go. Many of them were killed in the battles at Latrun, in the foothills and in the Negev, before they learned to love the country they were defending.

Then, for a long time, there was no sign of them. But now they were back.

Now I know who the people around us are, and I begin to understand the makeup of our population.

31. Overseas Recruits, an adjunct to the Israel Defense Forces during the War of Independence.—Trans.

I don't see Shim'on Srebnik at the moment. He is to be the last of the three witnesses from Chelmno, after Podchlevnik and Zurawski. After him, we will move on to Treblinka.

Prosecutor: "What happened that Sabbath when you and your father went for a walk in the ghetto?"

Witness: "We had just gone out of the house, when suddenly I heard shots, and my father fell to the ground beside me."

Then he himself was arrested, put in a truck, and taken to Chelmno.

Presiding judge: "How old were you then?"

Witness: "Thirteen."

"Have you noticed that most of the survivors were children then?" one of the other reporters says to me. "Boys that age have a tremendous capacity to adapt and resist. They're quick and flexible. Their senses are sharp. And look how healthy and strong they still are. They made it."

It's hard to say, since 99 percent of their age cohorts are no longer alive.

They answer the prosecutor's questions. They speak softly, in measured tones. They answer the questions. They have phenomenal memories. They speak.

There is a large gray-and-black picture on the wall, a photograph of a maquette of Treblinka, Camp 1 and Camp 2, which Ya'akov Wernik made. Wernik, the elderly construction worker who looks so much like Maxim Gorky.

They hold a long pointer, like those used with architect's models and overhead projectors. They say, Here was the train station. Here was the selection area. Here they cut off the hair. Along this path, between the fences, they took them to the gas. Here there was a diesel engine. Here were the graves. And suddenly you begin to believe it really happened after all, that it isn't just a bad dream.

You lean back in your chair. You look at the speakers as if they were actors in a silent movie. You look around you and see people weeping bitterly or dumbstruck. Then you look back at the witness and tune in to what he is saying.

"Yes, it was exhaust from a motor. They used some kind of fuel oil. Those who went into the gas chambers last were jabbed with bayonets, because they could already see what was happening inside and didn't want to go in. Four hundred people would be squeezed into a small gas chamber. When the doors were closed, we were outside. Then we heard cries of Hear, O Israel, . . .'[32] 'Father!' 'Mother!' Thirty-five minutes later they were dead. Two Germans stood listening to what was going on inside. Then they said, '*Alles schlaft*,' everyone's asleep. We opened the doors and took out the bodies."

"What is your name?"

"Eliyahu Rosenberg."

"Where did these people come from?"

"At first," Rosenberg says, "they were brought from Warsaw, Czestochowa, and the little Polish towns. Later they came from all over Europe, from Austria, Belgium, Czechoslovakia, Holland, Serbia."

"How do you know this?"

Rosenberg says, "When I pulled the bodies out of the gas chambers, I could see that the people, particularly the women, had hidden all kinds of documents and money on their persons."

Here, he lowered his voice and told the court where they had hidden them.

There is a hush that stifles even the weeping.

"When we opened the gas chambers we would see children still alive. The Germans shot them."

I look around. The German reporters are gone.

Presiding judge: "Dr. Servatius?"

Counsel for the defense: "No questions."

---

32. Deuteronomy 6:4, the traditional deathbed confession of faith.—Trans.

But he does cross-examine Avraham Lindwasser.

Avraham the dentist, intelligent, bespectacled, one of only two out of a thousand who were spared on condition that they pull the gold teeth from the mouths of the dead.

The prosecutor: "And you did this?"

The witness: "Yes."

The prosecutor: "And you did this work until the time of the uprising at Treblinka?"

The witness: "Not exactly. I did it for a month, a month and a half, maybe more, until I came upon the body of my dead sister."

Servatius questions him as to whether Himmler, when he visited there, was wearing a coat with red epaulets or with red lapels.

The witness: "I claim, as I did before, that Himmler was wearing a leather coat, but underneath it you could see a strip of red."

More questions about the strip of red on Himmler's coat. Finally, Servatius raises his voice and asks, "And what about the tall, thin officer who was with him? Did he, too, have on a black uniform?"

The witness: "That's right."

Servatius sits down abruptly, saying, "I have no more questions." He says it in that meaningful tone that experienced attorneys use.

It all seems so ridiculous. Like the important matter of the belt and the pants in the Budapest cherry grove: "How could they whip the boy with his belt? Wouldn't his pants have fallen down?" And so on.

Such weighty, professional questions seem like a bad joke. You want to get up and walk out and go to a corner somewhere and lean against a wall.

What have we managed to convey so far? Nothing. The transcript makes our attempt to express it all look laughable. The stories always begin, "There was a forest there and a small train station." We know today what they did not know then. We follow them through their testimony and watch them take their seats next to each other. As if huddling together for protection until it is time to go home.

It is all well known. What is there left to write about? The glorious uprising at Treblinka? The statistics of people killed? It is all well known, well known.

Back now to Shim'on Srebnik, the one who was thirteen when they brought him to Chelmno. After showing the judges the scars of his bullet wounds, on the back of his neck and in his mouth, this burly, athletic-looking man sits down.

The prosecutor: "Have you managed to forget?"

Wiping away a tear, the witness says, "No. I can't sleep at night. Nights, I can't sleep. They're always after me."

June 7, 1961

THE PLANET OF ASHES

The ambulance goes to Gate 4. "Gate 3!" the guards there shout. The ambulance goes to Gate 3. Two policemen pick up the stretcher. Several officers run ahead of them, and Professor Asherman and Dr. Dworzecki follow along behind.

He lies motionless, his face the color of a light summer suit.

The ambulance doors open, and the stretcher with its occupant and those accompanying him are loaded in.

Why has he been called to testify?

He is standing there raving, as if he were reading aloud from his book *House of Dolls*, when the attorney general interrupts. "With your permission, Mr. Dinur, I would like to ask you a few questions, if you don't mind."

Ka-Tzetnik[33] went on raving.

The presiding judge, the assertive, dignified Mr. Landau, says, "Mr. Dinur, please listen to what the attorney general is saying."

The witness then collapses and faints, as if unconsciously trying to step out of his body and his life in order to reach the things he wants to say.

"I had not expected this," the prosecutor mumbles.

But I had.

Why, then, have they brought him to the stand? Did the prosecution really think that this man would be able to work a miracle

33. Pen name of Yehiel Dinur, ka and zet (K and Z) being the initials of the German words *Konzentration-Zenter*.—Trans.

and give us a real sense of the planet he had come from, a miracle that, just this once, could be achieved with ordinary words?

What happened was inevitable. His desperate attempt to break away from the courtroom formalities and return to the planet of ashes, so that we, too, could see what it had been like, had been too terrible for him to bear. It had broken him.

Others have spoken here, day after day, each one telling his story, gradually filling in the broader picture. He tried to go from broad generalizations to the very essence of that world, from which he had come like an alien. Anticipating what should have come later on, he tried to take a shortcut from one planet to the other, across the bridge that was his life. He tried to be more than just another person who had been there. He tried to speak for the vow that had, as he put it, kept him alive, to be part of the reckoning with the divine.

More simply, he didn't have the strength to stand before the court and describe the web of torture and death, although he had taken it upon himself to be its spokesman.

Or perhaps, suddenly seeing Eichmann, his mind had been short-circuited, and all the lights had gone out.

Then what happened, happened.

In fact, he said it all. The things he added afterward would turn out to be merely superfluous detail.

Those who follow him do the same, and they do it just as well.

There is Yosef Zalman Kleinman, who, in Mengele's "plank selection," filed across the soccer field with the other boys, his shoes filled with stones so that, with the added centimeter, his head would reach up to the plank, and he would live.

There is Yehuda Bacon, who spent frosty nights next to a fire in one of the gas chambers in which half the Jews of Europe were murdered.

Or Alfred Oppenheimer, the tortured Luxembourg Jew who came from the depths of the latrines. Or Dr. Beilin, the physician from the planet of the ashes.

Ka-Tzetnik-Dinur whispers a brief statement and leaves the dais. Those who follow him bring humanity a more detailed report. They are amazingly precise in their recollections, showing powers of memory no less impressive than those of the people from Planet Maidanek, Planet Treblinka, Planet Sobibor, and Planet Chelmno. There is a steady stream of them, each having his say and going on, past Ka-Tzetnik's prostrate form, as it were.

The mighty legal machinery ploughs ahead with a terrible ruthlessness that seems to derive from the realm being revealed to us, the land whose capital was Auschwitz.

The capstone of the case for the prosecution, the summation.

Sobibor and Auschwitz times a hundred, and then the cities and towns scattered all across Poland that were chosen as graveyards.

But there is always an additional element, unexpected even by those of us who thought we knew everything: the plank-touching test, the finger-pointing lineups, the attack dog Beri, the story of the mice, the march through the snow to Austria.

Something else unique to this event, like a final chord, like a cry from the very heart of the death industry, something frightening, too, because of the astronomical numbers of people murdered, tortured, and humiliated, the people who, at morning calisthenics, had to wave their hats in the thick, plague-infested air in unison when the order was given, like sailors saluting.

Yes, as if in conclusion all were being emptied out, leaving only the framework: the person sitting in a chair that is not there, eating nonexistent bread, reaching out to a life that is no more, to a substance that is fading away.

European Jewry no longer exists.

And here, with a force no less than that of the bloody annihilation itself, the still-living animal is recovering its strength.

Now those who returned from there are coming to Jerusalem, to the Eichmann trial, erasing the intervening time and giving the now-concluding prosecution a portrait of Auschwitz, of the planet of ashes.

June 8, 1961

POTATO POWER

Thursday, Session 71.

Mrs. Raya Kagan is speaking. An attractive woman in a white summer suit, now an official at the Ministry for Foreign Affairs. She is giving amazing testimony concerning one of the less-understood phenomena of the period (as we tend to say about the riddles passing constantly before our eyes), the Germany mania for paperwork. The kingdom of questionnaires, forms, registers, and reports. The wonder of German orderliness.

The question cannot be avoided.

Q.: "What about the people taken directly to the gas chambers? Were they registered too?"

A.: "There is no sign of this."

Q.: "It was as if they had not come."

A.: "No sign."

Presiding judge: "That is, straight from the trains?"

A.: "Straight from the platform."

Yet the registry turns out to include, for example, a file for one Bruno Jellinek from Vilna. On May 16, 1944, his record notes that he "tried to buy bread."

It turns out, in other words, that in the very camp where two and a half million European Jews received "special treatment," the Germans were also playing their paperwork games, with letters being sent back and forth and everything filed, numbered, and cross-referenced.

Not in vain, however.

It turns out that some of these files are to resurface today as exhibits for the prosecution. Eichmann didn't often have his photograph taken, but his department was meticulous in its orderly, German correspondence.

Kagan was one of the most important witnesses at this trial in terms of the indispensable information she furnished the court. But she also introduced us to figures of great heroism and brotherly compassion, their strong, free spirits illumined by the light of the ovens, the light of legend.

And perhaps this is the place to say and say again that in that world devoid of meaning, between the wholesale, impersonal killing on one hand and the relentless roll of the German paperwork machine through the void on the other, human greatness once again shines through.

We pause for a moment to contemplate the figure of Mala Zimetbaum, the young Jew from Poland, well known among the women in Auschwitz, who ran messages between the blocks, organized things, and lent a hand. She escaped in an S.S. uniform and was caught, interrogated, and sentenced to death.

Q.: "Did you speak with her?"

A.: "Yes, I asked her how she was."

Q.: "What was her reaction?"

A.: "She said quietly, bravely and with a touch of irony, 'I am doing fine, as always.'"

The prosecutor: "How did she die?"

A.: "They took her to Birkenau. There was a mass lineup. They had to make an example of her. Mala had tucked a razor blade into her sleeve, and at the lineup she opened her veins. An S.S. man came over and began mocking and cursing her. With a bloody hand she slapped him across the cheek. It could be just apocryphal, but she said to him, 'I will die a heroine, and you will die like a dog.' Afterward, in this horrible condition, they put her on a wagon and took her to the crematorium."

She finishes testifying and, red-eyed, steps down. She takes an empty seat on the side of the auditorium and sits sobbing for some time.

In between Raya Kagan and the documentary films there is

Esther Goldstein, of Kfar Ruppin,[34] who is shown photographs in which she identifies relatives and neighbors from her home town in the Carpathians. Her mother, father, brother, and sisters, and her sisters' children. "And here is the doctor, Dr. Kellerman," and "Belsher, our pharmacist, " and "Zager, the grocer," and "Mr. Kremer," and "Mr. Roth."

It was a German in an S.S. uniform who took them. Unlike Yitzhak Nehama, from Salonica, who shouted, "That's me! That's me!" this witness identifies herself in a near-whisper. She is asked to get closer to the microphone.

"Which one is you?"

"The one in the middle, with the white kerchief."

Her lips are pressed together, as if she were testifying under duress.

The auditorium is cleared, and, after a break, the lights are dimmed and films are shown.

The sound is not played ("so that the narration will not influence the court"). We are back in the age of the silent movies. And it is a good thing for us too, because it allows us to supply our own narration or to experience on a preverbal level what is being shown.

The actions of the Einsatzgruppen in the East. Blurry, distant. A truck stops, discharging Jews. They run, then stop at the edge of a deep pit. S.S. men are walking to and fro. There are also German onlookers in civilian clothes, wearing Bavarian hats with feathers. No shots are heard, but people can be seen falling into the pit. Then dirt is shoveled over them. We see the slope of a hill, the edge of a forest. We see a big German standing with his legs apart.

The films provide the corpus delicti. You multiply the number of Jews shot by a certain factor and you get the end of Jewish life in the occupied areas of Russia and the Baltics, "places where the grain was nourished by corpses," in Vercors's words.

Auschwitz, Landsberg, Bergen-Belsen. "*Arbeit macht frei.*"[35]

34. Kibbutz in the Jordan Valley.—Trans.

35. German slogan posted over the gates of the concentration camps.—Trans.

All those familiar scenes: the nightmare visions of death, the personal belongings, the dolls, the hair, the *musselmaenner* staring, motionless, at the liberating troops of the Red Army, the Americans, the British, the French.

But even more chilling are the scenes from a German newsreel: a train arrives at a camp platform; people in suits and coats climb out, carrying their suitcases, they and their children; the purposeful bustle; the dignified man who stops and looks around, as if trying to find a porter to carry his bags; the man who lights a cigarette, the one who looks at his watch; the diligent woman inspecting her new home; the thick trees in the background.

As in the movies, you have the impulse to warn the hero, "Look out behind you! Look out behind you!" The audience, after all, always knows things the actors do not.

Suddenly, the German camera comes to rest on the face of a Jewish girl in a dark-colored scarf, who undoubtedly guesses everything.

That face will haunt you for days afterward, and sometimes, at night, you may see it as a negative: a dark face in a white scarf.

Aside from the photographs of the "action squads" in the East, taken from a distance, I think I have already seen most of these pictures in other documentary films.

But now they are being screened at a closed session of the Jerusalem District Court, where Adolf Eichmann is on trial.

He is not seeing these films for the first time. Clips were shown to him during his interrogation by Section 06. Through the defense attorney, he was asked to be present at this showing as well, "so that he could identify the military units by their uniforms."

He is still playing games, and Servatius follows his lead. He sees great significance in the fact that, after twenty years, one of the witnesses is unable to remember what color uniform the murderers of his children wore. Was it black? Green? Brown?

Some reporters thought the films would "break" Eichmann. They thought, for some reason, that "seeing things with his own eyes" would affect him more than witnesses had. He had many opportunities to break down. But so far he has not done so. He is still scribbling notes to his attorney, rifling through files, defending his right to live and be treated as a decent human being.

Today we hear the last of the witnesses for the prosecution.

In the afternoon, Nahum Hoch and Gedalya Ben-Tzvi testify.

As a teenager, Hoch found himself in one of the gas chambers, together with hundreds of others like him. The door was shut, and he waited. Suddenly it opened again, and there was a hasty "selection." Fifty boys were chosen and taken out. The others were sent back in.

There is a strange, puzzled silence in the hall. Hoch clears up the mystery: a shipment of potatoes had arrived, and they were shorthanded.

He who dwells on high owes us answers to the following questions: (1) Why, of all the members of his family, was this boy spared? (2) Why was he given twenty-five lashes on the soles of his feet ("To this day I have sores there")? And (3) why did he have to stand in the dark, in that room from which there was no exit, until summoned back to life by a sack of potatoes?

It was the German writer Goethe, if I am not mistaken, who said, "When you come to a strange city, ask the children. They know everything."

Gedalya Ben-Tzvi's testimony is among the most impressive. The explanation, that he has a "good memory," explains nothing. Today, he is a teacher of painting in Ein Hod.[36] Then, he was a child. Had he been the only one to testify about Auschwitz, we would still have learned everything about that "planet." He builds it from the ground up, specifies its dimensions, describes its various camps, lanes, departments, and ovens. He lays it all out with matchless precision, to the point where you have the feeling something

36. Artist colony near Haifa.—Trans

supernatural is taking place before your very eyes. But when you put his own life together with the comprehensive picture he is painting, what comes out of it is a cry like none heard before, since the first cry a human being ever uttered.

I am afraid to touch his testimony. Even seeing the man, I am rent by pain.

June 9, 1961

IN VINO VERITAS

It is 6:15.

The prosecution rests, Hausner announces. No more "new material" will be heard.

Monday, June 12, 6:15 P.M.

We came to the afternoon session, which began at 5:00, to hear the court's ruling on the Sassen document, which contains Eichmann's recollections as published in *Life*.

Evidently the decision was made only after a prolonged debate among the judges, and it was postponed several times. By a majority vote, it was decided to allow only those portions of the text that had been annotated by the defendant, and only after the annotations had been authenticated by Inspector Hagag as being in Eichmann's own handwriting. Dissenting, Judge Halevi insists that other excerpts, not commented on but scattered among those that were, be admitted.

The ruling is also preceded by a lengthy battle between the prosecutor and the counsel for the defense. Hausner asks the court to admit the document *in toto*. The defense attorney wants to summon Sassen, to confirm that Eichmann in fact made the annotations, because otherwise Sassen could have written whatever he wanted. Again, Servatius maintains that the statements were made under the influence of alcohol and that he later added to them. The defense attorney also claims that his client wrote additional notes that are not in the possession of the prosecution and without which the entire document would be misleading. He cites paragraph 37 (2) to the effect that a defendant's confession must be written and signed in his own hand. The prosecutor claims that in this case the situation is different, in that the paragraph refers to a defendant who has already been charged, whereas here circumstantial evidence is sufficient. Furthermore, Eichmann confessed to Inspector Less that the interview did, in fact, take place. There is therefore no need to be so formalistic as to cite paragraph 37 (2). And so on.

Dusty old tomes of English common law are hauled out and similar cases and precedents cited by each side. The court, which has been listening day after day to the endless story of the genocide of the Jews of Europe, shifts its attention to the nitty-gritty of procedure, paragraphs, and sections. You forget for a moment where you are and what is actually happening here.

In the end, you have to remind yourself that this is a court of law. The power of the trial arises, in part, from these hours that seem to be wasted on dry, long-drawn-out arguments, on technicalities.

But the trial will eventually return to the substance of the case, and you will once again be enveloped in that atmosphere that is so difficult to convey.

"Concerning the tavern," the defense attorney says, "I must point out that it was not actually in a tavern that these things happened but in a tavern-like atmosphere. The defendant had been given wine. It was a tavern type of conversation, the kind that takes place in a tavern."

It is only with great effort that I switch back from the tavern to the courtroom and the defendant, "who had been given wine by the interviewer" to get him to share his recollections "for the history books."

If I'm not mistaken, it was in a basement beer hall in the city of Munich, in early 1920, that it all began.

Some thirty-five years had passed from the time of the meetings in the Munich tavern to the meeting between Sassen and Eichmann in a "tavern-like atmosphere" in Argentina.

Now, in the course of seventy-four sessions, these years have been passing before our eyes. One hundred and eleven witnesses have had some six hundred thousand words to say about them, in Hebrew, Yiddish, English, German, French, Polish, and Hungarian.

The prosecution's final day. With a little effort, one can imagine Eichmann sitting around a table with Sassen and Fritz, a bottle of liquor in front of them and cigarette smoke all around, as he gives his version of events, making comments and corrections.

A different version was supplied by the 111 witnesses. Not in a tavern but in a court of law. Beginning with Hershel Grynszpan's father and ending with Attorney Ahrou Hoter-Yishai.

One hundred and eleven witnesses for the prosecution.

They came forward following Hausner's opening speech of accusation and lament.

You want to know our version of things? Here it is!

And we heard them in seventy-four sessions, morning and afternoon.

Now we know "the truth, the whole truth, and nothing but the truth," as if for the first time.

And those who say it's a pity the last day of the prosecution had to be devoted to the Sassen affair don't grasp its real significance or the significance of what the portly counsel for the defense says about his client having been "given wine in a tavern-like atmosphere."

Try to imagine the scene: the story of the genocide of the Jews is being told by the very person in charge of carrying it out, the specialist from IV-B4. Imagining it, you also see clearly in your mind's eye all the witnesses who have appeared here and all the documents dug up by the Promethean Section 06. Gradually, you come to understand what this trial means.

The prosecution's last day.

Did anyone expect it to be climactic? How often we thought we had reached the trial's height and could go no higher. How often we thought we had reached its depths and could go no lower. But it became clear, again and again, that the prosecution could easily have called another 111 witnesses. After all, the subject is the murder of an entire people.

When was it that the old man Grynszpan testified? When did Benno Cohen talk about the pitch-black shop windows, about *Kristallnacht*? When was it that the Chief Rabbi of Vienna had scrubbed the sidewalk of the Hotel Metropole? When had they burned books in the public squares? When had the torchlight parades illuminated a vengeance-intoxicated Germany bent on war?

When were the signs of the apocalypse first seen? Who saw them? Who understood? When was it that the *Judische Rundschau* had hoped for "better days"?

One hundred and eleven witnesses, an endless procession now receding from view, sinking and rising in a miasma of blood and smoke. One hundred and eleven proxies, each taking his or her turn on the witness stand and leading us across the desolate landscape.

"Why so many?" the cognoscenti asked.

The prosecution was well aware that only a number this large could convey anything at all of what happened in those years, in the length and breadth of that world that was and is no longer. And as the last of the witnesses prepares to conclude, the prosecutor announces that "we have been inundated with requests from people who want to come and testify," and the presiding judge announces that the court, too, has been inundated with hundreds of such requests. And you know that each of those who has asked to speak has a story that simply must be told, that at the prosecutor's door stands a long line of people pushing noisily toward the front, saying, "What could you possibly know?" and "You haven't heard what they did to me!" and "Oh, what they did to us!"

You remember the witnesses who begged, "One more anecdote, your honor, one more incident." Yes, you remember the testimony that had to be cut short, the warnings of the presiding judge that the court would have to be harsh in insisting on a certain framework.

You saw the case for the prosecution burst out with tremendous force. You confronted the nightmarish scenes, in which heaven and earth had played a role, the unparalleled chaos in which whole peoples and countries had had a hand. You saw the fire that lit up the faces of the murderers and their innumerable victims alike. Surely, you thought, this trial will never come to an end, because it is infinite. But then you saw that, miraculously, it was, in fact, contained within the framework, within the four walls of the Jerusalem District Court that was judging Adolf Eichmann.

The prosecution's final day.

Bringing up the rear of an unparalleled parade, two witnesses are called today.

The next-to-last, as if to confirm everything that has not been said, tells the story of the Jews in the forests, the story of the partisans. This witness was added to the roster at the last minute, by special request of the prosecutor. Of the hundreds who did not get to speak, he asked the court to hear "only him."

Unfolding the tale of the glory and suffering of the tens of thousands of Jewish fighters in the forests and swamps, Shalom Cholawski concludes, "When I entered the little town of Lachowicz, I didn't see a single Jew, not even a Jewish child."

"How many Jews had there been there?"

"Some three thousand. I passed empty streets, empty houses. The wind was howling. There was death in that town."

Attorney Hoter-Yishai winds up the case for the prosecution. The last witness. 1945. The Jewish Brigade has finally made it to the "planets."

"When I stopped to ask if there were any Jews in the camp, my car was suddenly mobbed. They looked like strange creatures, but they were human beings, struggling with the last ounce of their strength to get near the soldier who had come into their midst and touch his Jewish badge. If they couldn't, they kissed the Star of David on the car instead. Others bent down to kiss the soldiers' dusty boots."

Presiding judge: "As I understand it, this concludes the testimony?"

Attorney general: "We have no more witnesses."

June 13, 1961

THE KEY?

"TELL THE DEFENDANT to rise."

"The prosecution has finished presenting its case, and the defense is about to begin. Do you wish to make a statement in your own defense? If so, you can do so under oath or not."

"I wish to do so under oath."

It is 11:00 o'clock. Today is Tuesday, the 6th of Tammuz, 5721, June 20, 1961.

This moment, too, has arrived. In the glass booth, the defendant/witness stands erect. There is silence in the hall.

The presiding judge, to the bailiff: "Pass the New Testament in there." To the defendant: "Place your right hand on the New Testament."

There is silence in the hall, as in a dreamt ritual. There is silence in the hall, the silence of one who always believed such an hour would come, one day, one year.

"I am not swearing on the Bible. I am swearing by God. I do not belong to any church, but I do believe in God."

The word "God" is the last to be heard. We can hear it quite clearly. "God." "*Gott.*" For a moment, it seems to have been taken from the motto on the brass buckle of one of those heavy German belts: "God is with us."

"I swear by God that my testimony at this trial shall be the truth, the whole truth, and nothing but the truth."

The right hand does not rest on a book but is raised to shoulder height, the way scouts do when they take their oaths.

"I swear by God. . . ." Rivka Joselewska, too, swore by God.

God is not to be seen in the hall at this moment. But He is still God. As always.

Is this one of those moments that, with some effort, can be grasped as unique, one of those moments that, effortlessly, hold the entire world in their grip?

The official photographer, poor fellow, is holding his head in his hands. He has failed to capture the scene of the defendant standing and being sworn in. He came seconds too late. Only the television cameras, which are concealed like machine guns and watch the proceedings uninterruptedly, caught that moment.

A climactic moment.

Why?

Because up until that moment he, the man from the other side, had not spoken.

Many witnesses had spoken, telling us where, when, how and by whom the Jewish tribe of Europe had been exterminated.

And he had kept silent.

This time he rises to speak. It brings on an almost intolerable mixture of feelings, if I may be forgiven for saying so: a tense, morbid curiosity, a strange anticipation, a fear. After all, you expect some great riddle to be solved here.

Something unanticipated is about to happen, you think.

Despite the down-to-earth atmosphere in which this play is being enacted, you expect something unexpected, either the "nervous collapse" he is said to be on the verge of, or something similar, some kind of breakdown, to balance out that of Ka-Tzetnik, whose stretcher bearers had to fight their way through the throng of reporters rushing to send their dispatches.

But it all turns out differently, turns out to be within the bounds of normalcy, although the present writer is still wandering in a no-man's-land between the real and the surreal. The man who has just sworn by Almighty God is not mad, or so the doctors, after examining him thoroughly, have determined. Still, is it conceivable that his erect posture, his raised hand, his deep voice repeating the words of the oath belong to the realm of sanity?

What, after all, is going on here?

At this point, a certain power asserts itself, the power of the time and place, the power of non-chaos, of non-hallucination.

Now everything comes back into focus: the three judges in their black robes, the shining brass seven-branched candelabrum,[37] Servatius's broad back, the secretary at his side, the prosecution team, the stenographers, the translators, and the defendant, standing erect, raising his hand and finishing his oath with the word "truth."

There has been a lot of discussion of him lately. They've tried to figure him out. There are different opinions, of course. Some have said that the man before us is "homicidally aggressive," "schizoid," incapable of empathy," etc. In their view, he gives only the appearance of being a "minor official," a "good father," a "bureaucrat." What is more, had he been given the task of growing potatoes instead of exterminating the Jews, he would have produced record crops throughout the Third Reich.

We must be forever grateful to the court for its constitutional aversion to impressionism, "in-depth analysis," and psychologizing. It is in the ruthless clarity of the machinery of the law that you find the most exalted capacity to bring order out of chaos, to give stubborn facts some meaning again, to free the energy of the truth brought to light by the law's special modus operandi.

Now we can sense the power that is gaining sway over those desolate lands, those distant planets, that is connecting us to them with brief utterances like "Tell the defendant to rise" (and he rose) or "Now answer the questions of your defense attorney." This last sentence is spoken in the court at exactly 11:06 A.M., and not in the tortured dreams of the persecuted and bereaved.

Clearly, what is being said represents both worlds.

And, indeed, the defense counsel is right this time when, rising heavily to his feet, he says, "Honorable presiding judge, honorable

37. Emblem of the state of Israel.—Trans.

members of the court, in this trial two worlds stand juxtaposed, the world of the sufferers and the world of those who wielded power, the lowest of the low and the highest of the high."

"He does know what he's doing," people whisper. Yes, he knows how to begin and how to approach, intuitively, the task that brought him here, to prove that "Eichmann was not among those who gave orders but among those who were given them," that "it was the country's leaders, without whom the defendant could not have lifted a finger, who bear responsibility," that "the whole system was devoted to sowing the seed that produced this harvest," that "the defendant neither ordered the exterminations nor carried them out."

We are informed by the defense attorney that the defendant, "to show good will," will relate to us "the most important thing, his knowledge of the killing processes," and that the defense will "put it in the proper light."

Yes, that is its task, its obligation.

Now Eichmann is to speak.

Is it because we think he has the key to the riddle that we are so desperately anxious to hear what he has to say?

What happened, when and how, and who did what—these things the prosecution has told us. Are we expecting Eichmann to explain *why*? No. He cannot be asked this question. Better to ask God, in whose name the Obersturmbannfuehrer took his oath. But if the man is too small to answer such a question, he was big enough to discharge his duties as head of Section IV-B4, the one that "finally solved the problem of the Jews of Europe."

The key! Now you begin to understand the world this man represents, as he sits there answering the questions in detail and at length, "putting them in the proper light" in his deep, calm drawl.

The key! Note down, as a point of departure, the story of his Hebrew lessons with the rabbi. "I asked my superiors to allocate three marks per lesson, so that I could study with Rabbi. . . . Of course it would have been easier to arrest a rabbi and force him, in jail, to teach me Hebrew. But I was not then inclined to do this, and so I looked into the price of private lessons and made my proposal."

A decent man.

"I read Herzl's *The Jewish State*. It was a great discovery for me, an obvious solution, because only in their own state could the Jews overcome their difficulties."

We recalled the inscription "the Jewish state" over the entrance to the gas chamber.

JUNE 21, 1961

THE POWER OF THE IMAGINATION

What is happening at the trial?

It continues.

Yesterday, when he stood and took the oath, we spoke, as I recall, about the heavens being rent asunder and the earth opening under our feet. What about today?

Q.: "On page 8, we see a listing for Section 2a, the organizational and legal section, headed by S.S. Oberregierungsrat Dr. Bilfinger. Did you work with this section?"

A.: "Yes, Section 2a—that is, Section A of Department 2 of the Reich Security Head Office—dealt with all the legal questions. Sturmbannfuehrer Suhr, who is listed here under Division III-A2, joined my department after Regulation 11 was issued and was given a great deal of autonomy. He could always get instructions and orders directly by going to see the head of Division IV, Sturmbannfuehrer Regieungsrat Neifeind, listed here on page 2, in Division II-A2."

Then, ten minutes later: "Division III-B3, the Division of Race and Folk Health, dealt with questions concerning Jews, especially the offspring of miscegenation and mixed marriages and matters of definition, and this division, or, more precisely, section, worked primarily in conjunction with other offices, on the basis of its authority over matters of determination and definition [of racial identity], for example, determining who was to be considered the first-degree progeny of miscegenation and who the second-degree progeny. And more important, it determined what was to be done with them. The processes I was given the opportunity to describe earlier provided an important basis for the work of the State Police, of Division IV, not only within the division or the section but in interministerial contacts conducted by the Reich Security Head Office or the Chief of the Security Police and the S.D. or the Reichsfuehrer S.S. with the Chief of German Police, the Ministry of the Interior or the Economic Ministry."

And three minutes later: "If one sees that all police matters within the purview of a senior officer of the S.S. and the police were subject to his authority as a representative of the Reichsfuehrer S.S. and the Chief of German Police, and, on the other hand, that the evacuation of Poles and Jews from the newly occupied eastern territories in 1939 was delegated to the district officers, called Landraete, and if the preparation of timetables for the transports was the responsibility of the local authorities, such as the Central Offices for Transferred Inhabitants, and if, in this respect, a special status was conferred on this role by the establishment of a special division within the Reich Security Head Office, under his direction, then the participation of the Central Offices for Transferred Inhabitants, through contact with the local authorities, including the district supervisors, the local police, and gendarmerie, on one hand, and, on the other, ongoing contact with my special division, part of the responsibility of which was providing them with transport schedules, with the aim of directing them, so as to ensure orderliness in the transmission of orders—this orderliness, in the final analysis, facilitated the transfer of the residents, if one can use that term at all."

Presiding judge: "The witness's style is his own affair, but if he wants us to understand him he will have to speak in shorter sentences. It is true that in German the verb comes at the end, but here it is just taking too long."

Servatius: "I have already instructed him in this regard, but evidently, once he started speaking, it escaped him."

No. Let us not be hasty. Let us pause here. We have been quoting at length. I have a personal request for the reader: go back, if you will, and read the above passages carefully. This is the key. Later, we shall analyze the intentions of the defense, although they are already clear: a small cog who acted on orders, who, in a roundabout way, worked with a thousand other offices and divisions and departments and administrations and authorities, a minor vehicle officer. We'll come to this. But not now.

Let's get back to our subject. Slowly, patiently. It is boring, I know. Half the reporters are out for coffee.

I must admit I am not interested right now in the lengthy German sentence structure, full of tangents, in which the verb comes last.

"I have already instructed him in this regard," Servatius said, apologetically.

This is very important. But less important, it would seem, than another instruction the witness was given. "The defense attorney's secret weapon is boredom," they are saying here. He wants to put us to sleep.

Others are speaking of an "anticlimax." They say the suspense will return when it comes time for the defendant to be cross-examined by the prosecution.

But I, for one, do not doze off. I sit hour after hour, listening, thinking.

Let us get back, then, to the testimony cited above. We have chosen these excerpts at random. We could give hundreds, even thousands, of examples.

As we have learned, "Section 2a, that is Section A of Department 2 of the Reich Security Head Office, dealt with all the legal questions."

One of the reporters finishes his coffee and comes back upstairs. As he takes his seat, he hears the words "legal questions." For a moment, he stops listening to the witness, who is "explaining and putting things in the proper light," and asks himself what "legal questions" mean.

He has to use his imagination. "Legal?" he asks himself. Then he begins to grasp that what we have here is a special way of formulating things, a uniquely German lexicon. Artur Levi, after all, did not have the option of applying for an order *nisi*. No! Had he done so, he would have been seen as a Jew with a sense of humor, wouldn't he?

He would given everyone a good laugh, wouldn't he? But the court would not have summoned Rudolf Hoess to give cause why he should desist from stoking his ovens with the plaintiff's relatives.

We are also told that Sturmbannfuehrer Suhr joined the defendant's department and "was given a great deal of autonomy."

It would then have been easy for Mr. Suhr to tell Mr. Cohen, "Your house is being transferred to the jurisdiction of my department. You must sign here. And on the other form, too."

The power of the imagination. In the evening, Mr. Cohen goes home. His neighbors knock on the door, but there is no answer. They break down the door and find Mr. Cohen and his wife hanging in the living room.

Then you learn that Division III-B3, the "Division for Race and Folk Health," dealt with the "offspring of miscegenation and mixed marriages" and was the one that decided "what was to be done with them."

Try to imagine a young man of twenty whose grandfather is a full German but whose grandmother is "a German of the Mosaic persuasion." "Please understand, doctor," he says politely, "this is not my fault. My father was killed at Verdun. He got the Iron Cross. I want to join the German army. I am a German. This is my homeland. Please, doctor, please!"

Then you find out that this man underwent a "small operation" at the order of Division III-B3. Thanks to his grandfather, he was not sent to the "state of the Jews" in Auschwitz, but thanks to his grandmother the aforementioned division denied him the possibility of having any children.

The "evacuation of Poles and Jews," which, as we now know, was dealt with by district officers at first, the "transportation" being provided by the local authorities, such as the Central Offices for

Transferred Inhabitants, was later, in the name of greater orderliness and efficiency, handled by the defendant's department.

We are forced to break up the long sentence that aroused the presiding judge's ire.

Yes, the sentence does have 207 words. It's really too many. But for some reason I am thinking about the associations: "the evacuation of Jews and Poles from the newly occupied eastern territories," "timetables for the transports." Two minor matters connected with the defendant's department, this defendant who constructs lengthy sentences.

The power of the imagination. We have to use our imagination, because if not, we will gradually be lulled or mesmerized into this man's world. This man who explains the system, the orderliness, to us with the zest of a professional.

One more scene that has to do with the imagination and with the terms "transferred inhabitants" and "transport timetables":

A convoy of trucks makes its way along a dirt road, goes through a forest and across a field, and stops.

Only then, only then do you remember something you once heard about a family of eight Jewish souls. About a grandmother carrying a year-old infant in her arms and tickling it so it wouldn't cry. About a father gathering his children around him and pointing to the sky. About a young woman who says, "I am only twenty-three."

"They lay side by side in the pit." "Another group arrived."

"Between November 2 and 8, 1941, inclusive, Einsatzkommando Unit 5 shot fifteen political officials, twenty-one saboteurs and looters, 10,650 Jews, and 414 hostages."

You remember a forgotten episode from a forgotten report about the "action squads" in the East.

You connect it with the boring, mind-numbing replies that send the reporters downstairs. You connect it, but with great difficulty. You, too, find yourself weary and lost among the numerous names, with their Roman numerals and Latin letters, the authorities and departments and bureaus and sections, and on and on.

All at once you realize that all through this testimony, which has been going on for two days, not a single cry of terror has been heard. Not one man has been seen embracing his only daughter, a young woman who is to be sent to Dr. Carl Clauberg's experimental station instead of the wedding canopy.

He goes on, uninterrupted, in his Austrian patois, churning out prepared answers to prepared questions, answers that make him smaller and smaller. Soon we'll need a magnifying glass to see him.

We haven't really told a thing. The reader is asked to see the attached report. I am tired. My head is filled with numbers and letters and abbreviations.

Servatius does his utmost to load us down with the names of additional functionaries. He does his utmost to demonstrate what a small role the defendant played, how negligible his influence was.

The judges will deal with this. Meanwhile, he is performing a valuable service.

We have returned to Germany itself, as it was then. We go from him to Germany and back.

The power of the imagination. We are really going to need it for the next two days, until Thursday, when the man who chose to testify under oath will have to answer questions.

"It's going to be boring until then," they say. True. But perhaps now we shall begin to understand what an important role that "boredom" played in the death of Europe's Jews.

June 22, 1961

THE "LEGAL BASIS"

Today, we crossed into the realm of humor. It is a nameless person in the audience who expresses it. When the court takes up the issue of Account W and everything connected with it, someone bursts out laughing, loud and long.

It is at 12:30, if I'm not mistaken.

Servatius: "Can you tell me, sir, where this large sum of money the commanding officer of the shipment was carrying, 47,750 marks, came from?"

The witness: "Every Jew who was evacuated had to pay fifty marks."

At this point, the nameless person gives a chuckle and falls silent.

Not a bad idea: to pay your own way to the next world!

Today's session is accompanied by laughter. That's just the way it is. Why did he issue instructions that the deportees were to bring along provisions for eight days? Wasn't he concerned only with the timetables of the transports? It was clear: those who came with food for only two days would be turned back by the "local authorities," who refused to feed them. As a result, there would be "traffic jams."

Someone gives a snicker, stands up, and says, "I've had enough." Then he walks out.

Or when Eichmann says his "final solution" was Madagascar, says he "wanted to give the Jews some solid ground under their feet." Again there is laughter in the hall, and the presiding judge asks for quiet.

When the prosecution was presenting its case, many wept.

Eichmann!

He makes himself smaller and smaller, forcing us to laugh or embarrassing us, the way a ham actor does when he gets into trouble on the stage.

We turn all the spotlights on him. We want to see him as the chief executioner of Europe's Jews. And, in fact, the prosecution has proven that this man, the "specialist," held a key position in carrying out the Final Solution, that his department, IV-B4, had only one meaning for those unfortunate people: deportation, expropriation, humiliation, torture, and death.

Each count of the indictment states explicitly, "the defendant and others." The counsel for the defense turns the "others" into the main perpetrators and his client into a minor accessory.

The judges can be counted on to put him in his proper place. But it isn't merely a legal question.

The trial is being conducted in Jerusalem, in the State of Israel, which stands before the peoples of the world as the heir of all those who were murdered.

Adolf Hitler is dead, and so are Himmler, Goering, Streicher, Heydrich, Kaltenbrunner, and hundreds of other Germans whose names will not be forgotten.

We haven't caught Dr. Mengele yet. Mueller's trail has been lost. Bormann is in hiding.

Tens of thousands of murderers of all ranks, uniforms, and departments are scattered across Germany, wearing civilian clothes, *wunderkinder* in fedoras.

Eichmann alone is here.

The legal procedure, by its very nature, concentrates on him. It is to the credit of the prosecution that it has broadened the scope of this trial to give it its true dimensions, but the prosecution, too, is tied to the legal procedure in which Eichmann alone is the defendant.

I would like to touch on a point that is not limited to the court.

On January 15, 1941, a meeting is convened to set basic policy guidelines. It is called by the Interior Ministry, Messrs. Herring and Hans Globke. Those present include representatives of that ministry, the Reich Security Head Office, the Foreign Ministry, the Justice Ministry, the Finance Ministry, and others. "All the principal decision-making bodies," the protocol records. The representatives of the Interior Ministry suggest "depriving all Jews of their German citizenship, those living in the country as well as abroad, thus making them stateless persons."

This step leads automatically to the next: "The property of these people is to be confiscated immediately." Plain and simple. The suggestion is accepted and becomes "regulation number 11."

Eichmann's representatives are also present at the meeting.

Replying to a question from the defense counsel, he says, "This was the legal basis given to those who issued the orders and who carried out the deportations, and it made the juridical aspect of the deportation quite simple and easy."

"I would like to ask the witness," the defense counsel says, "how involved he was in these procedures."

To this, Adolf Eichmann replies in his own defense, "This is a direct result of Regulation 11. . . . It was not an order of mine. . . . They concocted it in Section 1 of Department I of the Interior Ministry, and if other departments were directed to carry it out, there was no choice but to do so. Principled reservations did not enter in. It was simply a question of jurisdiction."

Here we get to the heart of the matter.

He acted "within the framework of the law." Yes. "There was no choice but to carry it out." The "Interior," "Foreign," "Justice," and "Finance" Ministries, and the others. One could add the church (remember the brave words of Dr. Grueber), the professors, the writers, all of Germany! Except for those who were tortured and killed.

Stage by stage. The addition of "Israel" and "Sarah" to the names. The Nuremberg Laws. Regulation 11. A legal basis for the open pit, for the gas chambers.

Being so involved with the criminal we have in our hands, we can lose sight of that whole endless chain of crimes in which an entire nation, including its legislators and jurists and physicians and priests, took part.

The bullet through the mouth of a ten-year-old girl was the final outcome of the process that rested on this "legal basis." I believe the number of doctors who took part in the extermination of the Jews of Europe exceeded that of the privates and sergeants in the "mobile slaughterhouse" of the "action squads."

Out of all the voluminous material presented at today's session, we have dwelt this time on a single point, "the defendant and others."

Adolf Eichmann's testimony will yet supply us with a great deal of material to work with. Many will ponder how pathetic an S.S. man seems once you have stripped him of his boots and his Parabellum.[38] We shall come back to this. For now, we only wish to remind the reader of "the others," of "the gentlemen from the ministries," of the academic scum. By pointing to them, we do not take him off the hook, as the defense counsel is trying to do. We only remind ourselves of the real scope of the problem.

June 23, 1961

38. German revolver.—Trans.

ADDENDA AND NOTES

In an effort to save his own skin, Adolf Eichmann repeats the same lines over and over: "It wasn't me . . . Who was I, after all? . . . I saw nothing and heard nothing," and so on. Making it all the more shameful, all the more painful.

What makes it all the more shameful is that it is his fear for his own life, this mortal dread, that galvanizes his energies.

What makes it all the more painful is that every one of his victims was more courageous, more honest, more human than he is.

And as we have long known, this is how all the others acted, too, all his superiors and underlings, when at last they were called to account by those who overpowered them.

The case for the prosecution was a tale of woe and bereavement, a memorial service for the dead.

The word "pride" could well have been added to the lessons in language and arithmetic given in 1943 in one ghetto or another—alongside conjugations, declensions, and multiplication tables.

When I was in elementary school, a note on the back of my workbook said pupils were required to come to class clean, neat, and well fed.

In the Vilna ghetto, Abba Kovner told me, a workbook—a botany workbook—dating back to 1943 was found, and in it a Jewish child had drawn "the structure of a flower."

Later, when the pupils' lives were snuffed out, their words were left dangling in the air: "I am alive, you are alive, he is alive, we are alive, they are alive." "2 x 2 = 4." "Petals, sepals, and stamens."

A child who had forgotten what a loaf of bread looked like was practicing drawing flowers. That is why the term "pride" applies to this people, which went on educating its children to the very end.

Pride at having set a tank on fire with a Molotov cocktail, at having blown up a train, of having stabbed someone in the dark. At the glory of revolt.

"To our Breton comrades who lost their lives before their courage," I read some years ago on a marble plaque at Les Invalides, in the French army museum.

Where, on what marble or bronze plaque, will we find the inscription, "In memory of the Jewish children who refused the order to hang their clothes on hangers and tie their shoes together but instead threw their clothes on the floor before they were driven with whips into the gas chambers"?

Or, "In memory of the Jews of Grodno, who refused to die naked"?

Now that we have come to the arguments for the defense, there is no room for mourning or pride.

It is nausea that overcomes us.

Our people are not, by nature, cruel. As I sit in the hall, the audience I see following the testimony is far from rubbing its hands together with glee or clamoring for the hangman to do his work.

On the morning of the execution, the country will receive it, too, quietly.

The audience sits rapt, listening. The order of magnitude here is that of silent wonderment.

From time to time, there is laughter in the crowd.

It is a laughter that says, "What can you do?"

It has been said that he is determined not to go down in history as an ogre whose name will still scare children when they hear it a thousand years hence, that he is a very strong man with a surprising ability to withstand interrogation.

He might have done so if it hadn't been for the Sassen document.

Fifteen years had passed from the time Eichmann disappeared until the day he provided his Nazi comrade, journalist Willem Sassen,[39] with answers to his questions.

He could have vanished altogether, ceased to exist. Fifteen years. Half a generation. The graves were covered with grass. He could have repented. But the "quiet workman" Ricardo Clement[40] met Sassen fifteen years later and answered his questions, speaking the truth as he saw it. And in that room, filled with smoke and the clink of glasses, the past returned. A past of glorious exploits, of rank and command, of trains lumbering toward their destination from all directions. A thundering, purple past of "action squads" and conflagrations. A past of files and telephone calls and secretaries and black Mercedes automobiles. A past of boots and comradely laughter, of hard work, of flags, and trumpets. A past in which life had meaning.

And there, in the light cast by memories, he recounted story after story, coming back to life, setting things in order for future generations, waxing indignant all over again at the dead Krumey and Wisliceny for letting him down, so that there were still Jews left in Hungary "to make life miserable for the Magyar people."

What remnant of the Sassen document made it to the trial? Five or six pages. But every sentence was worth its weight in gold.

Now he had to tell a different story.

In one newspaper editorial, "Adolf Eichmann's Testimony," I read today, "What interests us at this moment is the *intellectual* level reflected in his testimony and explanations. For parallels can be drawn between Eichmann and other high officials of the Third Reich. . . . Eichmann, and apparently most of the Nazi leaders, were dangerous not only because they knew no moral inhibition . . . but

39. A Dutchman whose interview with Eichmann in Argentina in 1955 was published in *Life* and *Der Stern*.—Trans.
40. Eichmann's pseudonym while in hiding.—Trans.

because of their lack of education. . . . The picture we get is of a half-educated man trying to give the impression of being educated. . . . The world did not stop these uneducated, amoral individuals. . . . He is an ignoramus even in the field where he ostensibly became an expert."

I fail to understand why "what interests us at this moment" should be Eichmann's "intellectual level" or level of "education."

By presenting the Nazis as primitives, "dangerous" because they are "half-educated," the writer gives far too facile an explanation of those terrible events.

So Eichmann was uneducated, primitive, etc., and so were Hitler, the painter and corporal, and all his friends, who were "dangerous not only because they knew no moral inhibition . . . but because of their lack of education."

This is an offense to countless ordinary, decent people who can barely sign their own names but will pick up a crying child and kiss its forehead, will take pity on someone who is hurt, will open their homes to a fugitive from persecution; the many simple folk who live by the precepts of human brotherhood, warmhearted people who love their fellow human beings.

And supposing Eichmann had an academic degree and expertise and did not confuse Uganda and Madagascar, for example, would he then be any less an Eichmann?

They say the whole gang was made up of "simple people" with a deep sense of inferiority, and thus hatred, toward intellectuals.

We forget we are actually talking about an entire nation in a certain period of its history. Leaving aside the technocrats, the generals, and the scientists—all of them very well educated indeed—who created what was the mightiest and most efficient war machine in human history, we have to keep in mind the bitter truth that among those who marched at the head of this brown-shirted army were philosophers, writers, professors, and intellectuals, as well as a vast number of doctors, lawyers, and clergymen.

Say what you will about these people, they cannot be described as uneducated.

When France was liberated, hundreds of collaborators were brought to justice there, among them writers and poets who had seen National Socialism as a remedy for the spiritual ills of a "decadent, decrepit Europe."

It was an enormous body of educated people that paved the way for the Action Squads.

It was not for lack of education that Dr. Hans Globke played a key role in drafting the Nuremberg Laws, the first step toward the ovens.

Mengele was well versed in his profession. He even had a Ph.D.

It was not for lack of education that the bystanders looked on silently while blood was being shed, that the statesmen and heads of government saw a drowning man and did not throw him a lifeline.

This is a dangerous notion because it narrows the scope of the criminality, which hovers over an entire people. It blames the defendant's deeds on his personality, even though we know that those deeds were only part of a pattern of action taken by the people as a whole, a pattern that provided the legal, juridical, and philosophical basis for humiliation and murder.

As we have already pointed out, there were more Ph.D.s who had a hand in the destruction of the Jews of Europe than there were sergeants in the Einsatzkommando.

JUNE 26, 1961

"AN HOUR TO AN HOUR AND A HALF"

MONDAY, THE 12TH of Tammuz, 5721. Jerusalem. 8:35 A.M. You arrive five minutes late and find yourself in the middle of the Wannsee Conference. We learn from the witness that he "worked up Heydrich's presentation."

The word "presentation" is a bit awkward. "Presentation." Presumably, the protocol reports faithfully what was said there, but, according to Eichmann, "it reflects the content of the discussion at that meeting but smooths out the colloquialisms too much."

We do not know what "colloquialisms" were deleted in favor of "more official-sounding language."

Protocols, by their very nature, do not convey atmosphere.

Dr. Servatius asks the witness to convey the "atmosphere" to us.

We learn that "the atmosphere was well reflected in Heydrich's self-satisfied, uninhibited disposition."

Last week the witness told us that Heydrich, who stayed behind afterward with a few friends, smoked one cigar after another and drank one glass of brandy after another, then climbed up on the table and began to dance (a north German custom).

And what about the others?

"There was not only a cordial consensus among all those present but also a strong desire to work together to move this matter along, the solution of the problem of the Jews."

Now we discover that "the conference was quite short. I can't remember exactly how long it lasted, but it seems to me I would not be far wrong if I said that it took an hour to an hour and a half."

An hour to an hour and a half.

In an hour to an hour and a half, they wound things up. In an hour to an hour and a half, Heydrich gave his presentation, the others commented, and there was a summing up.

An hour to an hour and a half. At such a meeting, "people speak briefly and politely," the defendant told Inspector Less at the interrogation. "Waiters serve cognac."

Eichmann, too, probably sensed that this seemed like a very short time, and he added, "Of course, the gentlemen who participated had gathered earlier. They had stood about in groups and talked among themselves, undoubtedly about the subject of the conference as well as other matters."

You imagine the mansion in the garden suburb, the guest quarters, the mahogany furniture, the carpets, the waiters serving cognac to those who "stood about in groups," smoking and shaking hands with new arrivals ("How's the wife, by the way?").

Then someone—perhaps it is the witness, who, after all, organized the conference "clerically and administratively"—announces, "Gentlemen, you are requested to come inside." Everyone takes his seat. Then, after a moment of silence, Heydrich begins his presentation.

An hour to an hour and a half. An hour has sixty minutes. As a result of this "conference," the problem of six million Jews was "finally solved." Each minute, then, sealed the fate of a hundred thousand Jews.

It's too much, isn't it? Even at session 79, when we are long accustomed to hearing awful things. Even when the whole thing has begun to seem "boring."

I do not think this "hour to an hour and a half" will ever give me any rest.

"After the conference broke up, Heydrich and Mueller lingered for a while. I, too, stayed behind. I, too, was allowed to remain with this smaller group, where Heydrich expressed his gratification. Yes, he expressed satisfaction."

We could stop here. What else is there to say? We could go outside and mutter "an hour to an hour and a half," or we could shout "an hour to an hour and a half" in the middle of Zion Square. But no one leaves, not even we, for the proceedings must go on, and all of us are sober and sane, or perhaps we have crossed some kind of boundary and it no longer matters.

What do we learn next?

That "Heydrich was satisfied with the practical outcome of the conference. My satisfaction was with my own personality, in that it had been tested and weighed and not found wanting.

"I examined my own persona, and it left me content. I derived a certain peace of mind from the fact that I had done what I could, despite my low rank, to find a final solution that was not reprehensible, that was feasible and reasonable."

This brought us to a moment in the trial similar to the one when the words "an hour to an hour and a half" had been uttered. "So after all these efforts,"—in regard to Madagascar, etc.—"I could, in light of the Wannsee Conference, say to myself and tell myself that despite my wishes and not as a result of my planning"—his preparation of Heydrich's address had been merely a "clerical, administrative" matter—and through no fault of my own, and with a feeling like that of Pontius Pilate washing his hands of the matter, I could feel that I was not the one to blame. Because what happened at that conference was that the high and mighty, the peers of the realm, came and decided what was to be done. And I? I could only obey."

I think this passage is worth a closer look. We can leave aside, for now, the other matters raised in today's session: the deportees, the supply of skeletons to laboratories, the executions, the evacuations, etc.

He was a *major* player. He had authored the Madagascar plan: "solid ground under their feet." He had established a "state" for the Jews. He was satisfied with himself: after self-scrutiny, he concluded that his personality had been "tested and weighed and not found wanting." He is not blameworthy: "the high and mighty, the peers of the realm, came and decided what was to be done." He was a *minor* player: "I could only obey."

He obeyed and became, once again, a major player. The plan was changed. Instead of Madagascar, it was to be Auschwitz, and Heydrich appointed him his *referent* for the execution of the Final Solution. When it came time to implement the plan, Heydrich wrote Martin Luther, on February 28, 1942, "Please have your subordinate get in touch with my authorized *referent* Obersturmbannfuehrer Eichmann."

Judge Halevi: "Why, in what respect, or in what way were you Heydrich's *referent* in this matter?"

The witness's answer supplies the last piece in the puzzle of his personality ("the depths of the German soul"?): "Once the decision had been made at Wannsee, it had to be carried out. Since in Goering's letter appointing Heydrich he stipulates that the latter is to report to him concerning technical guidelines and the like for the attainment of the objective, . . . this administrative coordination between offices was assigned to Section IV-B4."

Conference, address, solution, decision, objective, technical guidelines, administration, office. . . .

Now everything is clear.

Now let us move on to the conclusion, to the name Pontius Pilate.

"With a feeling like that of Pontius Pilate washing his hands of the matter, I could feel that I was not the one to blame."

Adolf Eichmann says, "I could feel." He doesn't say, "I felt." He phrases it carefully, as if hinting that, all the same, there is a distinction to be made.

We go to the New Testament and reread what Pilate said (Matthew 27:24).

We ponder Pilate's words and Jesus' fate. We ponder Eichmann's words and the fate of the Jewish people, which was crucified in the twentieth century, during the interval between the two men's statements.

Suddenly, through the name of Pontius Pilate, the thing breaks the bounds of a closed world, a closed time, "another planet" that can only be imagined, and returns to the real world, to

Jerusalem, where both that Roman and this German said what they said. It returns to "history," to "culture," to Christianity.

Having traveled back into the depths of time, we return, to the accompaniment of the Auschwitz Symphony Orchestra.

JUNE 27, 1961

IVAN AND NIKOLAI

Once you see his line of defense you can predict everything he's going to say. It's a matter of principle with him: Section IV-B4 was just a way station, part of a conduit, within "proper channels." We've already seen the diagram: the Reich Security Head Office set up seven departments, one of which was Department IV, directed by Mueller, and under him were four sections, which, in turn, were divided into subsections. Eichmann was responsible for nothing more than one subsection, which, for some reason, is engraved in Jews' memories: IV-B4.

First we thought he had been a logistics officer. Then we had to demote him to sergeant. Now he presents himself as a clerk, a mere secretary who passed on letters and telegrams from his superiors to his subordinates and from his subordinates to his superiors, up, down, and sideways.

If he goes on testifying for another week, we will be reduced to tears and ask for his release, apologizing profusely for ever suspecting him and offering to pay damages.

"Servatius is brilliant," I hear people say. "Servatius's line of defense is stupid," I hear others say.

To my mind, there is more to the second opinion, although I wouldn't know what to suggest if he asked my advice.

He should be ready to give up a lot of territory so that he can hold on to that which is vital; that is, he should surrender parts of the front and concentrate his forces in a few main judicial strongholds, where his last battle can be fought. Instead, the counsel for the defense and the defendant have taken a different tack: to defend the entire front, from 1938 to 1945.

This approach cannot, by its very nature, concede that Adolf Eichmann was ever out of line. In principle, it makes no difference whether we are speaking of the personal cases of Mr. Wilner or Mrs. Cozzi or the timetables of the transports to Auschwitz.

Having said A he is obliged to say Z as well. He cannot admit to even a single mistake or failure or instance of "complicity in the destruction of the Jewish people," in the words of the indictment.

If he does, he will cease to be a logistics officer or sergeant or clerk or secretary or way station—the rest can be filled in easily enough.

On June 16, 1942, the Foreign Ministry calls Himmler's attention to a friendly request from Argentina that the Jew Wilner be spared internment in a concentration camp. The ministry forwards the request to the General Government. The General Government's reply is forwarded by the Reich Security Head Office to the Foreign Ministry by way of Section IV-B4 on July 9: "The aforementioned Jew, an Argentine national, died on April 12 of this year, despite treatment with heart-strengthening medications."

Eichmann claims he "could not have known what led the senior S.S. and police commander in Krakow to announce at the time that they intended to send this Jew to Auschwitz. All I could do was pass on to the Foreign Ministry the notice that Section IV-B4 had received from the General Government. This was another instance in which Section IV-B4 served as a mere way station."

It was the same in the case of Mrs. Cozzi, the Jewish widow of a non-Jewish Italian citizen. "The Italian embassy made efforts on her behalf, then the Italian Foreign Ministry, then the Fascist Party," according to Servatius.

That year some two million Jews were exterminated, but the fight for Mrs. Cozzi's life went on.

Were it not so very sad—Mrs. Cozzi, after all, wanted to go on living—it would be funny. But it was Eichmann who had the last laugh, however serious and disciplined he is here in Jerusalem. "On September 25, 1943, Section IV-B4, acting on instructions from the head of Department IV, was to notify the Foreign Ministry that, in view of the diplomatic circumstances, the Jew Cozzi was being transferred to a concentration camp."

On Mueller's instructions. Only a way station.

And on and on and on.

Presumably, there was no difference in principle between the case of Mrs. Cozzi and that of the Jews of Bratislava. As we have seen, Himmler gave orders to Heydrich, who passed them on to Mueller, who passed them on to Eichmann.

In the case of the Italian Jew, the instruction was not to release her; in the other case, it was to send them to the East.

So we shouldn't expect any change in the line of defense tomorrow or the next day, when we get to the liquidation of millions. Wc had a hint of it today in thc discussion of Theresienstadt.

This "way station" had no need for special forms. On the contrary, it was easier for our postal clerk to "solve the problem" of those Jews, because he didn't have to bother with a lot of correspondence. No ministries of friendly countries intervened to save their lives.

Two days later, too, the man would say, "It was not I, after all, who made the decisions. . . . I didn't have the authority to decide. . . . I only passed on the instructions and drew up the timetables."

We have already mentioned the power of the imagination, which helps us understand what these words mean.

Timetables: Dannecker in France, Richter in Romania, Wisliceny in Slovakia, and the others. And all roads led there, to the "state of the Jews."

Who, then, killed all those Jews? "Nikolai and Ivan," the two Ukrainians at Birkenau who introduced the Zyklon-B crystals into the gas chambers, according to the testimony of Eliyahu Rosenberg, a Jewish boy who served in the Sonderkommando and was tortured. "When everyone was inside, Ivan and Nikolai introduced the gas. . . . Afterward, we opened the doors."

Here was the last stop, the station at the end of all the proper channels, the terminal.

You didn't send them to the French Riviera, did you? Didn't

you know what would be done with them? There's no point in asking this question, because the day before yesterday we heard there had been a decision and there was no choice but to carry it out. Nevertheless, this game played by the little cog goes on, even though dozens of trials have proven that it is only hammers and sticks and pistols that are instruments or way stations, whereas human beings must take responsibility for their acts. For human beings are not just "a means to an end."

And, for heaven's sake, no more talk about "the regime" or "the times."

Yes, IV-B4 was one section of one department of the Reich Security Head Office, but what enormous power was wielded by this man, who, as a functionary in a "way station," sent millions of defenseless people from this world to the next.

So what do we have here? A game of honor, the desperate desire not to go down in history as a blood-drenched murderer?

German observers are saying the defendant has undergone a metamorphosis in Israel. He looks up to the court, respects the power that it represents. He wants to be seen as a different man, whatever the price.

Meanwhile, we are emerging from dreadfully long sessions in which we witness a phenomenon no less frightening than that of mass murder: a man's absolute refusal to take responsibility for his own actions. It is a phenomenon that recurs in all the trials, from that of the pettiest killer to those of the captains of the death industry, at Nuremberg.

I recall the last scene in the film *Night and Fog*. The Nuremberg defendants repeat, one after another, the refrain "Not guilty!" Then the camera leaves them for the silence of the empty camps, the fences, the barracks, the gas showers, the watchtowers. "Who, then, is guilty?" the French narrator asks.

It turns out to be "Ivan and Nikolai."

June 29, 1961

JACQUES STERN'S FACE

TODAY, I RECALLED the face of Georges Wellers, the head of the physiology laboratory at the Sorbonne medical school. The witness stand is on the stage opposite the glass booth. The defendant testifies from inside his booth. The witness stand is now empty.

Today, Georges Wellers sat there. He did and he didn't. It brought us back to France, to Drancy.

When Wellers first testified, on May 9, Eichmann maintained one of his prolonged silences, all the while taking copious notes.

Now Eichmann is speaking at length, and Wellers is sitting there mute, as people do when they are listening intently.

Servatius: "The next document, T/439, is a memorandum from Roethke, or more precisely from Dannecker, from Paris, dated July 21, 1942. It says, 'On July 20, 1942, Eichmann and Novak, from IV-B4, phoned. The deportation of the children is now being discussed with Eichmann. He has decided it will be possible to resume the shipment of the children as soon as deportation to Poland becomes feasible again.' I would like to ask the witness if he can explain this directive of his."

Eichmann: "Yes. Himmler had ordered the deportation of the Jews of France without reservation or limitation. The French police had arrested children, among others. And so they turned to us and inquired urgently what should be done with those children. In replying to this inquiry, I passed on what is written here. . . . If you read the document as its stands, without reference to any others . . ."

Wellers: "The children arrived in the camp in the latter part of August, in four transports of a thousand children each, guarded by French police. . . . Quietly, in groups, the children got off the trains. The older ones held the younger ones by the hand. Their clothes were tattered, and many had been left with only one shoe."

Eichmann: "One could get the impression that I decided right then and there what would be done with the children. As if I had the authority to make such decisions. But, as the document makes clear—it's original number was 64, and it is a telegram—on July 10, 1942, an inquiry was referred to me, to IV-B4, from Paris, informing me that the children had been arrested and asking what to do with them, whether to deport them or not."

Wellers: "Many children did not know their own names. Some of the camp inmates, including me, gave the children names and wrote them on tags, which were hung around the children's necks."

Eichmann: "The very fact that the matter was delayed eleven days until a decision was made and a directive issued shows that it went through proper channels to the highest local authorities."

Wellers: "The children were brought to empty rooms where the floors were covered with mats crawling with fleas."

Eichmann: "Eleven days later, when a final decision about the inquiry was finally taken, I passed it on to Paris by phone."

Wellers: "Many of the children were awakened at night by bad dreams and cried out for their parents. One child who woke up crying would awaken the others, and so the night passed."

Eichmann: "It must be pointed out that although Himmler's order had called explicitly for deporting the Jews, the inquiry was referred by Department IV to a higher echelon, the question being whether the order applied to children."

Wellers: "Then a teenage boy asked if he would be leaving the camp soon to join his parents. I knew that once they had been sent to Auschwitz they would never see their parents again. I lied to the boy and told him, 'Don't worry. You'll join your parents in a few days.'" Dr. Wellers wipes away a tear. "Then a boy named Jacques Stern took a half-eaten cookie out of his shabby coat pocket and said to us, 'I've been keeping this for my mother, and I'm going to give it her when we meet.' Suddenly, the boy burst into tears. We couldn't bear it and left the room."

Eichmann: "Here, in the documents relating to France, you see the intermediary role clearly, the clearinghouse role that my office played."

Wellers: "When the time came for the transfer, they would awaken the children at five in the morning. . . . They were loaded onto trains, in shipments of a thousand children each, and so they made their final journey, to Auschwitz. The children remained half asleep. Many of them did not want to get off and cried. They were pulled from the trains by the policemen."

Dr. Wellers is not there. The witness stand is empty. The defendant is still explaining and clarifying and shedding light.

Servatius: "The document the defendant is referring to is Exhibit T/613. The next document is number 962. The reference indicated is 'Ongoing Discussions with Eichmann.' In a letter signed by Mueller, in the last line on page 3, it says, and I quote, 'A general Italian position on the question we are dealing with . . . makes it absolutely impossible to fulfill the demand the Fuehrer has made in every speech, in every proclamation.'"

Judge Raveh: "Who, then, wrote this?"

Eichmann: "This letter, considering that it served as a basis for discussion . . ."

Presiding judge: "You have been asked who wrote this document. The answer to this is very short. You haven't been paying attention to my comments to you about this."

Eichmann: "I beg your pardon. I am only making an effort to explain the matter in detail, and I keep making the same error. I shall try to correct it."

Judge Raveh: "So who wrote the document?"

Eichmann: "The document was edited by the head of my office, and I elaborated on it and dictated it according to his instructions and according to the wording he wanted included."

Judge Raveh: "Who assembled the details mentioned in the letter?"

Eichmann: "Your honor, this I do not know. But certainly I would have gotten them from the head of my office."

And so on.

In such situations, I always bow my head. It is hard for me. Maybe it's a character weakness. There is a feeling of embarrassment and shame. He is lying. But it is hard to see a grown man caught in his own lies.

I do not always remember who this man is. I forget. I have an above-average imagination. But sometimes I forget. Afterward, I remember. A drop in the bucket: the phone call to Dannecker on July 20, 1942. The resumption of the shipments as soon as they can be "handled" there in the East. The face of Jacques Stern in the truck making its way across Europe. Dr. Wellers's story.

"I shall try to correct my error, your honor."

With great effort, he may be able to shorten his lengthy German sentences with the verbs at the end, to speak briefly.

There are things he cannot correct: that phone call to Dannecker, sending those children to Uncle Rudolf, who lives way off in Birkenau.

"Pardon me, your honor."

June 30, 1961

IN THE MADHOUSE

"I AM FINISHING the documents about Greece, and I hope I will have time today to discuss Bulgaria, Romania, and Slovakia. Perhaps I will even manage to begin on Hungary, so that by tomorrow I will deal with Hungary and the question of the concentration camps."

Yes, Servatius does manage to "begin on Hungary."

It goes quickly when you do it in hopscotch fashion.

I close my eyes and choose, at random, Exhibit T/973. It is a letter dated May 21, 1943, from a Foreign Ministry official named Wagner to the German consulate general in Salonica. The subject is "Jewish families of French nationality." It seems "the French government has inquired about this matter." Further on, he says that "neither the German embassy in Paris nor the Foreign Ministry is interested in these French Jews being returned."

It's simple.

"The embassy in Paris will therefore notify the French government two weeks hence that the deportation was required for military reasons and reasons within the purview of the Security Police and that it has already been completed, so that the question is moot."

What else is there to say?

"Please direct their units accordingly." And in a note attached to a copy of this letter sent to Eichmann, Wagner writes, "For your information. Emphasis on the issuing of appropriate instructions to the action squad."

Stop! Stop! Stop!

It is 8:46. The beginning of the morning session. Today, as promised, five countries will pass before you, along with hundreds of similar examples.

I wriggle out of my white straitjacket, so that I can go out to the lobby for a moment and sit down on a bench.

Why has Servatius chosen to cite this particular document, T/973?

He wants to prove that the deportation and extermination were initiated by the Foreign Ministry—this he does prove, with dozens of documents—and by local authorities throughout the occupied areas, and that Eichmann had to act accordingly.

Yes, the German Foreign Ministry has a respectable name. The Foreign Ministry. Von Ribbentrop. It is a name that now drips Jewish blood, drips ceaselessly. Alongside such names as "action squads," Maidanek, and IV-B4.

But what sort of defense is this?

It is madness, not a line of defense. Utter madness. The insanity has gone on for days. Since the witness first opened his mouth to answer the defense counsel's questions. One big fit of madness, a madness that does not vary, that does not smile. A very serious madness. A madness so profound that it regards itself as normal.

Exhibit T/973 is a "mild" document. We have seen even crazier ones today.

But what is the greatest insanity of all?

Let us repeat what is already well known: the counsel for the defense is turning all the incriminating documents into exculpating ones. Using this same method.

I cannot deal with any more episodes today. We have gotten to Hungary. The same method is applied there. The defense's method does not change.

Eichmann complains to the Foreign Ministry that the Romanians are expelling Jews across the River Bug. "There is a danger of further expulsions, . . . and we must act to put an end to the illegal shipments."

The witness, in full possession of his faculties, goes on clarifying and illuminating.

July 4, 1961

GHOSTS

It was one of the longest days of my life. When I left at the end of Session 85 and went out to Menora Square, I had no sense of what time it was.

The reason was the sudden turn the defense counsel's presentation had taken. Today, we heard testimony taken in Europe from Nazis who had not been allowed or who had refused to come here to testify in person: Wilhelm Hoettl, Walter Huppenkothen, Eberhard von Thadden, Hans Juettner, Horst Theodor Grell, and Kurt Becher.

This long day was a highly concentrated distillation of the entire trial.

The day began with quiet deliberation over procedural matters. "I think, Mr. Hausner, that the correct order would be as follows: since these are to be considered witnesses for the prosecution, let us hear, first of all, from Dr. Servatius what he wants entered into the transcript, and then what you are interested in," the presiding judge says. The prosecutor replies, "As the court wishes." And the counsel for the defense says, "I have no objection." They agree to begin with Wilhelm Hoettl.

In connection with the latter's testimony, I hear Servatius say, "In the view of the court, the significance of the Eichmann trial for world history demands, does it not, that we make use of all possible means to assist us in ascertaining the truth, to the best of our abilities."

This long day swings back and forth between hundreds of highly significant details and dates and fine points of procedure, on one hand, and "the significance of the Eichmann trial for world history," on the other.

Between 12:10 and 12:25, the court takes up a most important question: whether or not to allow the testimony of Kurt Becher, it having turned out that the questions sent from here had been given to him by the German judge only a few days before the interrogation.

There was a lively, interesting argument between the attorneys, and then the court decided, in ruling number 88, to allow the testimony. "But of course we will consider this fact in our evaluation of it."

A few minutes later, we hear Becher quoting Himmler: "Get whatever you can out of the Jews. Promise them whatever they demand. What we are actually going to deliver, we shall see." A quick transition, wasn't it?

We hear this man, today a respectable businessman, say, "I was opposed to it. I decreed that under all circumstances we should keep our agreements with the Jews."

The line "Eichmann murdered, Becher came into the money" sticks in my mind. There is a lot of nausea to suppress.

Following questions of hearsay about the relations between Himmler and Mueller and Kaltenbrunner, between Eichmann and Himmler, and others, which momentarily distract us from our subject (so, what were their relations like anyway?), we come to the Black Forest, near Trieberg, to the Reichsfuehrer's official railway car. "You might say Himmler was both rough and gentle in speaking to Eichmann. I remember his shouting at him, 'If until now you've been exterminating Jews, now you are the one who must take care of them. I am the one giving the orders, not you or Gruppenfuehrer Mueller!'"

Perhaps we should stop here and ponder this marvelous sentence. For the moment, everything else is less important. December 1944. Becher, the "rescuer," convinces Himmler to stop, complaining about Eichmann, and it has to do with Mueller and Kaltenbrunner, and they say Eichmann is circumventing Himmler and going on with the exterminations instead of "taking care of" the Jews. He continues to ship them off—but no, it isn't he who does the shipping. It's the Hungarians! It's Winkelmann! It's Veesenmayer! It's Geschke! Von Thadden says Veesenmayer played a key role in it. Then we find out that "the supremacy of the Reich Security Head Office over the Foreign Ministry was unambiguous." "Eichmann informed me of the contents of the plan. I was shocked. I was in full agreement with others in the Foreign Ministry that it should be blocked." The Foreign Ministry is in the clear. It is Eichmann who is guilty. No! Yes! "Winkelmann told us he had been circumvented, that he had nothing to do with the march to Austria." "Winkelmann knew about the transports." Wait a minute, what does Juettner say? "He is convinced it was the Hungarian government that was mainly responsible for deporting the Jews from Hungary."

And what does Horst Theodor Grell say? Yes, on page 7, at the bottom, fifth line from the end: "Late in the fall of 1944, Eichmann once said to me, when we happened to be talking, that the enemy powers saw him as the number-one war criminal and that he had the lives of six million people on his conscience. . . . Eichmann wasn't drunk, not even tipsy, at the time of this conversation." That's what Grell says. On June 20, 1961, in the city of Bremen.

He wasn't drunk.

"Then Eichmann began gulping down shots of whisky, one after another. I put a bottle and a glass in front of him. We were alone in the room," says Wilhelm Hoettl, the intelligence officer. "Eichmann got up and left, saying, 'I suppose we won't be seeing each other again. . . . The Allies regard me, because of my role in the extermination of the Jews, as one of the chief war criminals.' . . . I had always wondered how many Jews had been exterminated," Hoettl goes on, "mainly because I am a historian. . . . Eichmann said it was a deep, dark secret, but in his situation he could tell me."

And in that room, face to face, over a bottle of whisky, Eichmann said, "Six million have died so far. Four million by gas, two million by shooting and from disease. Himmler says there have been more."

We have learned that when he said these things, "Eichmann had drunk four or five double shots of whisky, but I did not get the impression that the figures he used were invented on the spot."

No, the figures were not invented on the spot.

A very long day. What exactly were the "normal channels"? There, in the maze of Roman numerals and Latin letters and Arabic numerals . . . Geschke, Winkelmann, Mueller, Mueller, Mueller, Veesenmayer, Eichmann, Eichmann.

The Jews died in the interstices between "areas of jurisdiction."

July 5, 1961

THAT DEAL

Today, as Adolf Eichmann was giving us his version of the Budapest deal with Joel Brand, many reporters downstairs learned that the Israelis had launched a rocket into space. I heard about it myself in the snack bar. At first, I was incredulous. When I learned it was true, I got excited and hurried to the press room. The cables that normally carried the horror stories around the world were suddenly saying something different. The air was filled with giddy amazement at the sensational development. People huddled in little groups talking about the missile.

A German reporter said, "Pretty soon you'll be encircling the globe with twenty-five hydrogen bombs."

Upstairs, Eichmann went on talking.

At the espresso bar, Joel Brand was standing alone drinking coffee.

"He's talking about you," a reporter said.

"To hell with him," Brand said and left the room.

I must say it wasn't easy to go back upstairs to hear and see what was going on there. Even more than before, the courtroom seemed unreal, like some strange dream.

Let's go back. The truck deal had always seemed like a fiction dreamed up by tormented, desperate people.

It had been written about, talked about. Long ago. The other party to the negotiations, Adolf Eichmann, had seemed so remote sitting there in the Schwabian mountains in his black uniform, at the far end of that mad world. "Give me ten thousand trucks, and

I'll give you a million Jews." Then Istanbul and Aleppo and Cairo. We knew there was something to it, didn't we? And yet we didn't know. Because it all seemed so unreal, like a bad joke.

When Joel Brand, a broken, nervous man, took the stand and gave a detailed account of the negotiations, he tried, with shouts and grimaces, to imitate Eichmann's voice and facial expression. The defendant kept silent. Even when Brand said, "It was a terrible proposal; it destroyed my life; I had a million Jews looking over my shoulder"—even then, the defendant kept silent.

Today, the "other side" confirmed the details of this unreal affair. Now things are quite clear: "Why did I choose Brand? He seemed to me an honest, idealistic man. Personally, I was very happy to see Brand testify here and give a description on the witness stand that was largely accurate, with a few minor exceptions that I would like to take up."

For a moment, I forget what is being discussed. It seems to me it is just a matter of two people who met long ago to make a deal, which for some reason went sour, and they both regret it.

The description of one of the "minor exceptions" brings me back to the reality of the courtroom: "Joel Brand is not correct in saying that I told him I would stop the mills at Auschwitz."

It is the word "Auschwitz" that brings us back to the matter at hand.

What Auschwitz? What are we talking about?

"If afterward this deal was blocked from abroad, it is I who was very sorry about it at the time, and I will permit myself to say that I can certainly understand Joel Brand's anger and pain. I only hope that Joel Brand, in light of the documents that now prove to him that it was not I who was responsible for the exterminations, will, for his part, understand my anger and rage."

These things were said at 11:30 yesterday morning. Joel Brand was sitting in the audience, listening.

"It is I who was very sorry. . . . I can certainly understand Joel Brand's anger and pain."

Yes, these two people were sitting across the table from each other. It didn't go well. A third party interfered. What can you do? It happens.

Then, once more, out of the blue, we hear the words, "it was not I who was responsible for the exterminations." And you want to ask again, What is he talking about? What exterminations? It is only Servatius's red neck and the prosecution's black robes and the faces of the judges and the bailiff scurrying about that remind you what, after all, we are talking about here.

Words fill the hall. "I couldn't imagine that nothing would come of it . . . I went back to the work I had been doing since 1939, and the peddlers, the profiteers got their due and were happy . . . I never touched any foreign money . . . I passed on every last dollar. I did everything according to the letter of the law."

An honest man. He didn't take any money. He didn't cheat at cards.

The deal fell through. "It is I who was very sorry."

Then you leave. It is hard for you to stay. You leave and go downstairs. You run into a friend. "Well, have you heard the news?" And he tells you about the rocket. And down in the press room there is the same frenzy over this sensational development.

It is 1:30. Servatius says, "Tomorrow I should like to go on to the question of the concentration camps."

July 6, 1961

ON ASSIGNMENT

"IT WASN'T WINTER yet, because I remember green trees next to two farmer's huts, trees with leaves on them. So I guess it was late summer or early autumn."

Who is speaking? It is Eichmann. It is the last day of his testimony.

His testimony is coming to an end, and these are the concluding words.

"Sir, you made several trips. On several occasions, you went to the camps where extermination was going on. Can you tell us what those trips were about? In what capacity did you go there? On what mission were you sent? What did you do there? What did you have done there? And what did you report?"

"May I be permitted to begin with the first trip I made in the performance of my duties?"

Yes, he is permitted to begin with his first trip.

He is summoned by Heydrich, who tells him, "The Fuehrer has ordered the physical extermination of all the Jews."

In the transcript, three lines intervene between this sentence and the following one: "I reached Lublin and presented myself there. To Globocnik." He is accompanied by an escort to "a place [he] hadn't known about." "I saw two farmer's huts there. A police chief told me these two buildings were to be sealed up 'so that gas from a Russian submarine motor could be piped in to kill Jews.'"

He goes back to Berlin and reports to Mueller and Heydrich.

"Green trees." Autumn, 1941.

The second trip is to Kulmhof. This time, it is Mueller who

gives the order: "Go to Warthegau, to Kulmhof. They are exterminating Jews with gas there. I want a report on how it is done."

"In Lodz I was assigned an official who knew the way. I went there. I observed what was being done. I took notes. I returned to Berlin and reported to Mueller."

His manner is businesslike. Almost telegraphic.

Kulmhof is Chelmno. Only three people got out of there alive: Podchlevnik, Zurawski, and Srebnik. All three have testified here.

When he heard the truth about Chelmno, Yitzhak Zuckerman had shouted, "Who could believe it? How could it be?"

Now there is silence in the courtroom.

We are still thinking about the name Kulmhof when the witness is confronted with documents showing he was there. "In that case, one could say, on the basis of this, that I was there at the end of December." He claims he asked Mueller to assign him to a different job. "'I am not the right person for this work.'" And the commander of the Gestapo told him, "A soldier on the front lines cannot choose where he is to be stationed either. He has to serve wherever he is told."

Then he does his "duty" by going to Minsk, "where they are killing them by shooting them." "I want a report about this," Mueller tells him.

"I arrived in the middle of an extermination operation. They were shooting a group of people standing in a pit. I saw them shoot an infant in its mother's arms." Mention of the Jewish baby compels him to add, "I have already testified what my reaction was at the time." He hastens to add when it was. "I was wearing a long leather coat, so it must have been the winter of 1941–42." The cold Russian winter.

"I was ordered to go to Auschwitz." You sense a tone of ownership in the way he says this word. Later, Eichmann disputes Hoess's version of the dates of his visit. Hoess says it was June 1941. Eichmann claims it was later. (This disagreement is important to him, because he is trying to prove that he did not initiate the extermination but that his job was merely to report on the actions being taken, without any connection to his trips.)

How well his memory serves him. "Hoess says that in the summer of 1941 he was burying the bodies in mass graves and that they had not yet begun burning them on iron grids. But when I visited there, I could see they were burning bodies on grids, and I included this in my report."

This last line is meant to serve in his defense. People are getting up and walking out. Those who remain behind have a similar expression on their faces. But no one cries out.

Eichmann goes on. "These were the work-related trips I was ordered to make. I was not asked to give advice or intervene. I was asked to look, to observe, to watch, and to write up a report without comment."

He tells us he carried out these orders "with the greatest reluctance," that he "asked to be transferred to a different job," "but I was ordered by my superior to do this, and I had to carry out these orders."

To round out his testimony—his last words?—he tells us of another trip he made to Lublin. He was carrying a letter to Gruppenfuehrer Odilo Globocnik "containing a directive or delegation of responsibility or endorsement for the killing of 150,000 Jews."

On this trip he thought it "a bit strange and funny for Globocnik to be asking for retroactive endorsement of the operation, since the operation was almost over."

Concerning this same trip he adds, "I passed through Lvov, and there I saw a geyser of blood for the first time. Jews had been killed there previously, and evidently the gas generated in the mass graves was forcing the blood upward, and it spurted out like a geyser.

"As I have read in Reitlinger's book [*The Final Solution*], that operation ended some time between the 10th and the 22nd of August, and during those days that was the treatment the Jews received there."

Eichmann says these things in the same tone and at the same pace that have characterized his testimony since the very first day.

When the presiding judge tells him to stop, he stops, and he rises briefly in gratitude. When he is told to go on, he goes on. "*It was to me that this happened, me, whose thinking was in an entirely different direction and who had devised the Madagascar plan and who hadn't the slightest thought of or inclination toward such a bloody campaign, such a solution by force."*

There is a faint smile in the courtroom. A person cannot incriminate himself.

And at this point the witness says his last, summary sentences: "I got involved in this against my will. I had to obey orders. I had to do it. That is all I can say."

When he spoke of the incident in the cherry grove he said, "I never killed anyone, never struck anyone."

JULY 7, 1961

THE CROSS-EXAMINATION

The court has taken a mid-morning recess. I am startled by the preliminary notes my own hand is making about Eichmann's final testimony.

I think I have just had one of those flashes of clarity with which we are so rarely favored, which banish the sloth that keeps us from grasping what we see happening before our very eyes.

The auditorium is packed today. I don't recognize everyone in the crowd. There are journalists, cabinet ministers, officials and their wives. There are Unit 06 people: Zelinger in his uniform, Hofstadter and others in civilian garb. Here is Inspector Goldman, the boy who survived eighty lashes and has come to take part in the prosecution.

I see Jewish tourists, black people from friendly countries, Israeli teenagers, soldiers and army officers, and all around them an anonymous crowd of people, many of whom were *there*.

Perhaps one of them is the man who saw his wife and children "go to the left." And perhaps next to him is the man whose sister fell into his arms when, "after thirty minutes," the door opened. And perhaps next to him is the man who is still alive thanks to the three centimeters he added to his height. And all the others, whose stories we now know.

The atmosphere is both solemn and unsettling. It is reminiscent of the morning the trial began, three months ago.

The defendant's summation. And the beginning of the cross-examination.

This morning the trial reached a climax, if I may use that expression. Let us backtrack to the last moments before the recess.

Servatius: "I have a question for the witness by way of summary. You arranged the shipments to the various camps. Did you know that at least some of those people would be put to death?"

You could hear a pin drop.

Eichmann: "My orders were to arrange the shipments. To tell the truth, I must admit I did know that some of those people would be killed."

Servatius: "You said during the police interrogation that you were hounded by guilt. Could you tell the court how you now see the matter of this guilt?"

The added word "now" is important, because since the time of the interrogation there have been several months of trial proceedings, during which Eichmann has seen and heard all the same things we have.

"Now," some time later.

Then the defendant says, in a firm, clear voice, as if lecturing, "I must distinguish here between juridical guilt and human guilt." (Between the poles of this Germanic distinction, I see the mass grave of European Jewry.) "The facts concerning which I have been called to account are those of my role in the deportations. But the deportations were at that time a policy directive of the regime, and the guilt devolves upon those who bore, or bear, responsibility for setting policy."

And here, far from breaking down and confessing his "human guilt," the Obersturmbannfuehrer goes on to expound his philosophy. "Where there is no responsibility, there can be no guilt. As long as human beings have lived together in society, no one has ever devised any comprehensive solution other than political arrangements grounded in orders and obedience to orders." Erect and animated, he goes on. "In order to strengthen its own security, the state finds a way of binding and obligating the individual, and this is the oath of allegiance." (See the Nordic swearing-in ceremonies in the film *Mein Kampf*.) "But responsibility and conscience"—this word, foreign and battered, interpolates itself here and is quickly lost in the onward flow of the declamation—"hang over the states' leaders. Those who get good leadership are fortunate. Those whose states are not well led are unfortunate, and I was unfortunate. My role in these deportations grew out of the directives of my legal superiors, the heads of the S.S. and the S.D."—Heydrich, and later Kaltenbrunner—"who passed them on to the head of my office, Mueller, who gave me my orders."

The prosecution would later focus its attack on this point. The Gestapo man goes on: "In the S.S., violations of discipline were punishable by death. I did all I could to obtain a transfer to some other job. I was unsuccessful. I had to obey orders. I was in uniform. It was wartime."

The monologue does seem to explain something.

But it is not enough to undo anything. Those who were killed because of this "concept" cannot be brought back to life.

The man continues: "Moral guilt, the inner sense of guilt, a human being's inner self, is something else altogether. But this takes us to more exalted spheres than the letter of the law."

The interpreter goes on translating word for word. I listen. There is no mistake. "Here, each person must judge himself and call himself to account. I myself have done this, and I continue to do so."

The hush pervading the room is one of astonishment. Not anger. Not pain. Not hatred. Just amazement. "A human being's inner self."

Now the man has no difficulty saying, "I can express condemnation and sorrow over the extermination of the Jews. . . . But I was merely a tool in the hands of superior powers and higher authorities, in the hands of a merciless fate."

The same silence.

This moment—allowing for the six-million-fold difference—reminds me of Dr. Grueber's closing words, spoken in a loud, pleading voice, about "a love that forgives and a wrong that is forgiven." It is a dreadful moment, in which anything can happen. But however much Eichmann tries to "explain" things and his own part in them—to rise above, to circumvent, to reduce to abstraction, to judge in hindsight, to juggle between the "human" and the "legal," between "self" and laws/orders/chains of command—the thicker and more intolerable is the sense of horror in room.

The defendant does not crack, does not forgo his dignity. He is prepared to express "condemnation and sorrow" for the extermination of the Jews.

The abrupt transition from this stance to talk of "proper channels" and the chain of command makes every allusion to change of heart and remorse seem farcical. No, the usual terminology doesn't fit this time or place. He could have come across as a real madman, another Hitler, or as a pathologically apathetic figure like Hoess, who in his "wayward youth" had been commandant of Auschwitz but who sat like an indifferent spectator at the Polish trial where he was condemned to death. But Eichmann is neither of these. He is a man of strong character engaged, he explains, in an unceasing struggle. He comes up with ideas like "superior powers," "fate," and the "self" in order to come back again and again to his well-known refrain, "I was only obeying orders." Then you see, for the thousandth time, that they were *all* obeying orders. Even those he says gave the orders and thus deserve to die.

"All rise!" the bailiff shouts. And everyone gets up and files out.

Forty-five minutes later, the session resumes.

Tension is at its height. The time has come for the prosecutor to cross-examine.

Every courtroom seems at times like a theater, an arena. Along with the ultimate seriousness you can find an element of histrionics, of professional role-playing. "Hausner's moment has come," I hear people say. Now, after all, he is not going to make speeches of accusation or lament, like his unforgettable opening statement. Now, as interrogator, he will have to prove his skill at cross-examination, his brilliance, his command of the material, his ability to jab and thrust, to surprise, to be forceful and unpredictable.

At the same time, he must keep in mind who this defendant is and what the interrogation is about, without letting his emotions get the better of him.

Presiding judge (to the defendant): "You must now answer the attorney general's questions."

Eichmann: "Yes, your honor."

Prosecutor: "Sir, during your interrogation by the police, at the end of the first statement you submitted, you said, 'I know that I shall be found guilty as an accessory to murder. I know that the death penalty awaits me, and I do not ask for mercy, because I do not deserve it.' Could you now repeat these words, here in this courtroom?"

Eichmann: "I stand by what I said in that submission, and this morning, while answering the defense counsel's questions, I repeated it."

Prosecutor: "You admit, then, that you were an accessory to the murder of millions of Jews?"

Eichmann: "This I cannot admit."

We stop here.

Everything has now been erased, and we have gone back to square one, leaving a trail of battered verbiage behind us.

The cross-examination has begun.

July 9, 1961

INSOMNIA

The morning session never took place.

Presiding judge: "I hereby call to order session 89 of this trial. The court has received a request from the counsel for the defense stating that because of the defendant's physical condition he is unable to withstand interrogation during the morning hours. We shall comply with the defense counsel's request, and therefore this session is adjourned."

"Insomnia," they say. The defendant lies awake all night despite the sleeping pills he takes. It is one of the first signs we have that he is human, other than his twitching lips and blinking eyes. It is a disquiet of the heart. He breathes uneasily. "I continue to call myself to account." So he said on Friday. Or perhaps it is a physical fear. The walls of the jail. No escape. A tiny particle of the fear felt by the victims of Section IV-B4.

"I should like to tell you," the presiding judge says in the afternoon, "that during the translation you can sit down to rest, even without special permission from me."

"Yes," Eichmann says.

"And if you feel tired, you can ask me and I will allow you to give all your testimony sitting down, should that be necessary."

He is not young, the defendant. He is fifty-four. For him, too, time has passed. Only the dead have not gotten any older: the children of Drancy, eternally youthful in the photographs.

"If you feel tired, you can ask me." I am filled with sadness. Accounts are being settled here in such a human fashion. Civility is being upheld. "You can ask me." It could all have been otherwise. One human being says to another, to the same man who sent a whole people to its death in railway cars, "You can sit down to rest." "Yes, I knew that some of those people would be put to death there."

"Sir," the prosecutor says, "when you joined the Nazi party, did you know the slogans 'Germany, awake!' 'Let Judah die like a dog,' 'When Jewish blood drips from the knife, our lot shall be doubly improved,' and so on?"

"In Austria, in the mountain valleys, I never heard such songs or slogans." In those places, the yodeling of the mountain folk in their leather breeches still echoed and re-echoed. He never heard.

It was not because of the war against the Jews that he had joined up. "What motivated me was the war against Versailles." That is why, between 1937 and 1945, he was dealing with the Jews.

"Did you know your Fuehrer had decreed that, in the event of war, the Jewish people would be annihilated?"

"Yes, I saw the Jewish people as a potential rival that could endanger my fatherland."

"And from that point on, you viewed the Jews as an enemy to be annihilated?"

"The word 'annihilated' is not appropriate," Eichmann explains to us, "because one does not always annihilate an enemy. One fights an enemy." He then goes on to explain that he did not understand Hitler to mean "physical annihilation."

"Are you aware of any kind of annihilation that is not physical?" the prosecutor asks sarcastically.

And here Eichmann says something very interesting: "Yes, the struggle against France or England was conducted with an eye to rendering the enemy harmless until the end of the war, and after the war was over, there would be no more hostility, no feeling of hostility."

Had they won, the next in line after the Jews would have been the Poles, the Czechs, the Russians, etc.—according to the plan.

As it turned out, others won, and there was, indeed, "no more hostility, no feeling of hostility." (The Jews, too, are beginning to forget. Some go back there. Some send Uzis and teachers there. Some spend their vacations there.)

The prosecutor is on the attack. It turns out the defendant still believes, or wants us to believe, that he wanted "to give the Jewish people some solid ground to stand on."

I assume that was not your own idea. Who were the other saints who had this idea? Heydrich? Himmler? Streicher? Rosenberg? Who!?"

"As far as I know, I was the only one to express this idea," Eichmann says. He refers to Adolf Boehm's book: "All the evil is the result of the fact that this people has no ground underfoot, no homeland."

We are getting closer to the Land of Israel.

"Your trip to Palestine was intended, among other things, to cement ties here with Haj Amin al-Husseini,[41] was it not?"

"The purpose," Eichmann says, "was, first of all, to get to know the country and how people lived here. Beyond that, it was meant to establish contacts and connections with people."

"I am speaking of Haj Amin al-Husseini!"

"Yes, with him too."

Returning from the Land of Israel, the author of the Radom and Madagascar plans writes a report on his trip in which, among other things, he says, "For want of Aryans in Palestine to cheat, the Jews cheat one another."

When he was interrogated by Section 06, he admitted to having written this report. Now he denies it. It was not he but Hagen who wrote it. And then he starts explaining why he could not have been the author. "Such ideas were put forward by *Der Stuermer*. I never thought that way."

An English journalist who recently interviewed Hans Globke writes, "The amazing thing about the Germans is their ability to

41. Mufti of Jerusalem, a Nazi sympathizer.—Trans.

espouse lies and actually believe they are true." ("The depths of the German soul.")

Eichmann also denies the authenticity of a whole series of documents showing that he tried to persuade Himmler to cancel his "harsh decree" allowing the Hungarian Jews to go to the Land of Israel. "You challenged the ruling and asked for a new one," said the prosecutor, "while at the same time trying to arrange it that by the time the formalities were worked out, the Jews would already have been deported."

The defendant is told to read aloud the document marked T/1215. He reads the passages that leave him a way out. But there is none. He has to read it all. "Read on!" the prosecutor says, raising his voice. "Read on!"

And he reads from Veesenmayer's report: "'S.S. Sturmbannfuehrer Eichmann has taken a position on this. . . .'" He mumbles. "'As far as he knows, Himmler has not agreed to the emigration of the Hungarian Jews. . . . They are biologically valuable material. Their emigration is undesirable.'"

"Read on!" the prosecutor shouts.

So Eichmann goes on. "'I intend, in light of the Fuehrer's decision, to give a report [directly] to the Reichsfuehrer and, if necessary, to request a revised ruling with the Fuehrer's backing.'"

The thirty-seven-year-old Adolf Eichmann, in his S.S. uniform and jackboots, is beating to death the fifty-four-year-old Adolf Eichmann, who stands in the glass booth in Jerusalem, looking pale and mumbling, "It was an order."

July 11, 1961

FALSEHOOD

"I SWEAR TO tell the truth, the whole truth, and nothing but the truth." Standing at attention, his hand raised, and speaking confidently, Adolf Eichmann took this oath. That was three weeks ago, on Tuesday, June 20.

What is left of the oath today?

This afternoon the attorney general got what he wanted. Eichmann reached the limit of his ability to reinterpret, and the truth was laid bare. It was the truth that the witnesses for the prosecution had unfurled before a weeping audience.

It had been hard work. Eichmann had fought back. Only this morning, the foreign reporters were asking when Hausner would give up.

We must remember that the Israeli justice system gave this defendant ideal conditions for his defense. (All the Nuremberg defendants would have envied him.) He was able to go over every document with a fine-tooth comb. He was given plenty of time to refresh his memory and to study the material, both during his interrogation by Section 06 and during the trial, when he was in close contact with his defense attorney.

He chose to undergo cross-examination rather than making do with a single statement. Did he really believe it was worth the risk? What did he hope to accomplish?

When he answered the defense counsel's questions, he was well prepared, practiced and drilled. Over the course of those two weeks, we watched him as he applied his German diligence to erecting an enormous, towering edifice of lies.

The prosecution's first blows shook the structure. Today its supportive pillars began to give way. He is now alone. At this stage he may no longer meet with Servatius. He must improvise answers to unanticipated questions. Not infrequently, the pauses for translation rescue him at the last moment. He takes a deep breath and quickly comes up with a phrase that will save him from an unambiguous reply. You are afraid you may not catch him. He has a phenomenal talent for evasion. But he, too—with all his cunning, experience, agility, ability to slide in between the lines, to skirt them and hem them in with lengthy interpretive discourses—he, too, finds himself, all at once, up against a blank wall, unable to pursue his tried and true tactics any further.

The documents will not leave him be. There were 111 witnesses for the prosecution in this trial. The long, tedious sessions devoted to documents were overshadowed by the living witnesses.

Now it is the turn of the documents to have their say. For the first time, abstracts of them have been submitted as incriminating evidence, submitted wholesale, by the hundreds, so many it is overwhelming. In his examination, the counsel for the defense makes use of some of them to bolster his case. Only now, in the cross-examination, do their awesome power and cruel, piercing accuracy become evident.

Exhibit T/164: the meeting held by Heydrich in his Berlin office on September 21, 1939. The commanders of the Action Squads took part, and Eichmann was present. His name, rank, and position are there in black and white. It was at this meeting that the extermination program in the East was decided upon.

"I was not there," he says. He is reminded that, under interrogation by 06, he said, "There can no longer be any doubt about it, since I do appear in the document as a participant." But then he withdraws his confession to the police.

There is murmuring in the courtroom, and the presiding judge pounds the gavel.

Eichmann denies and disavows, haggles and clarifies, trembling all the while with emotion, and he fights over every jot and tittle. Hoping a particular phrase will save him, will give him some sort of handhold in the world of falsehood he has created with such enormous effort, he suddenly runs up against two other phrases that knock him cold. And just when you think he is ready to throw in the towel, his amazingly quick mind comes up with a new lie. And when the lying approaches the absurd and the ridiculous, he says, "Mr. Attorney General, if I may be permitted to say so, one of the few positive qualities fate has granted me is truthfulness." And he goes on answering the prosecutor's sarcastic questions. "I am not fighting here to save my neck but rather to dispel the untruths about me that have accumulated during the last fifteen years."

The prosecutor asks, "And was it to dispel those untruths that you hid under an assumed name for those fifteen years?" Or, later on, "Was it to tell the truth, to remove this stain, that you told Sassen what you did?"

And then we hear again of "human" responsibility and "legal" responsibility. We hear that, "as years go by, you get older, and you learn to think differently." We hear, "My intention, standing trial here in an Israeli court, is to remove the stain of untruth which has been cast upon me."

But when the Sassen document, which hangs over his head like the sword of Damocles, is repeatedly cited as the harshest of the incriminating documents, he tells us that "these things were never said" or that he "didn't know what [he] was saying," and, later, in the afternoon, he comes back to the matter of the alcohol. He was under the influence. "We drank red wine." And you recall the conversation with Wilhelm Hoettl in Budapest just before the defeat, over a bottle of whisky, about the six million who had been murdered.

"Fate has granted me . . . truthfulness." Yet the packed hall is witness to a parade of fantastic lies. Finally, one of my neighbors says to me, "Now do you understand what a Nazi is?"

I do, yes. And I am feeling something strangely like pity for him.

While pondering this, I see his Madagascar Plan exposed. Four million Jews. One million a year. To an island. Isolated from the rest of the world. What will they live off of? "There were seven million head of cattle there, after all."

He knows how many cattle there were. But the number of native people living there is another matter—"two or three million?" "And what will be done with them?" "They will be transferred."

The fight over Madagascar is the longest, most desperate one he wages. At last it turns out that "the impending Final Solution" mentioned in his letters and memoranda is not Madagascar. At last he finds the documents persuasive. "On October 10, 1941, the deportation to the East was decided upon, was it not?" Pallid and weary, he replies, "Yes, and I have said that from the moment the transports began to roll, one could no longer infer, when the Final Solution was discussed, that Madagascar was meant."

Then comes the coup de grace: "On November 19, 1941, when you spoke of 'the impending Final Solution,' you no longer meant Madagascar?"

Eichmann replies, "Now that I have seen this date, the answer is obviously no. Obviously."

And from there to Wannsee. And on and on. It is all collapsing. Adolf Eichmann stands among the ruins of his edifice of lies, trying to muster his remaining strength for a battle that is already lost.

Falsehood.

A world of falsehood, without beginning or end, that does not begin with the defendant or end with him.

July 12, 1961

THE PUZZLE

The fourth day of the cross-examination has added nothing new. The battle between examiner and examinee went on for hours. No new weapons were introduced. There were new documents that forced the accused to admit, at last, that he had organized the transports of Jews to the "receiving stations" and notified them of this; that the "receiving stations" had received the consignments and sent him "receipts" for them; that he had been in constant contact with the camps regarding the pace, timing, and size of the shipments; that he knew what was done to those people once they got there and that he went on sending them.

It was shown beyond any shadow of a doubt that the defendant's claim that the concentration camps were under the S.S. Economic Administration, commanded by Oswald Pohl, and that he himself had no part in what went on there, was without foundation, in light of the fact that the camps used only for extermination, such as Chelmno, Sobibor, and Maidanek, did not report to Pohl but exclusively to Section IV-B4, and there the matter was laid to rest.

"How many times were you at Auschwitz?"

"Four or five times."

"Did you speak to Hoess?"

"Yes, I did."

"And did he visit you in Budapest?"

"Yes, he did."

"In order to determine the absorptive capacity of Auschwitz in regard to the Jews of Hungary?"

After fumbling a bit for an answer, Eichmann says, "That also depended on other things, of course."

So let us go on to the second point.

Q.: "There were transports that did not go to Auschwitz but directly to the extermination camps, were there not?"

A.: "I would not deny that."

Q.: "And so, when you issued a directive over your signature—I refer to Exhibit T/1399—for the deportation of Jews to Izbica, near Lublin, you were not obliged to report this to Oranienburg [Pohl's office] or Concentration Camp Auschwitz, but only to Lublin and Krakow, because this transport was headed straight for extermination. Isn't that so?"

A.: "The content of the document is accurate. It was under the authority of the Regierungssekraetar."

Q.: "I am not asking about authority," the prosecutor shouts. "I am asking whether, given a signed document to this effect, these people were being sent for extermination."

A.: "Yes, I cannot deny that at all."

Later on in the interrogation, this matter is summed up by Eichmann as follows: "Whatever happens, I, in any case, have never denied that, to my great sorrow, the deported Jews were sent to their deaths. I cannot deny that."

The words "great sorrow" give me pause. What is this? An acknowledgment of the connection most people make between such events and real sorrow? A sincere sentiment on his part? A conscious lie? An unconscious one? I do not know.

Later, in the afternoon, we would hear very strange things indeed, things that went beyond "proper channels," "receiving stations," "dispatching stations," and "freight."

The prosecutor: "In your conversation with Sassen in 1957, you said, 'This difficulty, the matter of the victims and the bodies, affected me less during the war, because it could not be avoided. And of course, in the last analysis, I was not allowed to react emotionally. The bombing of German cities, in which women and children were killed, was perhaps—the only thing I felt.' Did you say that?"

Four years later he explains, "This has to be understood in the following way: if I saw bodies of women and children in the streets after the bombings, it superseded . . . it was like—how to put this?—like seeing the bodies of Jews for the first time and not being able to grasp it. I was astonished and shocked, and afterward I couldn't understand it. But when you see many such sights, a person—how to put this?—is brutalized more and more by such sights of the apocalyptic chaos of war. And if I may say so—it is hard to say this, but all the same—the sight of corpses may still be new, but it is less shocking. It can happen to a person."

After that, when he comes back to "the mutilated, burnt German bodies," he says, "Death lost its horror then. One stood, after all, in the midst of death. . . . That was the way one's mind responded to this terrible business."

This long monologue is interrupted sharply by the question, "Didn't it bother you to be the great expediter of death?"

And the man who said he would gladly jump into his grave at the news that five million Jews had been exterminated replies, "It did bother me. It bothered me more than anyone can imagine."

There is something I feel I must explain to the reader. In my ongoing reports on the trial, I am afraid to depart from a certain framework, because every such departure will be seen as presumptuous by some, simplistic or reckless by others.

The figure of Eichmann is too complex to sum up with hackneyed terms like "minor bureaucrat," "filthy murderer," "liar," "hypocrite," "cynic," "coward," "murderously aggressive simpleton," or "schizoid."

The ongoing questioning adds nothing to our understanding. It adds some details to the proof of guilt. Each passing day brings us closer to the end of the trial and enriches our knowledge without helping us to understand what we have not understood until now.

The process thus moves in two opposing directions at once. Every day that brings us closer to August also takes us back to the beginnings of our amazement and mystification. The duration of the trial is not necessarily proportional to our ability to figure things out.

It goes back to the matter of orders and hierarchy. In any event, it turns out that one man named Hitler decided to annihilate the Jews. He gave an order to this effect, and the thing got underway.

At least formally speaking, it must be stated that, aside from any connection with Christianity, antisemitism, European history, or heaven and earth, it only took one sentence from Hitler's mouth to wipe out European Jewry, a sentence understood as an order and passed down through the chain of command.

Today, more than at any other time in my life, it was clear to me that a court that tries Adolf Eichmann is performing an important service for the human race, not to speak of the connection between crime and punishment or the meaning of the trial for the Jewish people as a nation.

But the puzzle is too much for us. We are overwhelmed by it.

July 13, 1961

"YES, BUT . . ."

TOMORROW, THE FIRST week of cross-examination will be over.

The prosecutor's key words were, "Yes or no?"

The defendant's key words were, "Yes, but . . ."

Has Eichmann been defeated by this cross-examination?

Yes, I think he has. But others disagree.

What more does the prosecutor need to do to convince the court that the defendant is in fact guilty as charged in the original indictment?

I'll be damned if I know. It seems to me prolonging the trial only raises doubts as to whether the body of proof presented so far, proof extracted from him at great effort, is sufficient to incriminate him.

It's over and done with, isn't it? The man has confessed to the fundamental charges against him, hasn't he? Yet the questioning goes on, with its many ups and downs, as it did this morning.

But in the afternoon, just when it looked as if the end were coming, we once again witnessed a prolonged, tiresome exchange, concerned with the most picayune details. We seemed to be going around in circles, nearing the mark and then pulling back from it. What was to have been the damning final summation, hitting with maximum impact, has given way to "additional clarification." It reminds us of a continually recurring nightmare.

The prosecutor, who has remained cultured and refined throughout the week's battle, had to restrain himself this morning from attacking Eichmann frontally. As he began his barrage of questions, he could not anticipate that the answers would be couched in such a way as to be utterly useless.

Hausner's interrogation is on the factual level. "Yes or no?"

Eichmann replies on the level of interpretation, with answers beginning "yes, but." When the "but" is meant to clarify the "yes," it can be tolerated as part of an answer. When it is drawn out and, in effect, turns the "yes" into a "no," it creates an interminable spiral that can drive the most patient of examiners to distraction.

Hausner obviously lost his patience more than once.

The prosecutor, with his complete mastery of the material, was attacking someone whose mastery of it was no less thorough. We anticipated that the contest would be decided once and for all by "stubborn facts," but what ensued was the strange interchange that gave the cross-examination its nightmarish quality.

Eichmann was facing a threefold enemy: the wartime documents, the Sassen document, and the record of his interrogation by Section 06.

Confronted by the prosecutor with these three things, he was defeated on the basic points.

Having stood his ground in a desperate battle against the wartime documents, he was stabbed in the back by his 1957 conversations with Sassen. And when, in response to the prosecutor's questions, he tried to rationalize these conversations away, the things he had said to 06 came along and disarmed him.

The real disaster for him, though, was the Sassen document, because this was one he had brought upon himself. When he got up to make his "moral," "human" pronouncements, we, in a moment of weakness, found them persuasive: as an expression of shock by a man who had suddenly come to realize what was at stake, as a heartrending expression of remorse by someone who had decided to do penance. But just then the Sassen document appeared and turned all this into a stomach-churning horror. For there, over a bottle of red wine, calmly and freely, under no duress, he had said just the opposite—after thirteen years; after all his heroes, both superior and subordinate, had been hanged or committed suicide or vanished to the ends of the earth; after a new age had dawned on a changed world; after Israel had arisen from the Valley of Dry Bones.

Like a ghost, he goes back to the scene of the crime and is caught up again in the world that was once his, the only world left to him, the chaotic world of the past, a blood-drenched world where he once, briefly, had the good fortune of being among those in power. He returns to "the best years of his life," to the days when he was somebody. There he recovers his sense of belonging; there he has friends and is no longer lonely. "Hoess was my comrade in arms, a dear and admirable man."

He basks in the light of his memories.

But now, this smoky, drunken conversation is killing him. Because of it, he can no longer ask to be believed.

Now it doesn't seem so smart.

"Yes, but." It is maddeningly intriguing. When he applies his "yes, but" to the facts, he can be dealt with by legal procedure. When he takes his "yes, but" into the realm of the "human," the realm of his "confessions," we reach the point where every word he utters is a horror.

The interrogation goes on.

What are we waiting for, a "yes" without the "but"? He is full of self-pity; he, too, is a victim.

I don't feel up to quoting him just now. He has provided us with fantastic new material: confessions of "serious crimes" (the extermination of the Jews), of "the worst crime a human being can commit" (violation of the S.S. oath of loyalty), of his inability to say whether the commandant of Auschwitz was a criminal, because he does not want to "betray his innermost feelings." And he continues his profound debate with the prosecutor concerning the "higher spheres," a debate full of "yes, buts."

July 14, 1961

DID YOU GO TO MAIDANEK?

In the illustrations that graced our storybooks when we were children, the good people were always beautiful, the bad people ugly. The "wicked aunt." The "witch."

Perhaps that is why it is so terribly difficult to connect this man's external appearance with deportations, transports, trains, hunger, beatings, shootings, gas chambers, and the smoke of burning corpses filling the sky like the smoke of great factories.

"No," a police officer remarks to me, "Eichmann hasn't been broken. So the only thing left is to shrink him, bit by bit, to squeeze him dry."

As I listen to what is being said each day, hour after hour, I fail to comprehend it all. But in the evening, going over the written material and making my notes, it all comes into focus.

What was new today?

IV-B4 is getting steadily larger, approaching its true dimensions. It is the shadow that follows the Jews wherever they go. It has no boundaries. They determine its role and function, in every detail. It determines how they will die. It is the Final Solution, wholesale and retail.

It sends them on their way still alive, and they come back as numbers separated from their bodies.

When Globocnik needs retroactive authorization for the murders he committed early on, he turns to Heydrich and Mueller, but it is Eichmann who gets him the authorization. He can take him straight across the border to the General Government if it concerns the Jews.

This is where Hans Frank's omnipotent rule ends. The killing is going on nonstop in his sovereign territory. It is true that this is the extermination area. But it begins in Berlin, with Heydrich, Mueller, and Eichmann. The extermination cuts across the territorial bounds of all the "local authorities."

Where and when does a Jew's death begin? If we don't trace the process all the way back to the moment when the name "Israel" was added to "Curt," it begins when he is put on a train. A train wheel is no less a corpus delicti, no less relevant, than a heap of spent cartridges next to a machine-gun nest or an empty canister of Zyklon-B.

But we've forgotten about the telephone. "I sat at my desk in Berlin," Eichmann says over and over. So we must look upon this desk as the heart of the extermination process. Today, this desk took on monstrous proportions.

Seen now behind his death-desk, in charge of a department governing the fate of an entire people, Eichmann is at the lowest point of his self-abasement. But all at once he draws back and puts up a fight, in which the horrible and the ridiculous are mingled unrecognizably.

Note: when he says he was nothing but a stenographer, a Dictaphone, a conduit, a minor middle-level official, he debases himself. When he says he was more than that, he incriminates himself.

Today we witnessed some fantastic exchanges among the prosecutor, the judges, and the defendant.

After Eichmann says once again that he "didn't initiate" and "didn't suggest" but only "passed on directives," Hausner asks him, "Couldn't a Dictaphone have sufficed in place of you?"

Eichmann takes offense. "Absolutely not, because, after all, I was able to make myself a digest of a large number of files."

And how did Mueller react to this?

Eichmann: "He knew me, and he understood that I was not going to take any decisions."

Judge Landau does not let up. "He tried to elicit your opinion and you refused. Is that how I am to understand your answer?"

Eichmann explains: "At first, he undoubtedly expected me to

volunteer an opinion, but afterward, when he saw that I wouldn't, he got used to it."

Here the prosecutor intervenes again: "You were completely passive, in other words?"

But the defendant is outraged at this insult. "Not exactly passive. I obeyed and carried out my orders."

"And that is why Mueller said, 'If we had fifty Eichmanns we could win the war'?" the prosecutor asks mockingly.

The one-fiftieth-of-the-victory replies, "It was just an expression. You must realize that he was a Bavarian, and it sounds different when a Bavarian says such things. . . . It was customary among men in uniform. We called it latrine humor."

It turns out his superiors thought highly of him. Himmler sent him to Hungary, with the message, "I am sending you the master himself."

Again and again, we hear, "I did not initiate anything."

Finally, Judge Halevi interjects, "As head of a department, as a *referent*, you say you had decision-making authority, but in principle you did not use it?"

Eichmann understands the question and tries to find some way of holding on to both his dignity and his life. "Your honor, I did, it is true, have certain administrative powers, but I was not a great devotee of making decisions, nor one who took pleasure in making them." If he had been, he adds, he would have been promoted.

Judge Halevi continues very quietly: "The way you are describing your function here, it would seem that you did not do your job properly. You should have been removed from your post, for your office would not have operated efficiently."

Deeply offended, Eichmann replies: "That is not correct, your honor."

As the trial proceeds, what is going on inside of him becomes clear. "I did my job according to the oath of allegiance I had taken, and I did my duty as ordered."

Halevi goads him. "You did less than you had the authority to do."

The Nazi continues. "I was entitled to ask my superior officer for instructions."

And Judge Halevi ends on a note of bewilderment. "How can an office be run with such a director?"

These exchanges distract us momentarily from the subject and make us smile. Sometimes, when we forget for a moment, we laugh. It's human nature.

Later, discussion turns to the details of his reports about the hangings and killings of Jews. The prosecutor asks him, "Why did it go through you?" "I don't know. I have no idea," he answers. Then we hear the following sentence, as if for the first time: "Because the murder of innocent people always went through you, didn't it?"

"No, I must deny that."

But it turns out it is true. He, more than anyone else, is linked to the death of the Jews. We hear the following quote: "Jews can also be put into Nebe's and Rasch's camps, as has been agreed with Obersturmbannfuehrer Eichmann."

A sentence from the report on the Action Squads.

Nebe and Rasch, two well-known murderers who specialized in the slaughter of Communists.

After a lengthy argument about this, the prosecutor says, "So it was suggested that they be sent to places where death awaited them. That is what you said, is it not?"

Here we come to one of those moments when the confession is scarcely audible, but it is clear enough: "Yes, that, too, is correct."

He was in Warsaw, too, when the uprising was being put down. "I was there mainly for the sleeping accommodations, because the best accommodations were to be had in Warsaw."

"And did you go to Maidanek?"

"Yes."

And "so that our people don't turn into sadists," he agreed to switch to gas, the more "elegant" method.

IV-B4 is still following us.

July 18, 1961

PATRIMONY

AT 8:30 THIS morning the hundredth session opened.

One hundred courtroom sessions. Let us observe a moment of silence, then go on.

Today the courtroom is packed. I have never seen it so full. Some of these people, I know, waited in the Russian Compound[42] from 2 o'clock in the morning on to get in.

At the mid-morning recess, the crowd escapes into the open air. When they come back, they find that others have taken their places. There is shouting and pushing. Those who decided to keep their seats take out sandwiches, fruit, and chocolate, but then the police tell them it is not allowed.

For a moment or two, there is a carnival or theatrical air in the auditorium. Then the bailiff makes his announcement, and the judges file in. They pause and bow slightly to the audience, which has stood up out of respect, and the hundredth session resumes.

The prosecutor's interrogation continues. The defendant's answers continue. Endlessly. Meaninglessly. And the interrogation, which was meant to break down the defendant's resistance and lead him to a confession, becomes a prolonged nightmare. "Yes" and "no" are replaced by Eichmann's way of "clarifying things." At times you almost get the impression he is answering questions put to him by his own defense counsel, not the prosecutor. Hausner has not broken him. He has forced him to compound his lies, to say

42. The usual seat of the Jerusalem District Court, where tickets to the trial were distributed.—Trans.

"after twenty years I cannot recall"— that is *the* lie, because he has an outstanding memory—to repeat the refrain about obeying orders, to blame his subordinates once again for acting "without my knowledge."

There are moments when the end seems quite close—when every line of the documents screams "guilty!"—but they pass, and we go back to the all-too-familiar routine. Finally, the presiding judge intervenes. "When I see that we have already been in France and Holland and are going back there, I say to myself, This interrogation could easily go on for quite a few more days. But the prospect worries me."

The two men confronting one another here represent such different worlds that the prosecutor's repeated attempts to get the defendant to confess "moral" culpability, using concepts alien to the man, seem painfully incongruous.

Q.: "Who gave the death sentences at Theresienstadt?"

A.: "It was the commander of the Security Police and the S.D. in Prague."

Q.: "Did he have the authority to do this?"

A.: "Yes, if the commanding officer of the S.S. and the police had given it to him."

With this the matter is concluded, as I see it. But the prosecutor continues with his questioning, in a normal tone of voice. "Was there a German law authorizing the commanding officer of the police to grant authority to pronounce death sentences?"

Eichmann replies, "I do not know. It was probably done by the State Secretary for Security."

At this point a question is asked which, as we have said, takes us back to the root, to the beginning, and it, too, has moral implications: "Was there a law authorizing the commandant of an extermination camp to exterminate human beings?"

Eichmann brings the question back into his legal frame of reference: "There was certainly no such law. The rest I do not know, because it was not my concern." Now he says it all, how it all began and how it was all justified: "The Fuehrer's word was law."

It is the kind of sentence that gives you pause. "The Fuehrer's word was law." But another question has already been asked, one that cannot break the vicious circle to which this Nazi answer gives rise: "Was there a law allowing Globocnik to execute 150,000 people, then another quarter of a million, then another 150,000, then another quarter of a million?" The question is addressed directly to Eichmann, who had a retroactive authorization for this slaughter. "You had a hand in this!" the prosecutor shouts. "You dictated the authorization. Was there a law permitting him to do this?"

The circle is closed. "Yes, I had an order to this effect." Orders are law. That is clear as day. But the prosecutor, feigning amazement, goes on and on: "There was a law allowing you to carry out mass deportations?" Then back to the beginning: "I got my orders from my direct superiors, and I had to carry them out."

What else is there to ask, what else? Does he really hope that Eichmann will say "the Fuehrer's word," understood as law, was not legal? Does he really want to take Eichmann back to the ground of all human law, which is the basis for this murderer being tried here to begin with?

"Weren't you at all interested in knowing whether it was legal or illegal according to the laws of the Reich itself?"

But how could it be seen as "illegal according to the laws of the Reich" if those very laws derived from "the Fuehrer's word"? Consequently, Eichmann could state for the ten-thousandth time, "When directives came from the chief of the office . . . it was he who bore the responsibility. He must have known with whom, among his superiors, the orders had originated. It was not my concern to worry about this or to look into it." This, for Eichmann, was where things began and ended.

Yet Hausner, for his part, cannot stomach such an answer, and so the nightmare goes on. "In other words, whether it was legal or not did not interest you?"

And the Nazi gives a brief answer. "This question did not come up, because I had been given an unequivocal order."

Enough! We've heard this already! No more! But I hear the

prosecutor pressing on: "That is why I am asking whether you had any interest in this, and whether it was legal or not. I want an answer: yes or no." Then, without waiting for the answer which the S.S. man has already given a dozen times, the prosecutor poses the question again, but this time in what seems like a man-to-man tone: "Didn't you ever ask on what basis things were being done, whether there was any legal framework, whether there was any kind of mandate, or on what grounds millions of people were being deported to the East? What law are we talking about? Didn't you ever look into it?"

Finally, this time, the Gestapo man gives an answer the puts an end to the questions: "I was not a legal scholar. I had to obey. I had only learned how to be a soldier."

Now, reading over the questions and answers, I cannot fathom what the prosecutor wanted. Had the defendant admitted he had wondered about the matter, admitted that these things were probably not legal, he would have found himself out of his bunker and a sitting duck for the first bullet to come along. His whole defense was based on the kinds of answers he was giving.

"The Fuehrer's word was law." That's all there was to it. There he stood on solid ground. Remember, if you will, Regulation 11, which was, in Eichmann's words, "the legal basis of our activities." He was right, because the lawyers in the Interior Ministry had given it the status of law. Move a Jew a hundred yards past the borders of the Reich, and you take away his German citizenship and property rights. Everything becomes simple and straightforward.

And what was the legal foundation of the Nuremberg Laws?

Obersturmbannfuehrer Adolf Eichmann can claim, quite rightly from his point of view, that he was acting within the law. Professors, experts, legal scholars, intellectuals, priests, and teachers had drawn up the law for him.

We have dwelt at some length on the matter of legality. It is here that we begin to understand the full scope of the horror.

Now it is easier to take up the matter of the children of mixed marriages, in which Eichmann was involved, and the matter of the skeletons sent to the laboratories.

The skeletons. Is this the climax? No. Why not? This trial will not have a climax.

We know that the S.S. had, in Strasbourg, a center for anthropological research called Ahnenherbe, the Patrimony Institute, and that this institution was in need of skeletons. The skeletons of Jewish commissars, to be more exact. And since these were not to be found, 150 other Jews had to be reduced to skeletons. To whom did the heads of the institute turn? To Eichmann.

"You recall the skeleton affair in Strasbourg? You recall that Sievers contacted you and that you told him to get you an order from the Reichsfuehrer, do you not?"

"I do not remember this. But I have read about it."

Then he is reminded, and it turns out that they did not apply to the S.S. Economic Administration but to Section IV-B4, to Eichmann. "Why to you?" he asks for the umpteenth time. He still has no answer. "What reason would Sievers, a Standartenfuehrer in the S.S. who was knowledgeable about these things, have to come to you for skeletons and skulls?"

The reply was lengthy but did not answer the question that kept coming back like a boxer's fist: "Why to you?"

Let me make it short. "Guenther was at work behind my back . . . I myself knew nothing . . . I didn't deal with it . . . I passed it on."

Still, we now know about the Patrimony Institute and the skeletons that were found there.

"Patrimony." The name "Patrimony." How is it that we connect this word with the word "culture"? Didn't one of the Nazis say that hearing the word "culture" made him want to reach for his gun?

"Patrimony." Now that the name has been given to that institute—where it referred to the Germans' barbarian Nordic ancestors—you can no longer smile when you hear the questions about legality that we have heard.

"Millions sent to the East." Suddenly we remember them. After "Patrimony" and "special treatment." Suddenly we recall that what we are talking about is the "millions sent to the East."

July 19, 1961

THE BEAR, THE DOG, AND THE MAN

The trial is over. It's enough. The thought of more cross-examination by Servatius makes me smile. In fact, today we were already smiling wearily and sometimes even laughing, more than before. Even the presiding judge somehow seemed relaxed and almost lighthearted, and the translator came up with some brilliant turns of phrase that people found amusing. It's enough. There's a limit.

Last week, we got angry when he denied, clarified, explained, forgot. I had thought he was a "complex, interesting character," that there was something demonic about him, that he was "articulate," that he had "nerves of steel" and a "sinister mind," that he was "riven with contradictions," etc.

Now it's enough. It's really enough. It's the third degree. From here on, it begins to be sacrilege.

It's probably good that things have been taken this far, to this limit, beyond which spreads the wasteland of weary smiles, of being fed up.

The audience anticipates his answers, which then elicit laughter. The presiding judge warns that he "will not tolerate this." Questions that in their import should be earth-shattering disintegrate into disconnected Hebrew words with no soul. In the simultaneous translation, they turn into German words. The prosecutor asks his questions, then waits quietly. Up above, in his booth, the translator catches up with him after a delay and passes them on to Eichmann, who collects them and then rises to answer. It is now that the questions are completely transformed. While he is answering in German, the prosecutor remains silent. When the second translator, sitting next to the judges, is rendering his answers into Hebrew, the prosecutor is still silent. By the end of the process, when the question has come back as an answer, there is nothing left of it. When he confines himself to yes or no, Adolf Eichmann is doing us a favor. When he makes do with *jawohl.* You want to thank him from the bottom of your heart for having spared you the suffering. You aren't angry. It's enough. It borders on meaninglessness. His answers begin to remind me of the officer who shot a little girl in the head or the professor or doctor who peered into the gas chamber and said, "They're all asleep."

Then comes the silence. Rudolf Hoess looks at his watch and says to his wife, "We should get to bed. It's late." And his wife goes into the children's room in their apartment at Auschwitz and rearranges a blanket or a pillow or moves a child who has fallen asleep crosswise on the bed. And the radio is turned off in the middle of a Viennese waltz.

I thought of this when he first said, "Hoess was a dear man."

Let us be done with the legal process. In this hall, it will soon be over.

Let us finish before it all becomes distorted.

Meanwhile, the session goes on. It is the last day of the cross-examination. What is the subject?

Somewhere in the endless wilderness of denials and corrections and reservations, the prosecutor catches hold of him: "Did you say these things?"

"I certainly did not say them in quite that way." No, let's not give rein to our anger. We are used to this. The matter he is being questioned about is a passage in the Sassen document concerning the visit he made to Bratislava just after Heydrich's murder. There, he had said some forceful things about "removing the last Jews from the area of Slovakia."

This page is black with editing marks. A relevant page. There's no going back. For the first time in three months, he loses his composure. "I do not know this. I only know one thing, that from now on I shall not take a stand or answer any questions, because I regard all these documents as inauthentic and inaccurate and unfair."

It is his idle comments to Sassen about "historical truth," coming back for vengeance.

Here the presiding judge intervenes harshly. "You will continue to answer questions until I release you from answering them."

A moment of high tension. But order is maintained. Eichmann has great respect for the presiding judge. He looks up at him and says, "Yes, right, your honor, I shall be prepared to do so, but I feel as though I am being roasted to a crisp here."

But what can you do? The Sassen document provides the prosecution with such treasures: all that arrogant prattle, straight from the murderer's mouth, recalling those "good years"?

Later, in relation to the "illegal" deportations from Romania to the other side of the Bug, the prosecutor quotes another brief passage in which every word is like a nail in Eichmann's coffin. "Did you say these things?"

What we are hearing is an interesting passage from Sassen, which Eichmann only elicits laughter by trying to explain: "In principle, I should have replied to Sassen, in each instance, that I did not know or remember these things, but [he] said to me, 'If you do that, we won't get much of a book out of this.' I had to put things in a more suitable way. What I wanted to do in the book was to describe the spirit of the time. It is a journalistic work and thus different from the official documents we have here, which tell the truth down to the last detail."

As for "literature," his approach was to make things interesting, using slang: "I knew some sort of cur in every village."

And when this excuse doesn't work, he goes back to the red wine.

But there was a moment of sanctity in the auditorium, which otherwise was pervaded with the presence of Eichmann. It was when his story about visiting Globocnik in Treblinka was read from that document. "I was once on some sort of trip from east to west, and

I passed through some camp, and in that camp Globocnik was carrying out exterminations. It was near Lublin, a place called Treblinka." Later on in the story, after telling about the little armored car that he learned to drive (he had the time), he describes arriving in Lublin, where Hauptsturmfuehrer Hoeffle, sitting by the fireplace, recounts to him the following: "One fine day, an S.S. man went to the tailor shop. Suddenly a Jew burst in and killed him with the pistol he had laid on the table while his measurements were being taken. Immediately, as if by order, they stormed the guardpost, killed several S.S. men, seized their weapons, started the armored car, and fired at the watchmen. After a certain number of the watchmen had been shot, a large number of these Jewish prisoners fled."

Yes, most of them were later recaptured. But the story has the effect of a roll of thunder from the realm of truth.

The name Treblinka brings us back from the endless wild-goose chase, from the "vulgar expressions," from "they're roasting me."

It's hard for me to go on now. I am jumping ahead to the afternoon session. (Those with the necessary fortitude can consult the transcript.) "You yourself visited the ghettos. We have heard the testimony of Sapir, from Munkacz."

"I did not go to the camps. I went bear hunting in the Carpathians." (More of the dolce vita. "The accommodations were better in Warsaw.") "I was never in the Munkacz ghetto. Endre[43] went about his official duties. I stayed in the hotel."

Later on we learn that he had a good friend, the commander of the 22nd S.S. Volunteer Division (Freiwilligen-Division),* General August Zenther, whom he wanted to help. The division was in a bad way. He wanted to give him ten thousand trucks. "If we could

43. Vitez Laszlo Endre, a deputy of Eichmann.—Trans.

*I want to thank Prof. Omer Bartov of Brown University for providing name, rank, and military position of August Zehender. —H.G.

have gotten rid of a certain number of enemies of the Reich and secured a military advantage in the bargain, it would have been a good deal, in my view." Further along in the Sassen document we hear, "I am convinced that if we were hard pressed we would even have given them two million in exchange for the ten thousand trucks. . . . This is further proof that not all the Jews were fed to the ovens."

We go on to Kurt Andreas Becher. He is angry with Becher for interfering in his affairs. Asked by the presiding judge whether he had been in favor of the truck deal, he says, "Yes, of course."

"Why?"

"It was a way of taking the business of immigration away from Becher."

The little "Dictaphone" is capable of wheeling and dealing after all.

July 20, 1961

THE CATEGORICAL IMPERATIVE

> Act as if the maxim of your action were to become by your will a general law of nature. . . . Act so as to treat humankind, in your own person as well as in that of anyone else, always as an end, never merely as a means.
>
> Immanuel Kant, *Metaphysical Foundation of Morals* (Modern Library ed.)

SERVATIUS: "THAT CONCLUDES the cross-examination, and I have no further questions." What? I look at my watch. It is 5:30. Unbelievable! The prosecutor's examination took ten days, the defense counsel's return examination an hour and a half.

Before we can figure it out, we hear the voice of the presiding judge: "The defendant will now answer questions put to him by the judges."

A new day. So different. The prosecutor has finished. The counsel for the defense is done. The judges begin.

Judge Raveh: "Do you recall that during your interrogation by the police you mentioned something about 'the Kantian demand'? You said you had tried all your life to live according to 'the Kantian demand.' There is no need to show it to you. Do you remember this?"

A.: "Yes, I remember it well."

Q.: "If so, do I understand correctly that you always kept Kant's categorical imperative in mind?"

A.: "Yes."

Q.: "Could you tell us, then, if your activities in the relation to the deportation of the Jews were congruent with Kant's categorical imperative?"

A.: "No, that was not at all the case. I did not have in mind the kind of life I was leading then, when I was under pressure and constraint from a third party. What I meant when I spoke of living according to Kant's principle was a life where I could judge myself, my will and my aspirations, not where I was subject to a higher power, forced to act according to its dictates. In that case, one can no longer speak of free will. On the other hand, I can include in this principle the concept of obedience to authority. And I must do this. Then the authority becomes responsible for one's actions."

Q.: "Do you mean to say that you are fulfilling Kant's categorical imperative even when obeying blindly the dictates of a higher authority?"

A.: "Ever since Kant formulated his categorical imperative, no head of state has ever issued a directive as destructive as this one . . . It was wartime. I had to obey . . . And so all I could do was place my life as much as possible in the service of the imperative."

And again, later on: "It could not have been in the framework of the Kantian categorical imperative to kill people by brute force, because it was not God's will."

Q.: "In other words, there was a time when you did not live by the Kantian categorical imperative?"

A.: "I could not live by it, because a higher power denied me the possibility of living by it."

Q.: "When did this begin?"

A.: "It began—to be strictly accurate—the moment I was transferred, against my will and desire, to Berlin."

Q.: "And how long did it last?"

A.: "Until the end."

Q.: "And it was clear to you the whole time that you could not live then according to Kant's categorical imperative, much as you would have liked to arrange your life around it?"

A.: "At that time I was reading Kant's *Critique of Practical Reason*."

Q.: "For the first time? In other words, it was then that you first learned of the categorical imperative?"

A.: "No, I knew about it before that, but only in an abridged form. You could, perhaps, sum it up in simple words: Be faithful to the laws, be disciplined, live an orderly life, and do not go against the laws. That is a digest for popular use."

Q.: "Where did you get this definition of the Kantian categorical imperative for popular use? Later, when you read Kant's original book, did this formulation sit well with his definition?"

A strange way to begin.

Judge Raveh is emotional but soft-spoken. He addresses Eichmann in German, and the latter answers standing erect like a pupil in class or one who is confessing. Now the same odd thing happens: you are suddenly aware that something momentous is happening right in front of your nose. No, it isn't the philosophical argument, from which the judge later turns to consider the numbers exterminated. What is it then? All at once, the examining judge is confronting the defendant with questions that do not allow him to take his usual line of defense, the one that empties the world of all meaning.

These questions take us back to the beginning. To our first encounter with this subject, a one-time event. It has a strange, grating sound, this academic debate in a slaughterhouse. But this beginning thrusts the trial powerfully forward, toward its closing moments, its summation.

After yesterday, which was swallowed up in Eichmannesque confusion, we feel as though a great force is bringing us back to the real issues. That is why Judge Raveh shifts to a discussion of the numbers of people exterminated, as if to say, It's time to put aside abstractions and get down to concrete, bloody facts.

Tomorrow the judges' short interrogation will continue. So let us wait.

Up to now, Servatius has been doing the interrogating. Why was he so brief? Was it that he didn't have anything to ask or that he wanted to make a big show of conciseness in contrast to the long-drawn-out interrogation by the prosecutor?

He doesn't add anything new. He explains, among other things, that the vulgar expressions "contra" and "milk me" have to do with card games. Yes, this transition, from "grilling me" and "bear hunt" to Kant's categorical imperative is very remarkable indeed.

On the death march to Austria, he does not remember "details about individuals." He remembers "images of people falling down." Who ordered it? He says it was the Hungarians, Winkelmann, Veesenmayer, etc. But we know that to mark the success of the death march in the snow, these evil men drank "brandy made of mares' milk."

There, in the shell of an empty factory, a Jewish woman gave birth to a baby boy under a flashlight held by an S.S. man who wanted to see how a human being is born. A human being who would live half an hour. Aviva Fleischmann, the mother, made her appearance and sent Servatius's questions of clarification up in smoke.

Let us sum up: (1) Today the prosecutor concluded an interrogation lasting ten days. (2) Today the defense counsel concluded an interrogation lasting ninety minutes. (3) Today the judges' cross-examination began. (4) Today we heard the last cry of the documents and witnesses for the prosecution. (5) Today the counsel for the defense tried to shore up his claim, familiar to us for three months now, that his client was "one who took orders, not one who gave them" by contending that the Sassen document was "unreliable evidence." (6) Today Eichmann vehemently denied taking part, directly or indirectly, in the murder of the Jewish boy in Budapest, so that his hands could be clean of that poor lad's blood when the judges asked him about his involvement in and responsibility for the murder of an entire people.

July 21, 1961

ONE LAST CHANCE

Judge Raveh: "We now come to the Wannsee Conference. In the minutes it says that at the end of the discussion the participants gave presentations about various possible ways of carrying out the 'solution.'"

Eichmann: "I remember, your honor."

Q.: "What were those ways, then? You might look at the end of the page there. Do you remember what they were talking about there?"

A.: "They were speaking about various possibilities of killing."

Q.: "Now, I do not understand why, at the end of the Wannsee Conference, three people, Heydrich, Mueller, and Eichmann, stayed behind to celebrate what had happened."

A.: "To celebrate?"

Q.: "I can understand about Heydrich and Mueller, but why Eichmann?"

A.: "Because I had to take the minutes."

Judge Raveh's eyes widen in amazement. "Wait a minute, wait a minute. This is a new version. Up until now I understood that the three of you stayed behind"—he gropes for words with his hands—"how should I put this?—to rest from the deliberations. Heydrich was content. He smoked. The three of you sat by the fireplace."

Eichmann remembers. "Yes, at that moment they were not talking about the proceedings."

And does this point have any legal significance?

It turns out it does. The reader will, I hope, permit me a brief comment. Once he had made his "philosophical" remarks about

Kant's categorical imperative, which seemed so strange, not to say ridiculous, to us, Eichmann had to admit that his actions concerning the deportation of the Jews were not compatible with that imperative ("No, under no circumstances"). What then? "I was subject to pressure and coercion by a third party. . . . Killing people by force cannot be done under the categorical imperative, because it is not God's will."

It now turns out, in light of the cross-examination, that the third man drank cognac with that "third party," toasting the Final Solution that was not God's will, or Kant's.

"Then," he tells us, "Heydrich explained how he wanted the minutes to read, and the three of us were left alone. We sat down, and they offered me a glass of cognac, or two, or three."

"After that," he concludes, "everyone went home, and I sat down to write up the minutes."

Then he washed his hands, like Pontius Pilate in relation to his "inner self." "I said to myself, All the top brass were here . . . I did try to get excused from my duties."

But he did not ask Heydrich to be transferred.

"No, no, I never asked that. I could not ask such a thing of Heydrich. . . . I thought it over and decided I had done what I could." Had he made such a request he would have been sent "to a regiment bound for heaven, perhaps, or to the nuthouse."

So he celebrated the Final Solution with his superiors—to whom he had never suggested a thing—drinking cognac with them, three glasses of it.

It is 10:45 A.M.

Judge Halevi: "Sir, you said in your deposition that you had been brought to Israel against your will, but now that you were here you welcomed the opportunity to tell the world the truth about what you did. Is that correct?"

And Eichmann, standing erect and very tense, replies, "From my own human perspective I am even glad this prolonged cross-examination has afforded me a chance to tell the truth and dispel the lies about me that have accumulated over the last fifteen years."

Speaking very softly, Judge Halevi asks, "So this trial is important to you, not only for its own sake but also because you are a famous man?"

And Eichmann answers, "Not only because of who I am. Yes, I am concerned, first of all, that my family and my sons be able to say, Look, he stood up to the longest cross-examination ever conducted and told the truth."

This would be a good place to mention what Nathan Alterman wrote last Friday, in an article entitled "The Meaning of Justice": "The fact, real or imagined, that 'Eichmann has not broken down under cross-examination' should not cause wonderment at the defendant's 'resilience' but rather, first of all, the thought that what he has suffered during these long days of interrogation is, in fact, paradise compared to a single moment of 'interrogation' by his Gestapo."

Judge Halevi gets Eichmann's point. "Your desire to be seen by your sons in the best possible light could lead you a long way from the truth."

Eichmann bristles. "No, under no circumstances."

And he adds, "I am no coward."

And Halevi, an experienced interrogator, continues without raising his voice and gets to the heart of the matter. "As you see, it is not with secret-police methods that you have been interrogated here, nor does this court resemble a 'people's' court in any way."

"Yes, I have noticed that," the defendant admits.

"So it all depends on you, on whether you have the courage to tell the truth."

"Yes."

And, almost as though he were administering an oath, the judge continues, "No one is forcing you."

"Yes, I realize that."

Now the first blow. "Since you have spoken of cowardice here, I should like to call your attention to the fact that Wisliceny called you a coward."

"Yes," he answers in the same tone of voice.

"And that Winkelmann said that, unlike you, Endre had had the courage to stand before the Hungarian court and accept responsibility for what he had done and not pin the blame on others."

"Yes," Eichmann says, and tries to add something. But Halevi goes on in his quiet way, reminding him that Hans Frank, at Nuremberg, had the courage to own up to his guilt when "most of the accused tried to blame others."

And Eichmann says "yes."

Now Halevi appeals to the defendant's self-esteem. "You are proud of not acting this way and of having the extraordinary courage to disclose the whole truth before this dais and before the public opinion of the entire world."

The lengthy speech is meant to provoke the man, to remind him of his oath and appeal to his masculine pride, and it hits home. The defendant tries to answer, but Halevi goes on and on. "This is actually not a question. I am appealing to you directly. There is no prejudice against you. . . . We both have the same objective. . . . But you must be brave, setting aside your personal interests for the sake of the truth." But to avoid any unnecessary misunderstanding, the judge stresses, "Although this court is impartial, that does not mean we are naive enough to believe everything any witness, or the defendant as a witness, tells us."

The hint is unmistakable, and the judge concludes: "You said you wanted to write a book and that you wanted to serve as an example of atonement and remorse for generations to come. . . . You now have the opportunity to do this here, in the testimony you give."

"Yes," Eichmann whispers.

And just when the ceremony seems to be over, the judge warns him again. "You will, however, have to convince not only your sons but the court as well."

"I know that," Eichmann says, his words filling the silent hall.

Then the room resounds with the following solemn and frightening statement: "Today you will evidently conclude your testimony, and this may be your last and only chance to tell the public where you stand, what kind of man you are, whether you are a real man or whether you are trying to avoid the truth."

"Yes," Eichmann answers one more time.

JULY 23, 1961

FINAL QUESTIONS

The judges' questions concluded this portion of the trial. We had awaited them anxiously. To tell the truth, we expected a miracle. Today the judges finished their questioning, but the miracle never came to pass, because it could not. Because there, in the glass booth, sits a man who has chosen to avoid confronting what he did and what it meant. So the judges' questions did not bring him to any dramatic breaking point. What they did was provide further material for assessing his personality.

We could thus have anticipated that he would take a contrary stand.

The judges' questions were quite different, in both form and substance, from those of the prosecutor. But the defendant's answers were always the same.

The judges tried to pit Eichmann against himself. They gave him the opportunity of explaining himself and what he had done.

Little by little, the judges' questions, too, got lost in his responses, even when he seemed to have no alternative but to answer unequivocally.

Halevi: "Will you at least shoulder the burden of the facts?"

Eichmann: "What do you mean?"

Halevi: "For example, the Sassen document. You have expressed all sorts of reservations about it here, that you were drunk at the time, that it is a forgery."

Eichmann: "I told the truth."

Halevi: "Were you also drunk when you corrected the manuscript?"

Eichmann: "No, I was sober when I made the corrections."

Halevi: "Did you dictate them into a machine?"

Eichmann: "I admit that when it got late, I let loose and chattered about all sorts of things, but I snapped out of it."

One example among dozens.

And when the soft-spoken Halevi begins to get hot under the collar and tells him that "this line of defense is not worthy of the place where you are standing," he makes the magnanimous gesture of offering to assume responsibility for "sins [he] did not commit." Anything not to appear cowardly or evasive. The judges appeal to his mind, his conscience, his pride, his duty to answer for his actions. But he is less afraid of his own behavior than of what others will say about it.

His efforts, now, to condemn the crime so as to appear trustworthy and respectable compel him to explain why he took part in it. This takes him back, over and over again, to that well-known realm where boundaries are erased, where he can share the ignominy with "others in uniform" and be merely one of "those who take orders."

I think the key to understanding the Eichmann case is the following exchange:

Judge Halevi: "Pastor Grueber has pointed out that there was, in Germany, a lack of civic courage."

Eichmann: "Indeed, that is true."

Had there been such courage, "things would have been different," Grueber said, and Eichmann adds, "Had there been courage in the hierarchy as well."

The presiding judge, who interrogated him yesterday morning, is making a long excursus through the entire period under consideration. He touches on the important question of Eichmann's status as one empowered to make decisions. "We have now heard from Dr. Grueber that you always answered him with 'I' or 'I reject the request' or 'I have to think about it.' Is that correct?"

And Eichmann explains that "in negotiation one slips into

office jargon, the idiom of bureaucratic German." "I," then, means "my superiors," "the office," and the like.

The presiding judge continues, and after a long line of questions he comes to one that can have only a single answer: "Here in the Sassen document you say you saw the loading of Jews onto railway cars. Is that correct?"

Eichmann answers: "The loading of Jews. . . ."—he makes a great show of trying to recall—"Hard as I try, I cannot remember such a thing."

And the presiding judge, always restrained, cannot contain the next question, which bursts out almost angrily: "This is something I assume no one could forget once he had seen it."

"The loading of people onto railway cars—that I did not see," replies this man whom fate cursed with "the unrewarding trait of always telling the truth."

"How, then, did that get into the Sassen document?" Judge Landau wonders.

"It was just meant to spice it up," he answers.

"You saw loading operations, but in fact you didn't see them. Is that not a distortion of the facts?"

But Eichmann does not attribute any importance to such details, especially since this approach gives him a flexible line of defense that can never be breached.

Back to Wannsee, and the words pop up once more: killing, annihilation, extermination. He wrote them in the minutes. But the essential, about "methods of killing," escapes him.

He is ready for the next question.

Everything can be explained. He was a Nazi, but he was no antisemite. "That is paradoxical," the presiding judge says. "Ostensibly, but not in fact," Eichmann explains. He read the *Voelkischer Beobachter* to keep informed. He was concerned with "the plight of the nation, the economic distress."

"But didn't the antisemitic propaganda draw a connection between the economic situation and 'international Jewry,' as it was called there?"

"I was absorbed then in my job at Socony Vacuum Oil, and I didn't have time for things of the mind."

But Judge Landau gets him to admit that he joined the party of his own free will, that he knew it was based on the leadership principle, that its leader was an extreme antisemite, and that in 1935 the Nuremberg Laws had been passed.

After that, his attitude hardened, in view of "the Jews' own desire to leave."

"But didn't that desire spring from fear?"

"But it was not I who sowed that fear." What is more, "I dealt with the Jewish officials as equals."

This brings to mind his "joint efforts" with Brand and their "shared regret." He wanted to "work out a solution" together. Again, we find ourselves in a state of utter confusion.

Further on: "Couldn't you have given up your position in the Security Head Office and gone to serve at the front, against the will of your superiors?" The presiding judge was not talking about the formalities. "Had you said you wanted to go to the front, would anyone have stopped you?"

And from the exalted level on which this question was asked, we fall to the abyss of, "I would not have gotten permission to do so."

It turns out Heydrich and Guenther were tough and Mueller a bit tough too. But he, no, he was "too meticulous." "Mueller, too, was brought up on order and meticulousness." He "managed" to find a way out, between his lack of toughness and his efficiency, and that is why they didn't fire him. This is his response to Landau's ironical question as to why Mueller didn't get rid of him. And he joined his abused personality to that of Big Brother Mueller.

Meanwhile, we witness an interesting symposium on the Nazi concept of "toughness."

Following some additional questions from the prosecutor, we arrive at a point where we are taken back to the beginning, to the heart of the matter. In his confession to Sassen he admitted that he "sometimes did [his] work blindly, without any pleasure." But there were also times when he recognized the "need and rationale" for what he was doing, and then he did it "with pleasure and alacrity." For example, in the emigration office in Vienna, where he acted as a "veteran National Socialist" against "the people who were guests of the host people."

The presiding judge asks him, "By 'guest' you mean the Jews, and by 'host' you mean the rest of Europe, correct?"

"Yes," Eichmann replies.

In the end, the "host" sent his longtime "guest" through the chimney-gateway to heaven.

July 25, 1961

THE LAST DOCUMENT

On August 3, the attorney general will begin summing up for the prosecution. On the 9th, the learned counsel for the defense Dr. Servatius will present his summation, which will, he has promised, be short. The trial will probably be over around the 11th or 12th.

That will be that. The defendant will be taken back to one of the other rooms here in Beit Ha'am, or somewhere else in the city, or elsewhere in the country. The reporters and observers will go back to their countries and cities and places of work. And Eichmann's name will be forgotten for a while.

During that time, following the summations, the three Israeli judges will deliberate on 1,434 exhibits for the prosecution and 109 for the defense. They will deliberate alone, having heard and seen, face to face, 111 witnesses for the prosecution, having heard and seen, face to face, only one witness for the defense, the defendant himself.

They alone will be repeating his name over and over again during that time, because they have to pass judgment on him.

Today, Session 109 ended. The last testimony for the defense was read aloud, the last documents presented. It was announced that, at the request of the prosecution, there would be a ten-day recess.

This morning, Slavik's testimony was read. He was the last of the witnesses for the defense. Others had already been heard from: Six, Krumey, Winkelmann, Veesenmayer, Merten, Novak, Keppler, Bach-Zelewski.

The term "witness for the defense" is misleading. We can now sum up: this man has no witnesses for his defense, not one. And when he himself appeared as a witness for the defense, another Eichmann, wearing jackboots and a pistol, hit him in the face, as did yet another Eichmann, drinking red wine with Sassen.

In his desperate battle with these two, there in his glass booth, beaten and humiliated at his own hands, he sought the help of these other witnesses, but they kept their distance and did not come to his aid.

Strange witnesses for the defense.

Six: "Eichmann's department had a special status . . . He had more authority . . . He was not under Mueller's command but, in a sense, alongside him . . . The two complemented one another . . . His superiors regarded him as a veteran Nazi, well suited to his task . . . He acted according to the most extreme interpretation [of his mission]."

Krumey, speaking about the *Fussmarsch* of the Budapest Jews, describes a long line of marchers: "[They] gave the impression of being on their last legs." He thinks Eichmann could have intervened. Eichmann told him, "You haven't seen a thing."

Winkelmann: "I did not care for this officer, with his arrogant manner. . . . He was a man who wielded his authority without any moral or mental inhibition. . . . Eichmann was not under my command but got his orders directly from the Reich Security Head Office."

Veesenmayer: "Eichmann's unit dealt with the deportation of the Jews."

Keppler: "An S.S. officer named Dannecker, from IV-B4, came to me with full authorization to conduct sweeps for Jews."

Bach-Zalewski: "If Eichmann was one of those who were sent reports about the activities of the Action Squads, his office must have been a very important one."

Etc., etc.

Yes, even so, these witnesses have been summoned by the defense, and they do have some things to say in his favor too, such as: "It was impossible for a department head to issue directives that exceeded the limits of his superiors' orders without their knowledge." Or, "Eichmann acted with excessive caution and tended not to take responsibility." Or, "I do not remember if Eichmann's name was ever mentioned in connection with the death march." Or, "I did not think Eichmann cut much of a figure in the Reich Security Head Office." Etc., etc.

A ghost haunts this testimony, a spirit from that other world. These witnesses are all members of his family, his comrades: those who were hanged, those now in prison, those who have been released and those awaiting trial.

Men the sound of whose names alone had been enough to cause heart failure are here again, leaping over elapsed time, testifying under oath. They lie; they contradict themselves and each another.

Franz Watter Six says: "Every senior ministry official knew by the end of 1943 about the concentration camps and the gassing and persecution of the Jews." But Dr. Edmund Veesenmayer, of the S.S., the German legate to Hungary, says he first heard about the Final Solution at Nuremberg!

But it is Otto Winkelmann, high commander of the S.S. in Hungary, who goes the furthest: Eichmann acted "without any moral or mental inhibition," he says. It makes you sad. Their humorlessness. Evidently he, Winkelmann, was a "moral man," who did have inhibitions.

Witnesses for the defense, warped and defeated, who have come back from the dead. We cannot see them. We can only hear their feeble responses, their last attempts to be correct and loyal.

And then he is left by himself, with only his proper, overstuffed attorney by his side, plowing ahead like a bulldozer, piling up material and fighting over the details of one document or another.

Who is left? Slavik! I can't wait to hear his testimony. The testimony about the cherry orchard.

Testifying on July 6 of this year before a court in Vienna, he said the following in response to a question: "I do not know whether, during the period I worked with Eichmann, a Jewish teenager was beaten or bludgeoned to death in the yard of the Aschner villa on Apostles Street."

I shall dispense with the rest of his testimony.

These things were said by the man whom Avraham Gordon, of Timna,[44] had accused of murdering the boy for stealing fruit from the garden.

I remember Gordon's testimony. He was very precise about everything: there was a villa, there was a garden; they had been digging; there was Eichmann; there was Slavik; there was an amphibious vehicle with a driver named Teitel. His story checks out in every detail. But Eichmann denies the murder, Slavik denies the murder. I remember the moment when Gordon, the witness, said, "It was the first murder I had seen in my life." He told of a beating in the shed, about pleas for mercy, about groans, about a body that was brought out and put in an amphibious vehicle waiting there—as even Eichmann and Slavik had testified.

Another Jew said in Vienna that it wasn't Eichmann who committed the murder, but Slavik. Two witnesses tell of the boy's murder. Eichmann and Slavik say no.

Was it really just the imagining of a frightened Jewish boy? Or was there, in fact, a murder that these men are denying?

Eichmann will probably be acquitted of this charge on grounds of "insufficient evidence." "I never beat anyone." All right, let's assume that. But in his office he had a telephone, a clock, and a calendar. Genocide is not committed with a garden hoe.

The prosecutor questions the witness vigorously about every part of Slavik's testimony.

They continue submitting documents, now concerning the children of Lidice and Krumey's testimony in the book *Here Stood Lidice*, which the prosecution requests be placed in evidence.

44. Place in the south of Israel.—Trans.

The presiding judge: "Dr. Servatius, do you have any more documents to submit?"

"Yes." Servatius asks that pages 299–302 from Poliakov's *Red Book* be placed in evidence. Why? Because it was from there that Eichmann had quoted passages dealing with "special treatment" and his interpretation of it ("not only execution"). It would be exhibit N/108.

One more exhibit for the defense. The last. Servatius: "I would like to present an excerpt from the second volume of the proceedings against major war criminals in Germany, the things Keitel said about the elimination of the Jews."

Pay attention, dear reader, to this document, which is presented in a tail-end atmosphere before a half-empty auditorium.

The investigator at Nuremberg, Colonel John Amen, asks a witness named Lahousen about things he heard Keitel say: "Just for the record, what actions, exactly, were agreed upon then, according to Keitel?"

Lahousen: "According to a description given by the Commander-in-Chief of the Wehrmacht at that time, they agreed on the bombing of Warsaw and the execution by firing squad of the various nationalities and groups in Poland that I have indicated."

Amann: "Which ones were they?"

Lahousen: "They were, first of all, the Polish intelligentsia, the nobility, the clergy, and of course the Jews."

Later, the witness adds that the Wehrmacht high command issued a directive that it had received from Ribbentrop concerning "a Ukrainian revolutionary movement aimed at wiping out the Poles and the Jews."

The presiding judge assigns this exhibit number G/109.

We understand why Servatius has cited the document. Everything had been decided higher up, by the Wehrmacht high command, by the Foreign Ministry. It is the big shots who are guilty. His client took no initiative . . . etc., etc.

Here we see the familiar, paradoxical procedure: the prosecution trains the spotlight on Eichmann. The defense shifts the blame onto all of Germany.

And on this closing morning things get jumbled together, with only a few moments separating Teitel, Eichmann's driver, who was sentenced to death for robbing and murdering an old Hungarian woman, and the directive concerning "the destruction of the Poles and Jews," issued by Keitel, Commander-in-Chief of the Wehrmacht. Between Dr. Werbe, from England, who proves—and the prosecution asks to submit his research as an exhibit—that 2.5 million human beings were exterminated at Auschwitz, and the postcard thrown from a train, showing two children who were murdered there.

The prosecution has made copies of the postcard, which was presented by the witness Freudiger. The court accepts it as exhibit T/1433.

A friend of mine gets one of the copies. "June 15, 1944," it reads. "We are in a railway car, traveling from Komoron through Budapest. S. O. S." The signatures are of men, women, and children. On the other side, you see a little boy and girl sitting on a lawn, laughing.

The final document submitted by the prosecution consists of excerpts from the book *Here Stood Lidice*—refuting testimony—Exhibit T/1934.

The final document submitted by the defense, N/109, deals with the directives issued by the high command for "elimination" and "wiping out."

T/1433 and T/1434 deal with children, the children of Lidice, and in particular the brother and sister who went to Auschwitz instead of to high school. Because Eichmann had "received orders" and passed them on "through the proper channels" to his subordinates.

On the wall, next to the glass booth, hangs a map of Europe, unnoticed for some days now.

What number will it be assigned among the exhibits for the prosecution? Perhaps T/1435?

July 26, 1961

THE TRUE PICTURE

All superfluities gradually fade away. And here we are again, most of us.

Gherman Titov[45] has circled the earth seventeen times. Elections. A long break. And we are back in this auditorium, with its constant temperature and uniform lighting, bright and cold.

The attorney general is giving his summation. The true picture, the great structure, is being assembled out of well-known facts. Many questions still cry out for answers. This generation will bequeath them to the next.

Words are regaining their strength. They skip over passing concerns, things that are "very important" in one or another place in the world. Tired but angry, they are running after humanity to call attention to the difference between then and now, and they overtake it.

Then a promise is made: "We shall prove to the court." Now everything is known; now everything is proven. The structure is complete. The voice is the same. In the afternoon, the voice will become fatigued and hoarse, as if it had just returned from battle.

But in the morning, in the prologue, the prosecutor gathers his witnesses around him, taking each one's soul, the gist of each one's testimony.

I admit that at first his words hit a wall of incomprehension. "We have already heard about babies being thrown onto bonfires."

45. Pioneering Soviet cosmonaut.—Trans.

But then, with immeasurable power, they break through our resistance to any return to the subject.

Hausner isn't adding anything new. Hausner is summing up, putting things in order, restoring them to the real world. Hausner is putting Eichmann back in his true uniform, giving him back his power, giving his actions back their meaning, delineating his responsibility.

After long weeks of interrogation, of questions and answers, the prosecutor leads us back to the basic truths about the reality of murderer and murdered, crime and punishment, fact and meaning.

After the "tortuous struggle, rife with lying and evasion," we stand, at the end of this exhausting legal odyssey, before the following sentence: "A crime does not cease to be a crime merely by being wider in scope or more terrible. The law imposes criminal responsibility upon the murderer of one person according to the same principle by which it imposes responsibility on the murderer of millions."

And another simple truth: "Once an unholy alliance is forged, all the parties become Siamese twins, inseparable partners in crime."

And further on: "The relation between leader and led does not obviate responsibility here. People are not to be regarded as innocent on the grounds that Hitler made use of them, provided they knew what they were doing."

He proves that Eichmann did know, that he cooperated willingly, that he initiated and carried out his work with "pleasure and enthusiasm"; that he did not try to avoid doing it; that he had no qualms about this murder, about the deportations, forced migrations, evacuations, transports, or killings; that he was a central and very powerful figure in the German death industry. This was how he saw himself and how others, his comrades, superiors, and subordinates, saw him as well.

Hausner is giving him back his identity.

The glass separating him from us is now, once again, just bulletproofing, after a terrible, prolonged attempt to turn it into a reducing lens.

He puts him together with others but denies him the right to shift the guilt hovering over him onto their shoulders.

A mother does not have a limited amount of love that must be divided among her children. Her love increases with and is increased by their number. The guilt of accomplices to murder is not diminished in proportion to the number who take part in the crime. And, as others have pointed out, the fact that many are murdered does not diminish the loss of each one. They stand in a long line. Each of the murderers belongs to each of the victims and to all of them collectively, because each victim was murdered for being a part of a collective, which itself was murdered.

What is more, this defendant was part of the high command of the murderers, where he served as the great dispatcher to oblivion, the one with the power of life and death over the Jews. It began when the first of them was deported. It ended when the last of those who died in the forced march to Austria gave up the ghost. Even there it did not end; he went on murdering them long after that world, "the dry-eyed world of the emperors," had vanished, when he sat with Sassen and murdered them all over again in his unrepentant memories.

August 9, 1961

THE BLACK FLAG

The prosecutor went on with his speech today. Eichmann kept silent and did not move. At times he seemed to be dozing or daydreaming, but after a few minutes he would suddenly lurch, as if awakening, scribble something, and give it to the officer sitting next to him. The latter would pass it on to the defense counsel, and Eichmann would nod in thanks. The last moves of a game that has already been lost.

The prosecutor goes on with his summation. "With the permission of the court," he begins, "I would now like to move on to evidence proving that Eichmann was connected to and in direct or indirect control of the concentration camps and death camps."

No, his job was not done when the trains reached their destinations.

His face, which I have watched for many long hours, no longer explains what he did. I make a mental snapshot of his name, in Hebrew letters. It tells me more.

The prosecutor now draws all the facts together and ties them to his name. So it wasn't only a matter of the transports. It was everything!

It wasn't just a relay race, in which each runner completes his segment and stops. IV-B4 extended from Amsterdam, Paris, Oslo, Salonica, Bratislava, and Budapest all the way to the ovens.

"Eichmann evidently intended Terezin to be the place where the last remnant would be eliminated. . . . Complaints about the conditions at Bergen-Belsen were referred to him." He came to Treblinka to survey the estate of death. He drove around the camp in a small half-track that belonged to the commandant.

"How many hundreds or thousands of Jews suffocated in the gas chambers while Mr. Eichmann was driving around the death camp in that half-track?"

When the extermination operation at Chelmno was suspended, it was Kaltenbrunner who made the camp staff swear to secrecy. And Hausner raises his voice: "Kaltenbrunner, not the head of the S.S. Economic Administration [Oswald Pohl]." "The camp staff," he continues, "was responsible to the Reich Security Head Office," of which IV-B4, Eichmann's department, was a part. "The gas vans belonged to that office." The transports of Jews to death camps in the Lublin area—where the defendant admits he sent the Jews from the West—did not have to be reported to the S.S. Economic Administration, only to Eichmann. The chemist Gerstein, who was held in a French jail and committed suicide in 1945, supplied the poison gas in 1942 on instructions from Guenther, Eichmann's deputy.

As for Auschwitz, Rudolf Hoess testified at Nuremberg and in Poland that Eichmann had absolute control over the fate of the Jews he had sent there (*transportjuden*). Of course Auschwitz was a whole complex of camps belonging to the Economic Administration, but "directives concerning the fate of those deported there, their incarceration or release, their immediate or delayed execution—all this was in the hands of the authority that had sent them there." That authority was Eichmann's.

Here there is mention of the name of Yehuda Bacon. I remember that witness, a painter at the Bezalel Institute of Art, a lad from Czechoslovakia, who described in a very soft voice the *familienlager* and the soothing postcards sent to relatives right up to the last day. Hausner says, "Eichmann personally supervised the transports and even set the dates for their passengers to be put to death."

And Eichmann sits listening, motionless, like a rock or a person dozing, until the prosecutor asks, "What did he do in Auschwitz?"

And the combination of these two words, "Eichmann" and "Auschwitz," sends a familiar shudder through the audience, even though the reporters' seats are half empty and it is only Israelis who have crowded in and are listening intently in silence.

The summation has to go over everything one last time. And so we are back to the skeletons, to the Patrimony Institute in Strasbourg. "And when Sievers was asked at his trial why it was to Eichmann, in particular, that he turned in this regard, he answered that the overall commander of the concentration camps, Gluecks, had referred him to Eichmann, and two months later Sievers turned to Eichmann again."

Again, the skeleton affair in all its details, in all its twists and turns, to the point where we forget what is being spoken about and ask ourselves, along with the prosecutor, "Why, indeed, to Eichmann?" And despite his protestations that it was "not me," the prosecutor asks, "Are we really to assume that the high command of the S.S. was not aware of these matters or of who was in charge of them and that it turned to a secondary official with no connection to them?"

If you have been sitting there hour after hour, listening stone-faced to all the details, and you have the strength to follow them, you put the facts together. If you cannot follow them, you just sit there watching, half asleep, pondering the questions the prosecutor posed yesterday about ruthlessness, about callousness, about "bicycle riders" who defer to the heavens above while running over those below, about the noble Grueber, who chose to suffer, about Mt. Sinai and "Thou shalt not murder," about "the steely-eyed world of the caesars" and the world of the victims, who did not even have the right to cry.

But if you are following the prosecutor, he is taking you to Hungary for the fifth time. Eichmann is saying to Brand, "You know who I am. I am in charge of the operation in Europe, in Poland and Czechoslovakia. Now it is Hungary's turn."

Hungary as dessert, following the rest of Europe. Once again, the railway clerk, his face pale, gets bigger and bigger before our very eyes. The transports from there, the direct and indirect control there. Retroactive authorizations to Globocnik for additional food for the extermination operation. Deputies throughout Europe.

Now Hungary.

At this point, the ghost gives a shudder. He is wide awake, listening tensely, because Hungary is his last line of defense. But after a half hour that line, too, is in ruins, has gone up in smoke.

The thing began with lying and subterfuge. It was these that sealed the fate of the unfortunate victims even more than bullets, starvation, or Zyklon-B. Eichmann told the leaders of the Jewish community, "It will only be for the duration of the war. Then everything will go back to the way it was, back to normal."

But the promise was accompanied by the whiplash of a threat: "You'll have to cooperate. Wherever there is resistance, people will be killed."

The heroism of the Warsaw ghetto cast a shadow over Hungary. And to the battered, frightened people who wanted to believe right up to the last moment, he said, "I am being frank with you. You must speak frankly with me as well."

The Artist (*the Meister*) worked wonders in Hungary. The goal was clear: "The speedy evacuation and deportation of the Hungarian Jews to Auschwitz." These were the words of his own confession to Section 06.

The transports were sent at a mad pace. And when he encountered Hungarian resistance (in 1944, with an Allied victory on the horizon), there was the horror of the deportation from Kistarcsa.

And again the prosecutor utters one of those lines to which there can be no comeback: "The crematoria at Auschwitz were being stoked to the point of bursting. Day and night, Moloch went on consuming his victims." And we hear of an argument between the dispatcher, Eichmann, and the recipient, Hoess, who was only willing to accept fresh shipments up to the camp's capacity, and Eichmann went there to make sure the speed of the operations was synchronized.

A bloody merry-go-round. He refused to let up. The Fuehrer's extermination order was given to him orally. That was sufficient for him. But when it came to stopping, he needed orders in writing, he appealed.

His last refuge, the blood-and-trucks deal, was exposed as a fraud. He hadn't wanted it, hadn't believed it would come to pass. "A thing like that, involving ten thousand trucks, was out of the question. I didn't dare even imagine it," he had told Sassen.

But under duress he had been prepared to give "even two million Jews" in return for the trucks. After all, "not all of them were fed to the ovens."

The prosecutor quotes more passages in this vein, like "Get this pile of shit out of here."

Hansi Brand's question, "How can you be so ruthless? Don't you have any children?" is an echo from a world without meaning.

But Hausner gets to the heart of the matter when he says, "I will now take up a juridical problem, that of orders from on high." This, after all, is the root of all the horrors. Of the many quotations he cites, I shall choose one from the trial in an Israeli court of a crime committed here, the Kafr Kassem trial: "A sign of 'patent illegality' should fly as a black flag over [such] orders, as a warning message reading 'forbidden.'"

The prosecutor then turns to an analysis of the Nuremberg verdict and to quotations from law books and treaties explaining why illegal orders carry the seeds of crime and havoc. He insists on "the logic that underlies the obligation to refuse illegal orders," drawing an instructive example from Stephen's *History of Criminal Law*: "The doctrine that a soldier is bound, under all circumstances, to obey his superior officer would be fatal to military discipline itself, for it would justify the private in shooting the colonel by the orders of the captain." Stephen goes on to discuss "the murder of women and children."

This brings the prosecutor to Nuremberg: "The fact that the defendant acted under orders from a government or higher authority does not free him of responsibility."

And he cites the verdict of a Polish military war-crimes

tribunal: "Even if we were to accept the defendant's explanations as a basis for judging him, his defense would not lessen in the slightest his responsibility for the crimes that were committed."

"But above all," the prosecutor says, "it is clear that the defendant did his work wholeheartedly and willingly."

Eichmann listens drowsily.

Over his head, somewhat belatedly, the black flag is flying.

AUGUST 10, 1961

A CONCLUDING SPEECH

"And in the days of the return to Judah and Jerusalem, behold, a trial was held here on account of 'the violent crime against the Judeans' and the shedding of their 'innocent blood,' as the Prophet Joel foresaw.[46] I beseech you, O judges of Israel: Let your judgment be just and true."

It is with these words that the prosecutor concludes his speech.

It is 12:15.

He is a man searching for lofty words, words with a power that suits the occasion. Having begun his argument many days before with the words "I shall speak for six million who are silent," he now feels apologetic. "To properly mourn their torment and death," he says, "we would need another poet like the author of Lamentations, that he might bewail 'the ruin of my poor people.'"[47]

Standing before the judges at the end of an exhausting journey, emerging from a mountain of documents, a wealth of testimony and anecdotes and events, a tangle of legalities and citations from law books, he has built a comprehensive case for conviction. He senses this is his last chance to express grief in those words of scripture that say it all.

It is as if, at the height of his summation, standing before his people and the world, he has assumed, without anyone noticing it, the stance of the prayer "Behold, I am inadequate,"[48] of "Who am I?"

46. A reference to Joel 4:19.—Trans.
47. A reference to Lamentations 2:11, 3:48.—Trans.
48. Recited by the leader of the Musaf service on the Day of Atonement.—Trans.

He longs for a poet like the author of Lamentations.

But we remember the witnesses who spoke in this courtroom. In the course of the trial we heard words, verses, stories, testimony that taught us another language, stronger than any dirge, a special language in which familiar adjectives became revelations from afar, from a place other than German-occupied Europe, from a time other than that of the murderers.

And standing or sitting in our presence, they took us along with them. And when we, the living, returned home from those places, our faces had changed and we were no longer ourselves.

They taught us phrases like "special treatment," "transport schedules," "receiving stations," "action squads," "night and fog."

They quoted things they had heard in the camps of their killers or told stories about the camps in the first person. In their unpolished way, they created a language even stronger than that of the poet of Lamentations.

"My little girl had a red coat. My wife went to the left and was swallowed up in the crowd as it moved off into the distance. I knew where they were by the patch of red. But it got smaller and smaller, until, finally, I could no longer see them."

What more is needed to prove guilt? It has all been said. Everything. But the prosecutor, on the last day, is still trying to convince the judges. He relies on documents and testimony, on reports, on the transcript of the 06 interrogation.

Yes, Eichmann had said he would "gladly leap into his own grave if he were told that five million Jews had been exterminated."

The prosecutor demonstrates at some length that what Eichmann had meant was Jews and not just "enemies of the Reich." "Its enemies *were* the Jews." And again, he quotes the now-deceased Wisliceny and Wilhelm Hoettl, and we go back to Sassen, until the details are blurred, and only this number hangs once more in the space above the crowd. He told Wisliceny five million. To Hoettl, he said six million. And, used to such figures by now, we, too, turn away from the prosecutor and his analysis of the matter and wait for him to shift the focus elsewhere. A few minutes later, he does: "In the dreadful, dark night that fell over Europe after the rise of Hitler to power, there were bright spots as well, and the Jewish people will never forget its benefactors, just as it does not forget its enemies."

He begins with Cyrus the Great, "whom we remember even now with gratitude and appreciation." This sudden leap back in time to ancient Persia, only to return to modern Denmark, has a powerful emotional effect on the capacity audience. There is a heavy silence in the auditorium.

I sit watching these people, who belong to a nation with a fearfully long memory, a nation that has suffered throughout its history. "We still remember Cyrus with gratitude and appreciation for permitting the exiles to return to their homeland." Even then, there was an exile. I am reminded of the pupils at the Alliance Israelite Universelle school in Paris, Persian Jews whose Jewish identity Eichmann could well have learned about from Haman.[49]

"Pilate." "Amalek." But the prosecutor continues: "We shall never forget the decency of the Danish people, an entire people that risked its life to save the Jews of Denmark."

And as if performing some strange, awful ritual, the attorney general enumerates all the other "bright spots," in Belgium, Norway, Sweden, France, Holland, Italy, Poland, Lithuania, Yugoslavia, Greece, Bulgaria.

The crowd is quiet and close to tears, thinking of the good ones.

And again the names of Dr. Grueber and his wife come up. "Since we do not wish to mete out the same treatment to righteous and wicked alike, we must find a way to single out those who were righteous amid the wickedness of Sodom."

After recalling these brave, decent gentiles, he allows a few seconds of silence and then comes back to the Jewish people, "beaten, isolated, hemmed in on all sides by hatred and cruel foes, yet rising to heights of heroism not exhibited by any underground

49. The genocidal Persian villain of the Book of Esther.—Trans.

movement in Europe." Again, we are reminded of the rebellions, the underground, and the partisans, of those who went to their deaths singing "I believe with perfect faith in the coming of the Messiah."

"Now let us turn to the indictment and the law," Hausner says.

We accompany him to the last stage, while terms from the previous stage—like "mercy," "love of one's fellow man," and "faith"—still hang in the air of the courtroom.

The three judges sit motionless, listening to the arguments for conviction. From time to time, they intervene, asking questions and leaving nothing obscure. For it will be their task, when they are left by themselves, these three men who are also judges, to weigh the words of the prosecutor against those of the counsel for the defense. To render judgment.

This part is cruel and hard. Here all that counts are the facts and whatever words can serve to verify them beyond any shadow of a doubt. Other words must now be put aside.

The fifteen counts of the indictment stand separate from one another, then cluster together in groups, and finally line up shoulder to shoulder, monstrosities that grow out of one another and explain one another.

In four of the counts—deportation, torture, murder, and despoliation—it is as if "Eichmann and others" were being accused by a single victim, for so many suffered all four.

"Usually, your honors, when a man is charged with murder, the charge of assault is not added, because the greater crime encompasses the lesser one," the prosecutor says. "But what they did to millions of Jews while they were still alive. . . ."

And when the prosecutor lays out the indictment in its entirety, you see that "war crimes" and "crimes against humanity" and "crimes against the Jewish people" and "physical and mental harm to millions of Jews" and "looting of Jewish property" and on and on—still do not cover it all and are not, a priori, necessarily all one thing. There is, for example, a breakdown into "total or partial decimation" or "subjecting to conditions likely to result in physical decimation."

And, indeed, the counts of the indictment link up with the infinite variations on the theme of death described in the testimony of the witnesses.

And the court, which has heard both grief and glory, subjects each of these charges to a probing analysis, until it arrives at a complete picture, the sum total of the facts, which is the murder of one entire people by another.

The listener then reels with the impossibility of connecting this oceanic vastness with the ghostly figure sitting stark-still in the glass booth. And for a moment you think this will prompt the defense counsel to mount a counteroffensive of his own.

But then and only then do you begin to fathom the single truth that provides the underpinnings of this trial: "the defendant and others." These others are very numerous, yet their number does not diminish his guilt for being the central figure in this endless murder.

When he called Theodor Dannecker, when he ordered a transport "sent," he was guilty of the murder of all the children of Drancy and theft of their property, their shoes and shirts.

Every one of them can accuse him personally of being part of the criminal conspiracy.

Together, the number of the criminals and the number of the victims have a dizzying multiplier effect that is infinite and inescapable. In fact, this brings us to the main point. If it had been Mueller sitting in the glass booth, Eichmann would have been counted among the "others," and these others begin with Hitler and end with Ivan and Nikolai, who scattered the gas pellets at Birkenau.

We should be thankful to the concept of "others," that it does not exculpate him one bit from the murder, torture, deportation, and despoliation, yet allows us to see the full scope of the criminality. The spotlight shifts back and forth between him and them, and when he is momentarily in the dark they become visible: the nation, the regime, the system, people in the hundreds of thousands. The notion of "criminal conspiracy," which we tend to think of as a group of conspirators in a dark, narrow room, bursts all bounds with a wild ferocity, and the whole of Nazi Germany stands exposed.

From this broad background of land and people and forests, the Gothic cities and broad expanses of occupied Europe, flags and hands waving, boots and helmets, watchtowers and barracks, fire and smoke, there emerges the figure of the man who headed Section IV-B4 in the Reich Security Head Office, who was put in charge of the Final Solution, Adolf Eichmann, of the S.S., the Gestapo, and the S.D.

It has all been said, and more than this was not said. What else can *we* say about the prosecutor's powerful closing address? It took a supreme effort to tie together every last detail, the most prosaic passages in the law and the unrelenting nitty-gritty and pedantry of the legal process, with the vast scope of this unprecedented trial.

In the least of the documents and the most obscure of the legal passages, we come upon the face of a man who is weeping, an abandoned house, a train barreling down a one-way track to oblivion. From the humiliation and torture of an old man, from the helpless reply of a father to his son's cry of distress, from the testimony of that endless parade of witnesses who have come before us to tell their story, Hausner has ascended to the heights, where he is able to connect the red coat of the little girl who went to the left with the whole history of this people, its lonely valor and its death.

He left the defendant and has come back to him. On the way, he encountered "the others." Their people, their time, their doctrines. He had things to say to all those who had been "lights in the darkness," to those who had stood by and kept silent while blood was shed, to the soldiers from East and West who met at the Elbe.

And he has returned to the defendant.

August 11, 1961

DR. ROBERT SERVATIUS

THE DEAD CANNOT hear what the counsel for the defense has to say.

Only the living can hear him. Those who were there, and those who were here or somewhere else where death could not reach them.

Who is this man in the gray summer suit sitting next to me and listening?

He is a man who carries his whole family around with him in a little album.

And I, too, am listening to the defense counsel.

I am not the man in the gray suit. I was not there. I am trying to imagine what is going through the mind of a man who was left with no one.

I am trying to guess what the learned counsel might have to say in Eichmann's defense, what he could say here in Jerusalem, before this people that is sitting in judgment, the heirs of those who were murdered.

Through dreams and poems, we grant the dead the right and the power to come back to life. There is truth in that.

But also, in what we conventionally call the "real" world, strange things happen: a state that did not exist sets out to exact justice for the blood of people who were never its citizens.

Is that possible?

Yes, they were murdered *because* they were not its citizens. That is why, despite not having existed during those years that were filled with their deaths, it can try one of their murderers, as if it had existed and they had been its citizens.

The defense counsel finds this strange fact unacceptable. He says, "Every state is entitled, within the area of its sovereignty, to broaden the legal definition of its citizenry as it sees fit. It has a natural right to protect that citizenry. But when it comes to extending its jurisdiction beyond its own boundaries, the state is circumscribed by international law. Since at the time the acts were committed there did not exist a Jewish nation-state, no crime could be committed against it. This fact is not alterable, even by means of a legal fiction."

What the defense counsel has said is very important and very interesting.

True, "there was no Jewish nation-state." There was a Jewish nation without a state. It was this very separation that made the murder possible. But this separation, in the defense counsel's view, makes the trial impossible—a "legal fiction."

But the defense counsel makes these claims within the framework of that same "legal fiction," which is the trial of Adolf Eichmann in Jerusalem.

Were we able to tell the dead about that "legal fiction," they would smile at us from beyond the grave.

But Servatius would not be capable of understanding that smile.

He repeats the claim he made at the outset of the trial, that the State of Israel has no authority to adjudicate crimes committed against "foreigners" "before it even existed."

We have begun with this point, even though it only came up later in his argument.

Let us list his main points, then, in the order in which he made them:

(1) The defendant should be acquitted of counts 13–15 in the indictment: membership in organizations that have been declared criminal. "We deny the criminal character of the organizations. The political leadership used these organizations for evil purposes. But the members of the organizations themselves were not party to the guilt."

And to make it sound better, he adds, "Exacting justice from a group of people without proving their guilt should not be permitted. This, after all, is precisely what Hitler did to the Jews." (The "group of people" he is referring to is the S.S., the S.D., and the Gestapo.)

(2) "As for counts 9–12, which refer to offenses the defendant is said to have committed against aliens—Poles, Slovenians, Gypsies, the Lidice children—on alien soil," the defense counsel argues, "there is no principle permitting a state to extend its jurisdiction at will."

The learned counsel for the defense, who has often compared the Law for the Prosecution of the Nazis and Their Collaborators to Hitler's laws, is not above pointing out, in regard to the deportations in Europe, that, to his knowledge, "the State of Israel faced similar problems and had to find a way of dealing with them."

Dr. Servatius loves to make comparisons, and he never forgets to add that "in each and every case the distress and suffering were equivalent." The delicacy of his irony is directly proportional to the thickness of his skin.

(3) It should thus come as no surprise that "count number 8, dealing with war crimes, is, by the same token, invalid, . . . for, after all, there can be no war crimes unless the parties are in a state of war. The intervention of a third party, the State of Israel, in the warring parties' exercise of their sovereign jurisdiction is inadmissible."

Count 7, "Confiscation of Property," fares no better. "The defendant is not being accused of taking things himself. . . . If confiscation took place, it was done by the state according to law."

Developing his ideas along these lines, Dr. Servatius comes to the argument for the defense in the matter of Account W—where the victims' own money was used to buy the sandwiches given to them on their way to the grave. His claim is that "contributions made to Account W were for the good of the victims."

We are coming to counts 1–6, "Extermination in Camps, Killing by Shooting, Deportation and Other Offenses." (Counts 5 and 6 are presented as crimes against humanity.) Count 6 deals with "the persecution of the Jews on racial grounds or on grounds of national or state interest."

Here we blanch and are at a loss for words. "What the real reasons for the persecution of the Jews were is not for a jurist to decide. Even so expert a historian as Professor Baron could not give an adequate answer."

And the defense counsel adds, "Innumerable letters received by the defense from all over the world paint an embarrassing picture of the way people see things. The picture they paint is of a world that is itself sick."

But this sickness is not for the trial to deal with. "We need experts: philosophers, theologians, historians. It is they who should study this illness."

Dr. Servatius does not differentiate between degrees of sickness, between an antisemitic letter to the editor and the gas chambers.

"It is only indirectly that the defendant can be implicated in the sterilizations"—or in the other medical procedures, such as gassing and procuring skeletons.

At this point I experience a crisis, one that was bound to occur sooner or later. I feel as though I am having a bad dream, that only two hundred years hence will I grasp what these "medical procedures" were.

At the last moment, Judge Halevi intervenes. "Dr. Servatius," he says, "I assume it was a slip of the tongue on your part when you referred to the gas chambers as a medical procedure."

And the defense counsel clarifies: "They were a medical procedure only to the extent that they were designed by doctors." And to amplify, he adds, "After all, killing, too, is a medical matter."

Silence reigns in the auditorium. Something suffocating is spreading through the air, something unbearable, because what is happening here is that death is being denied its last privilege, that of respect. Instead, we are being given precise Teutonic definitions.

"Deportation orders were issued by a higher authority. . . . It was not he who decided who was to be deported."

As for crimes against the Jewish people, it has been pointed out to us that "no Jewish nation-state existed" and therefore "no crime could be committed against it."

Wonder of wonders, all is now in order, all is explained. "To what extent the defendant is responsible for what was done, in that he transported the Jews to the death camps knowing what their fate would be, is a special question."

Then up pops a sentence like this one: "No document has been furnished proving collaboration between the defendant and the death camps."

Wannsee is not mentioned. The defense counsel's ability to sidestep anything inconvenient matches his gifts for fine irony as well cynicism and bluntness. At times, though, he can wax emotional: "There is no reason to doubt the veracity of the general picture the witnesses have painted. Their sufferings are too sacred to me to subject them to petty criticism."

But the Jews' testimony is not accurate. And the Germans' is meant to shift the blame onto others.

The witnesses for the defense, on the other hand, were subjected to the pressures of a press campaign against the defendant—"contempt of court on a mass scale."

The one witness who has told the truth is the ever-candid defendant. He acknowledges his guilt. He is cooperative. He doesn't look for a way out.

And the Sassen document? "He was provoked under the influence of alcohol. He dressed things up to appeal to the reader."

The matter of obedience to orders and the responsibility of the state can be summed up in a few sentences: "What happened before or will happen after the execution of an order that is part of a larger operation is of no concern to the person carrying out that part . . . There can be no 'conspiracy' between a superior and a subordinate . . . One who is given an order cannot identify the actions of the political leadership as being criminal.. . . A basic principle of all states is trust in the leaders . . . It all depends on whether a given policy succeeds . . . There was no alternative but to comply."

Here we reach one of the trial's "high points." "It was possible to shirk one's tasks. This would not have been a refusal to obey orders but rather an evasion at the expense of others. It would have been a betrayal of one's comrades. The shirker would have been seen as a deserter by the state and a traitor by his comrades."

His comrades: Hoess and Globocnik and Guenther and Kaltenbrunner.

And to dispel any remaining doubts, the German adds, "The State of Israel, too, has had to take harsh measures when its very existence was at stake."

In short, the laws of the Jewish state are illegal. They are "retroactive laws aimed at particular people" and extend beyond the bounds of the state's sovereignty in both space and time. "There should be a return to the prior legal situation under the Argentine statute of limitations. . . , as if there had been a legal extradition. . . . The law must not avenge wrongs committed [not by the defendant but] by the political leadership."

Here the counsel for the defense makes a valid point: "The conviction of the defendant would not atone at all for the horrible things that were done."

At night, the relatives of those who were killed, and their fellow Jews, have similar thoughts.

The last part of the speech is meant as an appeal to us for a clearing of the decks, based on the moral principle behind statutes of limitation: "We are not asking that iniquity be forgiven or forgotten. We are calling for respite, for a pause to think. Let humanity distance itself from the exercise of unlimited state power. Let humanity distance itself from the mass depredations of an unrestrained public against a particular, ill-defined group. The passage of time is bound to bring peace and heal the wounds. Let humankind return to self-limitation and self-restraint, to humanity. Let a just verdict be issued that resounds beyond the Eichmann case, a

Solomonic judgment that will earn the admiration of all nations for the wisdom of the Jewish people.

"I propose that the principle of limitation that applies in Argentina be recognized and that the blemish of the abduction be erased. These, too, are the ways of peace. I propose that the court dismiss this case, that the defendant's file be closed and not be considered any further."

When he has finished, I get up and see the prosecution team and the officers of Section 06 politely shaking Servatius's hand. The auditorium empties out. Eichmann is taken back to his cell.

In November the verdict will be handed down.

August 15, 1961

THE JERUSALEM TRIAL

After a brief, forlorn respite, I now return to my unrelenting immersion in the extermination of the Jews, still feeling in my bones the residue left after giving my exact account of the proceedings to date.

I have no newspapers or books with me, only what remains stored in my memory. There, in my heart, there is a permanent place for the horrors.

A powerful wave of emotion sweeps back over me. The sea rises above the shoreline. It is floodtide.

Without any sense of sequence, of past or future, I stand in the maelstrom of those evil years, with only flashes of mad illumination to cling to against the swell of rage that threatens to engulf me.

For weeks on end I have sat in the Jerusalem courtroom as a news correspondent, reporting daily what I see and hear there, in the place where Eichmann is being tried. Back at my desk in the newspaper offices, even before putting pen to paper, I have rehearsed in my own mind my inadequacies and understandable limitations. And returning home at night, I have apologized to my subject at length.

No, I don't dare compare my distress to a single second of the pain and fear experienced by those who were there. In countless ways, they and I cannot be compared. But I believe this trial has been a unique tribulation for all of us, both individually and as a group.

The victims were murdered for belonging to this very group. Their personal calamities derived from this bleak fact, and the collective calamity of their people was both a reality in its own right and the sum total of all their individual calamities.

After hearing the witnesses for the prosecution, I groped about for ways to avoid betraying the distant, forgotten details of their tales of reckoning. At times I would doze off and then, upon awakening, notice one of the witnesses walking away. I would ask someone sitting near me, "What did this man say?" and the answer would be, "Don't ask! Don't ask!"

"Look what they did to me," one of the witnesses said. And by the time he had finished and stepped down, followed by the eyes of the entranced spectators, another witness was already beginning to speak, to let you know that there was yet more to say on the subject. He did not say "my story was the same" but told a story of his own, for he, too, had been there. His life had been different and so had his experience with death. "Now listen to what they did to *me*."

These individual stories go beyond the generalizations: so many humiliated, so many suffocated, so many shot. They go beyond the common denominator.

And we who managed to go on living by turning the extermination into some sort of abstraction or symbol or circumscribed event, in order to avoid the shock and speechlessness of a face-to-face confrontation with the victims as individuals—we have been forced this time to confront the totality the hard way, through encounters with the concrete details of their experience. We could not set up some imaginary, anonymous case and put words in its mouth.

People came up to us, grabbed us by the lapels and said, "You want to hear what happened there? Well listen, I was there." And the person speaking to you is no mere phantom or apparition but someone who lives today in Tel Aviv or Holon or Haifa or Ramle or Kfar Ruppin or Lehavot Habashan or Kibbutz Lohamei Hageta'ot.[50]

50. Urban centers and communal settlements in Israel.—Trans.

And you are afraid you may not understand them, because you weren't there.

The truth, then, lay in the uniqueness of each witness's testimony. No one merely repeated what had already been said. Other than the times and places, all the cases were different.

Each of the prosecution's witnesses was thus the hero of a rescue operation—the rescue of the testimony of the victims from the danger of not being heard or of being swallowed up in an anonymous mass.

As a result, the victory of the mass slaughter over them was reversed. The question "What did I do to deserve this?" was no longer lumped together with the other questions with which the torturers and killers left their victims. No. Each individual had the right to ask it as if for the first time, as if he alone were voicing it, without the other questions encroaching on his unique entitlement to cry out.

So it happened that an angry, heartrending chorus arose from afar.

What we faced was not a division table, allowing each of the murdered his portion in the catastrophe, his share in the silence of the great graveyard of European Jewry.

On the contrary, what we faced was an unending multiplication table.

Each piece of testimony was multiplied by the others and acquired an astonishing power by association with them, and though they all cried out, none drowned out any other. The similarity among them did not detract at all from their power. Each retained its status as an only child of the iniquity, the villainy, the divine compassion.

We felt as though we had come to console each of them, under the same sky filled with the souls of the dead, and like a silent honor guard we heard someone say, You see that pillar of fire? My wife and daughters are now part of it.

Many in the audience could not hold back their tears of

stopped-up grief, and when the court adjourned for a recess we went outside holding our heads.

Could we have given these people anything more than we did? We gave them back what their murderers had taken from them: the right to tell their stories in the first person singular.

The memory of each of the dead is now doubly preserved: in the letters and albums and memories of his dear ones and in the treasure trove of the people as a whole. In the list of the lost, which is as long as the way from a people's decimation to its redemption, there is a place for each of these cries.

On more than one occasion I have often heard people ask why the prosecution called so many witnesses. After all, most of them were not "relevant." The trial turned mainly on documents. Could the witness list not have been shortened by half?

True, the documents were the crux of it. Indeed, it is depressing to think that if, in the twilight of the gods that marked the German defeat, any archives beside those of the Gestapo had been destroyed it would have been hard to find evidence against the defendant. But it is important to understand and keep in mind that all this personal testimony was not meant only to increase the sense of calamity. A single refugee with his clothes torn and ashes on his head would have been enough to concretize for us what had happened there. The entire catastrophe could be conveyed by the words of a single individual.

Nor did the numerous witnesses come to add to the accumulation of suffering and rage. They testified in order to illuminate the destruction in all its detail. They did not come to compete with poetry or prayer in kindling emotion in our hearts. They were the very center of the trial, because they served as faithful proxies of the Holocaust. They were the facts.

When one person is murdered, the investigators ask who he was. They want to know when he was killed, how, by whom, and why.

When a people is murdered. . . . What do you do when a

whole people is murdered? You ask those same questions and call many witnesses.

And then they come, one after another, from all the different countries, from all the years, from all the nights, from all the days, and tell us very long, detailed stories.

The man who had been in the Sonderkommando at Chelmno saw the entire Jewish population of his home town pass before him into the gas vans, until one day, when he opened the doors, the bodies of his own wife and daughters fell into his arms.

I remember this witness, a big man with a grimace of suppressed tears on his face, the bridge between his personal calamity and that of the entire town.

So each witness was an essential part of the proceedings, for, besides being a symbol of fate and miraculous resurrection, he revealed an additional facet of the truth.

But we knew all this, didn't we?

Yes, we did. We knew it even before the Eichmann trial. Scholars and historians and archivists had labored endlessly, in Israel and elsewhere, to provide us with the documentation, which many shied away from reading.

And there was Yad Vashem[51] and the Museum of Holocaust and Revolt at Kibbutz Lohamei Hageta'ot.[52]

But when this material reached the table of the prosecution and was entered into the indictment, when these documents broke the silence of the archives, they seemed to be speaking for the first time, and the knowledge they imparted was a different knowledge.

What happened to this material was akin to what happens in nature when potential becomes actual: there is a great release of energy. It could be summed up in the words "Now I understand."

The Holocaust was taking place now and not at any other time between those years and the beginning of the trial.

51. The official Israeli Holocaust memorial and research center.—Trans.
52. The name means "ghetto fighters."—Trans.

The records came horribly alive, and for a moment we felt enveloped in chaos. But the chaos was replaced by the severe marshaling of facts and details. The catastrophe emerged in all its concreteness from a fog of generalities.

It took the capture of Eichmann to give this people the strength to ask, belatedly, "What did they do to us there?" This people in its multitudes, including those far away and cut off, those born outside the circle of destruction, and those who have tried to go on living behind a screen of forgetfulness.

Eichmann was caught and brought here. Despite statutes of limitations, despite the human weakness for allowing the past to die, it has been brought back.

The past has returned. Instruments meant to gauge the power of the earthquake that would befall us broke down at the outset, and the violent shock wave, we now recognize, has arrived. There is no escaping it.

Something strange and unparalleled has happened. The court has managed, in a remarkable way, to restrain the shattering effect of this seemingly new outcry, channeling part of it into the language of facts, numbers, and dates, while allowing the rest to hover, ghostlike, over the trial.

The transition from remembering and lamenting to investigating, indicting, and judging has brought the whole world here. The world has been brought to a screeching halt, forced to listen, to retrace its steps and give an accounting, but, equally, to recognize the change that has taken place in the relation between the murdered and the murderers.

Germany, the murderer, has been brought here, the Germany that, in those days, counted Eichmann among its favorite sons. It is a Germany that has been brought here against its will and forced to listen to things it wanted to forget, to see things it wanted to block from its own view behind the new stone walls it built with such feverish determination over the ruins of its scabrous past.

Consequently, this trial has trained a giant spotlight on the facts, laying them bare, while casting a deathly shadow over those watching and listening, so that they have lost all sense of time and place, and the light and darkness were mixed together in a way that has no parallel.

The deeper you got into this trial, the more it seemed to you that it would never end, for the subject was endless, and the murdered, the murderers, and the passive onlookers all were involved. Where one person was willing to help the victims, a hundred rejoiced at their calamity. You felt that the whole of Jewish history was spread out before you, explained and summed up at last in the light of ovens. It seemed as though the life and death of this people had passed by, this people that had wandered in the lands of others, without sword or king or capital city, its capital being far away and half in heaven, its dead kings being mere letters and words and names inscribed in the holy books, its heavenly King having abandoned it to its fate.

The balance sheet of this "guest" people—whose "hosts" had never accepted its presence and whose foreignness had always, unbeknownst to it, marked it for annihilation—was now open for inspection.

For few had left those lands. Most had stayed behind, held back by their love of the forests and fields, the spring and the snow and the gray cities—until annihilation came. It came at an unexpected time, when even the wise and experienced and well connected thought axes, fire, and smashed windows were things of the distant past.

It was the time of a murderous Germany, a country that deprived its victims of the two rights the weak hold sacred: the right to submit and the right to flee. It was the time of a murderous Germany, which, carried away by the zeal of its deeds and an exhilarating sense of destiny, took the murder of the innocent as its highest joy. This was the Germany of the Final Solution to the Jewish Question.

In this trial, a murderous Germany was brought before the bar of justice. Eichmann did not ease Germany's burden of guilt, nor did Germany lessen his responsibility. Just as each of the murdered belonged both to his individual death and to the death of his murdered people, so the murderers were bound together inseparably. Each of the murderers belonged to those he himself killed, but all belonged to Germany.

For it takes an entire people to annihilate an entire people.

And as everyone knows, that is what the German people did.

Here lies the truth that the heart refuses to accept. Gazing at the glass booth, I, too, ask myself the question so many others are asking: Can this figure behind the glass really be linked with the death of an entire people? Doesn't training the spotlights on him make it even harder to connect this shadow of a man, fighting for his mortal life, with the names of the camps, names that once again assault us? It might just be a bad dream.

But the Jerusalem trial was not meant to set him apart as the wizard of the Final Solution or as a scapegoat to appease the anger of a lynch mob.

One of the things that haunts me, like a riddle whose answer is lost in the depths, is the quiet way the trial has been conducted, the quiet workings of the accepted legal process, out in the open before the cameras and reporters, before the legal experts who have come to observe and never left even for a moment, before the court of public opinion.

And this legal process, though occasionally disrupted by the outcry of an incredulous spectator, went on with its work under the firm direction of the presiding judge, following accepted procedure the way courts do when they are serious about learning what can be learned.

And this quiet sometimes made the trial seem like a lengthy symposium, in which experts make presentations and argue among themselves.

And now that the defendant and his counsel have been given a chance to say what they have to say in his defense, and the testimony and the documents have been examined and reexamined, you know the truth.

You know, now, how the Jews of Europe were exterminated. You know that the defendant was not omnipotent, but neither was he just a little cog in a big machine. He has gradually taken his proper place in the overall picture as one of the chief exterminators.

But his role and position are now seen to have been an integral part of the German death industry as a whole, which employed hundreds of thousands of workers of various ranks and carried on its work among the German people without interruption.

Before the eyes of the world.

It is thus incorrect to say that Adolf Eichmann is being tried here as a symbol of Nazi bestiality. He is not a symbol. He was appointed *referent* for the Final Solution, and he must pay the price for his part in it. Had Mueller, his superior, or Guenther, his right-hand man, been captured, the workmen at Beit Ha-am would have set up three glass booths. Even if Hitler himself had been caught, his trial would not have closed the case against Germany.

If a new leaf has been turned over, it is inside us. We now see things differently.

We have set aside a Memorial Day for the Holocaust and Heroism and in doing so have drawn a subtle distinction between the two, as if we had juxtaposed them as complementary but different.

The Holocaust was a source of shame to us, like some awful blemish, visible to all. But the heroism we embraced as a shred of pride, giving us the right to hold our heads high.

Far be it from me to blur the distinction between one who dies without putting up a fight and one who fights back or tries to fight back, because a people that loves life will, by its very nature, always prefer those who try to exact the highest possible price for their own lives, those who bestow on themselves and their people the final honor of a fighter's death, because that also offers the only chance to go on living.

But we must ask the forgiveness of the multitudes whom we have judged in our hearts, we who were outside that circle. And we often judged them without asking ourselves what right we had to do so.

A survey conducted by *Ha'aretz*[53] among Israeli teenagers who

53. A leading Israeli daily newspaper.—Trans.

had never seen a whip with the swastika emblazoned on it showed that right up to the beginning of this trial there were those who said, "Had we been there we would not have gone to our deaths the way they did," or "We would have acted differently."

And some of those interviewed said it all too readily, in their charming native born–Israeli way, with no pause between question and answer for silence or apology.

Until the witnesses came and explained to us once again how hard it was for someone who "wasn't there" to understand what it was like.

And we began to understand, not from the abstraction that it "was hard to resist," but from the detailed stories that, at the end of the day, left us, too, close to the state of utter paralysis in which the victims had found themselves the whole time.

It is now clear to us how a person's mind and body are affected by prolonged hunger; by the exhaustion that wastes and slows one down; by the fear surpassing all fear; by the enervating illusion of "perhaps, even so"; by the flicker of "it can't happen"; by the bulldogs on every side; by the loaded Schmeisser[54] at one's back; by the weaker relatives hanging on one's arms and neck; by the responsibility for hostages; by the terror that an informer will turn in an escapee whose fate is written all over his face and clothing; by the foreignness of the landscape; by the lack of a "city of refuge"; by the feeling that "in any case, all is lost"; by the weariness that wants it all to be over, come what may; by the sense of being abandoned to one's fate without anyone else uttering a peep of protest; by not knowing what is in store; by despair that comes too late—to those who knew and didn't let on and to those who heard but refused to believe.

But above all, the deception. The murderers misled their victims. Trickery, camouflage. "You are going to work." "Go in and take a shower." "Deposit your money in the bank and get a receipt."

54. German sub-machine gun, named after its inventors, Louis and Hugo Schmeisser (father and son).—Trans.

It turns out that others acted the same way as the Jews when they got to the "planets of ash." They were no more heroic.

This, it appears, was the end of the road for the fugitive. Beyond this lay submission.

But here, too, we heard of innumerable outbreaks of resistance, only a few of which we had heard about at the time they happened and most of which had been swallowed up in darkness without their heroes attaining their final wish: that we, the Jews of the Land of Israel, would believe they died proud deaths.

And all too often we lumped those unfortunate souls together with the others in our peremptory judgment that they all "went like sheep to the slaughter."

We now know more than ever, and it is the most important things that we did not know about: the pity and the succor, the Hebrew and arithmetic exercise books at the brink of the grave, the light of prayer, the hand on the shoulder, the lips on the forehead, the loving farewells, the words spoken when all hope was lost and no one else was left, the assurance that "the shame is not yours but your persecutors.'"[55]

And we judged them instead of ourselves.

We had refused to judge ourselves, but we cannot refuse in their presence. Some day, if we can muster the strength, we shall examine why we did not do more to try to rescue them. We can hardly take the easy out of telling ourselves we did not know, because we did. We knew more here than did many of those sentenced to death there, even those whose fate was not sealed until the war was nearly over. All roads led here. We can repeat to ourselves till we're blue in the face that our hands were tied, that the war, the distance, and the refusal of others to help separated us from them, but we can never escape the voice calling after us, "And what about you?"

Can anyone put his hand to his heart and swear that the

55. Line from the Hebrew poem "My Sister Ruhama," by Yehuda Leib Gordon.—Trans.

Jewish community in this country did all it could to warn, to expose, to arouse, to save? Who can truly say that our rescue efforts were in proportion to the scale of the slaughter?

Yes, there is, in these things, considerable wisdom of hindsight, and we are only grasping belatedly what was not grasped before. But we cannot avoid asking ourselves these questions, particularly those of us who were on the watch and in positions of authority in those difficult years.

In judging so many of the unfortunate people condemned to die there—for the illusions they harbored, for hiding their heads in sand already soaked with their brothers' blood, for the silence that held them in its grip—we keep hearing that voice asking, "And you?"

Such questions were not raised in the trial, but it came near them and scratched them with its fingernails.

I do not see how we can do this reckoning today without going up a blind alley full of useless afterthoughts and accusations that have more to do with the present than the past.

Whether we want to or not, we shall be pursued by this ill wind for a long time to come.

Could we have done more than we did? At the time, we thought we were doing everything possible!

This brings us to one of the darkest chapters to come to light in the trial, that of the people who stood by when innocent blood was being shed.

This matter came up almost by chance when the witness Joel Brand told the story of the monstrous "trucks-for-blood" deal. Documents retrieved from the Weizmann archives in Rehovot and the Jewish Agency archives in Jerusalem were covered with layers of dust. The exchange of letters and telegrams between the leaders of the Yishuv[56] and the British Foreign Office tells an infuriating and shameful tale.

56. The Jewish population of the Land of Israel before 1948.— Trans.

The refusal of the British to try any sort of rescue is here exposed for all to see. They made no attempt at all. Their polite replies rejecting Weizmann's entreaties and proposals make one's flesh crawl, when we recall that these things were said when German fortunes were on the wane and the star of an Allied victory in the war was already shining brightly on the horizon.

For five long years the extermination of the Jews went on without the Allies lifting a finger to stop it. Only this combination of killing and indifference can explain the enormous number of victims.

Wherever attempts were made to disrupt the extermination process, to throw a monkey wrench into the works, many Jews were saved. Often in this trial the names of brave, compassionate nations and individuals to whom the survivors owe their lives have been mentioned.

In the last analysis, the extermination went unimpeded.

Not only did the British not try to help, but they prevented us from doing so, beating back with a thousand excuses the initiative of fighters here who were ready to go to the death camps and to intercept the trains headed toward them.

Despite having provided the British with tens of thousands of volunteer soldiers, the Yishuv was unable to win their consent to parachute its sons and daughters into enemy territory. No British blood would have been risked by this rescue effort.

This story of abandonment will be long remembered.

The trial is over. In November the court will return its verdict, which will begin with Eichmann but not end with him.

What has the trial accomplished?

The Eichmann trial has been conducted in Jerusalem, capital city of retribution, people tell us. How powerful and comforting this fact is!

It is true. The question is: What lesson shall we learn from it, what will the Diaspora learn, what will other nations make of it? Or could it be that there is no lesson?

The Jews topped the blacklist of the German-Nazi madness, but others, too, lie with them in common mass graves, and there might have been many more.

The extermination of the Jews ushered in a new epoch, a new era following the Christian era, which has ended. It is the era of the murderers. The era of "anything goes." And, indeed, this trial has shown us what a human being is capable of when he is not alone in committing murder and has authorization for his actions from on high. We are now living in this era, under clouds of fear.

The Jerusalem trial has proclaimed a different victory, that of the murdered over the murderers. But there can be no more bitter victory. A red-eyed, white-haired victory.

In all human history, there has never been a trial that plumbed such depths, for, along with Eichmann, nations and values and laws have also been in the dock.

The Jerusalem trial has addressed the world from the thick of this city's history, from this ancient place that gave humanity its prophets.

September 10, 1961

CONVICTED

"DEFENDANT, THE COURT finds you guilty of crimes against the Jewish people, crimes against humanity, war crimes, and membership in hostile organizations."

Adolf Eichmann is standing in the glass booth. It is this sight that greets me as I enter the auditorium and hear these words. A few seconds later I am pushed aside. Foreign reporters are rushing to send their cables: "Eichmann convicted!"

I sit down and look at him, at the judges, at the shiny brass candelabrum, at the audience.

The verdict has been handed down. Things always happen differently than you expect. He is allowed to remain seated while the judges' *ratio* is being read. He sits in his usual way, facing the dais. It is 9:05.

This was the first of the trial's final days, a day that was hard to anticipate. It unfolded in the course of three separate sessions that, together, were representative of the trial as a whole, to which we now returned.

The first part was an enormous body of evidence, presented by Judge Halevi, showing that the law allowed an Israeli court to judge the defendant and, indeed, obliged it to do so. The second part, a presentation by Judge Raveh, was a survey, year by year and country by country, of the stages of the Final Solution, out of which a sharply etched portrait of the *referent*, the defendant, emerges.

The survey lasted until six o'clock, when an hour-long recess was called. Then came the third part, presented by the presiding judge, a speech of primordial power that brought the trial back to its most fundamental and urgent point, the point from which the laws themselves derived. This part turned the day completely around, recalling its beginning but giving that beginning a whole new meaning. In the end, the day turned out to be unbearably long and almost incomprehensible.

It was the first day of the end of the trial.

We were back in the courtroom. At first I thought I was at one of those many earlier sessions.

But from the way people were dressed, you could tell time had passed.

This courtroom exists outside of time. The seasons do not intrude here. The light is always the same.

He has the same clothes on. He has not changed. It is the same stony face, contorted from time to time by the familiar twitches. The same huge hands.

Here comes the verdict. But where am I? I feel as though I am inside the trial. Now, in the early hours of this long day, it seems to me things are passing me by.

We have gone back to the trial's first day. Then, Servatius maintained that this court had no right to try Eichmann, and he gave his reasons. Now Judge Halevi is answering those objections, giving rationales that had been promised but were put off until now.

And the Honorable Binyamin Halevi, the presiding judge, begins.

I look at him, but something he said in his opening remarks still rings in my ears: "How could this have happened in broad daylight? And why was it the German people that wrought this great evil? Could the Nazis have carried out their designs without the help of other peoples among whom the Jews were living? Could the Holocaust have been prevented, at least in part, if the Allies had shown greater willingness to help the persecuted Jews? Did the Jews of the free world do as much as they could to rally themselves and their brethren to their aid?"

One by one, you hear the questions, and they sink silently into your soul.

Even now, on this day when question marks are giving way to exclamation points, these questions remain unanswered, like mouths agape. But the court knows that "in this maze of insistent questions it must not allow itself to be dragged into areas that are not its concern. . . . The legal process has its own rules, which are set by law, and these are unchanging, no matter what the subject of the trial. Were this not the case, justice would not be done."

He explains the cruel dilemma faced by the court: "There was an understandable desire to present, in the framework of this trial, a full, comprehensive picture of the events of the Holocaust—to highlight the great displays of heroism—and there were those who wanted this trial to provide a platform for clarifying certain deeper questions."

"But the legal process has its own rules," I repeat to myself, as I listen to Halevi speak.

And this is what is so astonishing, for the whole "steely-eyed world of the caesars," the whole reality known as the Final Solution, exists in a realm beyond law or measure, a surrealistic, fairy-tale domain. In dealing with it by "its own rules," the court seems to be undermining itself.

But in Judge Halevi's presentation, this quality of the trial gives rise very powerfully to a brilliant legal discourse on Servatius's three main points: "authority," "abduction," and "statutes of limitations."

A courtroom. Those who weep are not to be heard here now, and no one is hiding his face in his hands. The outcry seems to have faded away. And for a moment, I feel transported elsewhere.

A long discourse made up of legal citations and evidence, straddling times, places, and jurisdictions. It is as though the whole legal literature had been opened and we were witnessing an endless procession of precedents and practices and rulings that, over the course of generations, had shaped the meaning of sin and punishment in human thought and given humanity this body of law. He quotes constantly in English, French, and Latin, skips from era to era and continent to continent, dwells on the most obscure cases, and joins his voice to that of the human-being-as-legislator-and-judge that was heard at the Nuremberg military tribunal. He says, "There is no need here in Jerusalem, fifteen years after Nuremberg, to go back over the reasoning behind the principle of 'crimes against humanity,' for that reasoning is written in blood, the river of blood spilt by the people Israel. As Aroneanu said in 1948, this law was born in the crematoria, and woe betide anyone who would try to stifle it."

"The claim," he goes on, "that the systematic murder of masses of helpless people by a government and police force constitutes an 'act of state' for which its perpetrators are not responsible is an insult to common sense and a mockery of justice."

He constructs a splendid legal edifice establishing the authority of Israeli law to bring the Nazis to justice, hence the authority of this court to try the accused, and he proves that the circumstances under which the accused was brought to Israel are not relevant to the court's authority to try him. Here, he relies on the ex post facto agreement between Argentina and Israel concerning the violation of Argentine sovereignty, and he dismisses the argument concerning statutes of limitations.

Why does he have to do this at such length? Isn't it all obvious?

But "the legal process has its own rules." This part of the verdict is admirable. It is an impenetrable fortress.

Then, coming to the subject of Israel, the state conducting this trial in the name of the murdered Jews, he reaches the high point of his presentation.

Until now, everyone has spoken toward the dais, with his back to us. Today the dais is speaking, with its back to the brass candelabrum. Things seem different now that they are coming back to him and to us as a verdict.

The court believes the witnesses and the documents. The court does not believe him and does not accept the contentions of his defense counsel.

The witnesses are back. Judge Landau has brought them back. It was this stiff, exacting presiding judge who opened this morning's proceedings by saying, "The testimony of the Holocaust survivors who divulged their inmost thoughts to us will provide valuable material for the historians. But for this court," he stressed, "that testimony is only a byproduct of the trial."

What happened in the courtroom this evening erased the boundary between essence and "byproduct," and the "material for the historians" burst from the presiding judge's mouth with the full force of grief and horror, restoring to the verdict a dimension it had been missing, the part that had to do with affliction and rage, in which the true face of the extermination was revealed.

As opposed to the law books and citations and precedents and analogies, we now heard once again the names Chelmno, Sobibor, Belzec, Treblinka, Maidanek, Auschwitz, and Action Squads.

These are the names one approaches and flees, as from madness. It was for their sake that this trial was conducted.

The presiding judge takes all the various paths back to the "valley of the shadow of death," following in the footsteps of Eichmann and the witnesses.

The passages he reads from their testimony and from the Gerstein report are heartrending for the audience to hear, and once again I see people's faces change beyond recognition. "If this is how individuals suffered, the sum total of the suffering of millions, one-third of the Jewish people, who were tortured and slaughtered is certainly beyond human comprehension, and who are we even to try to express it? This," the presiding judge continues, "is a task for the greatest writers and poets, and perhaps there is some symbolic significance to the fact that even a writer who himself passed through the hell of Auschwitz did not have the strength to bear witness here but collapsed on the stand."

The presiding judge does not collapse.

December 12, 1961

WORDS IN THE FOREST

WHAT DOES YOUR heart weep for now, O nameless woman, and what are you saying to me from the remoteness of your soon- to-be-forgotten death?

My heart does not weep now, nor does my voice rise from the forest.

And what do your eyes see in the forest, if they see at all, O nameless woman?

The villainy which turned into grass, the cries that turned into rare and beautiful birds, there among the dull-witted trees, so wondrous to behold.

And what do your blind eyes see there in the sky, O nameless woman?

It is a glorious procession that my eyes see; the procession of the clouds of iniquity, tainted by the glory of twilight, is what my eyes see.

And what do your ears hear, O Godforsaken, nameless soul?

It is the river that my ears hear; the water carrying my life to the distant sea is what I hear.

And what can restore you to life and solace?

The one who did not show me a way out, the one who did not grasp my hand to take me with him into the air that day.

And what can restore you to life and solace?

No human being can restore me to life. And what did solace want of me?

I hear your voice at my back.

You hear my voice in your hand, as you hear the sea in a conch shell.

And what do you command me to do, if you command me, if you have anything to tell me now, O nameless woman?

That you give voice to my words, that you live by them, remembering me.

And what shall I do with your death, which haunts me?

Think of me without becoming like me, without losing your own life by becoming like me.

And with what curse do you afflict me?

I do not send a curse upon you, nor do my hands touch your face, which gazes at me. Relate to me as one of the living.

You have been among the dead, lo, these twenty years.

Death is vanquished by those who remain.

And where shall I bring your shame, O nameless woman; what shall I do with it?

Shame dwells not beside me. Here dwell those who were weaker on that summer day.

And what did those who were weaker on that summer day say?

No bird has brought us report of it.

Tell me, now, what they said on that summer day.

They wanted to give their death greater weight than the life that had preceded it. They wanted to set it out in some visible place. They wanted to deny time the right to make of them a beautiful spring.

Tell me about their death.

Their death that summer was self-evident and very lonely. Their death was as loathsome as their killers.

And what did they ask for before dying?

That those who belonged to them at least remember them, so long as their killers remained alive. That they think of them as they did the first time. That they refuse to falsify forgiveness.

Your death stirs within me.

My death belongs to your life.

My life ends in the same forest where your death begins. Your death has become legendary.

My death is not legendary. It is like the death of those who were shot. Clear as the sunshine on that summer day.

Just as I was told.

You now know more about it than I myself knew on that summer day. You know everything. I knew only my part.

Your death explains my life. I return to it as to a mirror.

My death belongs to my killers and to you.

On my way to you, I sink further and further into bewilderment. Does your death dwell in bewilderment? What must I do to decipher my life and approach your death?

He who approaches my death shall be burned to ash and rise like the phoenix, and there I am with you differently than I am with myself.

Do you seek vengeance even now?

I refuse to make things easier for you or for my killers.

Do you seek vengeance even now?

It is you who can restore my right to be shouted in your ears. Do you seek vengeance for me?

I return to that summer in order to deserve your life.

You return to that summer in order to deserve your life.

Vengeance falls at your feet. If you lift it up, your heart will break.

It is as weighty as you are.

I have a punishment, and you are unbearably weightier than it is.

It is as weighty as your right to speak in my name.

December 13, 1961

DESERVING OF DEATH

It is the final hour. After this, no one will speak in this courtroom except the presiding judge.

This is the hour that knows no mercy.

This is the hour for the prosecutor to ask the court to declare this man deserving of death.

This is the hour for the defense counsel to plead one last time that the death sentence not be imposed upon this man who, as the counselor himself put it, "embodies death."

This is the hour when all the loose ends are tied up, and the essential meaning of this whole legal procedure, of the countless hours when this court was preoccupied with death, becomes clear.

But that death is to be found there, not here. What we can expect here is the death of one man, like an answer beyond time, like a circle slowly being closed.

The prosecutor asks for the death penalty.

Today is a continuation of yesterday, separated from it, only incidentally, by a rainy night. The judges' verdict virtually echoed the words of the prosecution. He was found guilty as charged, on all counts. Now the prosecutor, in turn, echoes the words of the court.

What quickly transpires now before your eyes is what you expected. There is only one great unknown left, and that is what the defendant will say, now that his life is about to end.

The prosecutor is speaking before a transfixed audience, conducting the dismal ritual in which one man asks three other men, sitting, black-robed, high above him, to put to death yet another man, sitting next to them, because he is "a predatory, murderous, bloodthirsty beast," because "by his own actions he placed himself beyond the pale of human society," because he "took part in horrible acts that would efface the humanity of anyone who committed them."

What did this man, who has been summoned from there, do?

"The blood of millions is on his head. . . . He wanted them all killed. . . . He was distressed that a single Jew might be spared."

But here in the auditorium sit living people, dressed in dark, winter clothes. A heavy Jerusalem rain is falling outside.

There are no emissaries from there, no solitary survivors to catch even a glimpse of retribution.

I follow the prosecutor's voice to the end, leaving half of myself behind. Up in the balcony, I see the row of seats occupied by the representatives of the German Justice Ministry. Below, there is the press gallery. There, I spot Crossman, the man who, in April, called it "biblical vengeance" and shrank back. Later, he changed his mind.

A good speech? A bad speech? Notes, cigarettes, brandy. That's how it is. But Hausner pauses and reaches out for me.

The doubts he voices about the death penalty provide him with his greatest moments.

The prosecutor cites the words of poet Hayyim Nahman Bialik about avenging the death of a small child: "I knew there was no point in exacting even a tiny part of the retribution appropriate for what he had done." And all the rest of it. A whole world.

These things are well known. I am repeating them. The prosecutor is right: "Clearly, if this were his punishment for killing one person, it should be no less for causing murder on a mass scale. . . . There should be no pulling back from the maximum penalty prescribed by law just because it is impossible to exceed it."

In his wrestling with the angel of death, I sense his forefathers coming back to life in his veins, they who termed "ruinous" a

Sanhedrin that handed down a death sentence even once in seven years."[57] He is caught for a moment between Saul and Samuel, demanding the head of Agag.[58] The comparison is ridiculous. "The man before you is a mass murderer. I ask you to pronounce him deserving of the death penalty," the prosecutor says and sits down.

The presiding judge: "Dr. Servatius, if you please."

And Servatius stands up.

It is a desperate, moving attempt to snatch from the jaws of death—heaven forfend—the very angel of death, the man from IV-B4.

"The spirit of our times is opposed to capital punishment . . . There was nothing he could do . . . He acted to please others . . . He was part of the world around him at that time . . . He tried to protect himself, but his spirit flagged when he saw how those in power were acting . . . Political hypnosis . . . Certain groups were guilty. . . The times were guilty . . . What happened with the German people could happen with any people . . . The crime of a government . . . The defendant is not important to the world . . . By convicting him the court has already achieved its purpose . . . The punishment is appropriate for this-worldly revenge, but it has been said here that 'vengeance is mine, and recompense, says the Lord.'[59] This points us toward the realm of grace, where all the contradictions of this world are to be resolved."

There, Jacques Stern, of Drancy, will give the cookie he saved for his mother to little Martha in her Sabbath dress.

No death sentence, then, for the defendant, who now rises to say his last words.

A deathly silence, the silence of death, fills the auditorium.

What now? The verdict identifies him with the extermina-

57. Mishnah Makkot 1:10.—Trans.

58. The Amalekite king whom Saul captures but spares, angering the prophet Samuel; see 1 Samuel 15.—Trans.

59. Deuteronomy 32:35.

tion. He cannot now say anything that implies less. Whether or not he thinks he is guilty.

And he stands up and says what he has to say.

I shall stop here for now. I cannot absorb any more of this. I'll deal with it tomorrow. Anyone reading and rereading Servatius's words will understand why he said them in Jerusalem on December 13, 1961.

December 14, 1961

NO REPLY

"I SEE THAT my hope for justice has been disappointed," he begins.

Good, now it will be easier for me to listen. I was afraid he would begin differently.

I do not understand German, but if the translation—"I am coming to understand the demand that the crimes against the Jews be expiated"—is accurate, I think I am beginning to understand him.

"My hope for justice has been disappointed."

One quickly gets used to things being "normal," in the commonly accepted sense. He has been wronged.

"I cannot accept the conviction." He may still be debating with his innermost self, but not on legal grounds. "No."

Now an interesting question arises, if I may say so. Does he think he is innocent? I believe he does.

On the other hand, he is "coming to understand the demand that the crimes against the Jews be expiated." He says this as if he were, for the most part, just a bystander.

"I found the witnesses' testimony bloodcurdling, as I did those horrible sights I had to look at"—and he remembers to add—"under orders."

Professor Gilbert explains that such statements, uttered by a schizoid, have no meaning.

Now comes a sentence made up of the words "obedience," "submission," "duty," and "oath," with the word "service" worked in three times.

So it is hard for me to maneuver between "my oath of loyalty to the flag and the service" and "I did not want to kill people."

Only the damned Sassen document, of which file 17 alone was admitted, intervened: Who are you trying to fool now?

"I did not persecute Jews out of blood lust."

True, Section IV-B4 could not have been run on the basis of "blood lust."

"Such obedience was not easy." Look at poor Adolf, still hard at work, the light still burning in his windows, at two in the morning.

"Those in power" abused his obedience, and now he pins the blame on them.

Some of them were hanged a while back. You can find them in the *Nuremberg Diary*, "those in power," so much like him, word for word.

If only one could hate them without being contemptuous of them. Contempt makes them human, and that makes things very hard. It was people like them who persecuted the Jews.

The word "obedience" is used five more times before we get to the heart of the matter: "I should thus be permitted to ask that consideration be given to the fact that I was obedient and not the fact that I obeyed particular people.

"They were responsible for the victims. . . . Those given the orders were themselves victims. . . . I was such a victim."

My last attempt to figure him out falls apart in the face of this obtuseness, which is expressed with an eloquence the obtuse usually do not command, the above-average eloquence instilled by Central European schooling. Why doesn't he acknowledge his guilt? Why can't he do it?

"People say I could and should have refused to obey orders, but that is the wisdom of hindsight," he says, without realizing that his very appearance here is a matter of hindsight, and that on a previous occasion, in 1957, he chattered to Sassen for days on end in hindsight.

I personally expected him to behave more like Hans Frank,

who really broke down, at least for a few moments, and tried to get out of the circle of the damned before he died.

In Eichmann's view, Frank and Hoess were both guilty. One was a superior officer who "confessed his guilt," and the other "actually carried out mass murder."

"My situation was different," he declares. Had he been in Hoess's shoes, he would have "put a bullet through [his] head."

There is no explanation of why the "dispatching station" was less guilty than the "receiving station."

But the fact that this goes unexplained explains everything.

Then his frightening little speech turns to "ethics" and "values."

Disastrously for him, he is stranded in a no-man's-land between the terrible remorse of one who awakens from a dream and sees what he has done and his attempt to cling with all his might to the "steely-eyed world of the caesars."

"My superiors shifted the blame onto me . . . by mistake, . . . and this bothered and upset me."

"He's crazy," I hear someone say.

He isn't normal! No, he *is* normal! It is the supernormalcy of an *uebermensch*. He is really offended. "I do not have blood on my hands."

It's just as well we aren't sure he murdered the boy in the cherry orchard. That would put him in the category of those who acted out of blood lust. Now we have one last chance to understand the other type of killer.

The raw fact of the death that took place is becoming more and more abstract, expanding upward and outward until it takes on the dimensions of an entire civilization.

"I never took part in the executions."

There are a few lines in Eichmann's speech that stand out from the rest. With a certain effort one can get a handle on the Germanic sentence structure.

It is a sentence in the subjunctive mood, spoken in hurt tones. "On my own initiative, I would now like to ask the forgiveness of the Jewish people and to admit that I am ashamed to think of the wrong that was done to the Jews and what was inflicted upon them by those who inflicted it. But in light of the reasoning behind the verdict, that would, evidently, be construed as mere hypocrisy."

A subtle, ironic construction. Why bother . . . ? You have decided anyway. . . . They have insulted me.

Oh, the indignity.

This "but" is only one of his innumerable "buts" and "howevers," except that this time it is not being used to explain facts but to express sorrow: You have denied me the possibility of making this gesture.

It was just about the worst thing that could be done to a person. "In Buenos Aires, they jumped me, tied me up, took me off in a state of shock and jabbed injections into my arms."

And this happened "because some people who had been National Socialists during that period spread falsehoods about me." They made him a scapegoat, and, astonishingly, the world believed it.

He thanks his defense attorney perfunctorily, as if merely discharging an obligation, and says he is "ready to pay for the deeds of others, . . . to bear whatever fate has in store." He says he will appeal the verdict.

I dare say the question of how it all happened is at least partly answered by the defendant's speech.

It is partly answered by his speech and by the eloquent remarks of Servatius, whose restrained, concise manner, at times inspired, and whose faith in the power of the word come to him as a legacy of the culture of the West.

Is Eichmann still an enigma? Not necessarily. Not if we can assume that the great murderers are not always monsters, that he is not, as he claims, "the monster they make [him] out to be," and that our notions of monsters are, in any case, outdated.

Beyond this trial—with its books and ideas, its hundreds of thousands of words, its living protagonists, its enormous scope—

and beyond heaven and earth and hell and the precious minutiae of the everyday, there stretches a field where people are standing alongside a pit, and other people are shooting them at close range with machine guns.

There stands a boy whose head does not reach up to a plank taken from an old cross, and he has to go to the left.

For the salvation of our souls, let us go there now, to the place where we can confront the death of the Jews itself. Let us leave here in order to take hold of what is real, to meet actual people and see what was done to them.

Let us meet the Jews, who for ages had not taken up the sword or shed blood but were singled out to be the first to die and whose death was the loneliest of all. Let us go to meet those wretched and noble people, in a place where the line is clearly drawn between murderer and victim, in a place where things can be called by their true names.

DECEMBER 15, 1961

THE SENTENCE

He enters the glass booth at 8:58 a.m.

The auditorium is packed to the rafters.

There are reinforced contingents of police in dark wool uniforms.

Now it is nine o'clock. The bailiff is at his post. There is a heavy silence in the crowd. No one ventures to speak above the faintest whisper.

Those who are sitting on the right side of the hall can see his face. The others, only his profile. Even on this last occasion he does not turn to face the public even for a moment.

It is 9:05. The dais is empty. Silently, we wonder. The silence is becoming palpable. Latecomers, hurrying in, encounter it and make their way on tiptoe.

It is the silence of a time bomb. The silence, too, of what has turned out to be a civilized crowd, putting things into perspective, rethinking the whole affair.

It is 9:15. Nothing has happened.

It seems to me this is the longest silence I have ever experienced in a crowd.

It seems to me I can hear my own heartbeat.

I gaze at him, trying one last time to decipher the face of a man who has been convicted of murdering an entire people.

I do not succeed. His face appears unchanged. Yet it is different. It is more than pale.

"All rise!" The bailiff's terrible cry rings out. The three judges suddenly emerge and pause briefly before taking their seats, as if bowing to the stony-faced audience.

It is 9:18.

"I call the 121st session of this trial to order," the presiding judge says. "The court will now pass sentence. The defendant will rise."

Adolf Eichmann gets up and stands to attention, facing the judges.

The presiding judge: "Now, having reached the end of the lengthy deliberations of this trial, we must pronounce sentence on the defendant."

He explains that the sentence about to be pronounced is not mandatory under Israeli law, but "we have proceeded on the assumption that it is left to our discretion."

In this courtroom, which has been defiled repeatedly by terms like "higher authority," "required" and "orders," these words—"reached," "proceeded," "discretion"—carry a great deal of weight.

These men are taking full responsibility for their decision.

The presiding judge speaks clearly and forcefully but with great restraint and no histrionics. Now and then his voice seems to catch in his throat, and he trembles before going on.

The defendant stands motionless, listening with his entire body to the voice of the man sentencing him to death.

The judge gives a brief summary of the court's reasoning. Much of this trial will one day be forgotten, but these words will remain as a distillation of the tens of thousands that have been uttered here.

"The purpose of the crimes against the Jewish people of which the defendant has been found guilty was to wipe an entire people off the face of the earth, and in this respect they differ from crimes committed against individuals.

"But in determining punishment we must consider, perhaps first and foremost, the harm done to individual victims"—it always comes back to one person—"and the untold suffering"—here the judge's voice seems to crack—"that they and their families endured and continue to endure to this very day.

"Every train carrying a thousand people that the defendant dispatched to Auschwitz or any of the other extermination sites was tantamount to direct participation by the defendant in a thousand premeditated murders. . . .

"This court condemns Adolf Eichmann to death. That is the sentence of the court."

The defendant listens without flinching. Only his throat is perspiring heavily.

He has never been so close to the many people whose deaths brought him here.

"All rise!" the bailiff shouts, for the last time. The judges leave by the right-hand exit.

He remains standing there for a while, as if waiting for something. Then he takes off his earphones and, surrounded by his guards, disappears through the narrow doorway on the left.

It is 9:29.

"This court condemns Adolf Eichmann to death."

Without specifying how he is to be executed and without adding, as the British do, "May God have mercy on his soul."

But the words "to death" strike dread into the hearts of the crowd, which has risen silently to its feet. Anyone's death is a dreadful thing, even that of "death's great dispatcher." But this dread is unique.

There are those who hurry off to cable and phone and spread the news. Most of the crowd moves more slowly toward the doors. Gradually, they regain their voices.

Thus did the trial end.

We have seen the last of a man whom we never believed we would see again, in later life, when he was no longer the smiling Sturmbannfuehrer in the peaked cap of the S.S., the *referent* of the Final Solution.

Thus did the trial end.

Long after those events, far away across land and sea from where they took place, his pursuers, the Children of Israel, caught up with him and dragged him back to their capital, where they tried him before the living and the dead, before the entire world.

He was given every opportunity to defend himself, and he made the most of it.

He spoke and spoke. He made pronouncements and was photographed. The world took far more notice of him than it had of his victims.

Now he is to be taken back to the domain that gave him his nickname. The life he stole by evading punishment has come to an end with the sentence pronounced on him in Jerusalem on the 5th of Tevet, 5722, according to the Jewish calendar, the 15th of December 1961, according to the Christian.

It is not for us to say more.

December 16, 1961

"HUMAN RIGHTS"

Appeal of conviction in criminal case 40/61 of the Jerusalem District Court of 12.12.61 and sentence in said case of 15.12.61, handed down by Hon. Moshe Landau, Hon. Binyamin Halevi, and Hon. Yehuda Raveh.

In the Supreme Court, sitting as the Criminal Court of Appeals:
Criminal appeal 336/61, before:
Hon. Yitzhak Olshan, presiding judge
Hon. Shimon Agranat, deputy presiding judge
Hon. Moshe Silberg, judge
Hon. Yoel Sussman, judge
Hon. Alfred Vitkon, judge

Session 1
Appellant: Adolf Eichmann
v.
Respondent: the Attorney General

THERE ARE FIVE judges on the dais.

The prosecution and defense teams are unchanged, except that Servatius has a new secretary.

In the glass booth, Eichmann. In the auditorium, the same audience.

Has Dr. Servatius brought any new arguments with which to appeal the conviction or the sentence?

Several hours later, it is clear that the answer is no.

The large crowd sits quietly, not expecting anything new. It seems we will have to endure one more, unavoidable, stage in the trial. The defendant-appellant cannot be denied the right to exhaust all the legal remedies available to him.

What a strong will to live "death's great dispatcher" has.

"The primary argument in this appeal," the defense counsel begins, "is the question of the [lower] court's competence to try the accused. This court, in the exercise of its authority, will have to make that determination." And he explains, "The district court responded in the affirmative to the question of its competence, basing itself on precedent. . . . But since the factual situation here is entirely different, the laws it cited cannot serve to draw an analogy."

The rest is not new: "In all the cases cited, the offender was brought before a court that was competent to try him at the time of the offense. He was brought before the same court whose jurisdiction he had fled. The present defendant, Mr. Eichmann, did not flee the jurisdiction of an Israeli court."

Further along he argues that the Israeli judiciary cannot "make the citizen of another state a fugitive from justice retroactively."

This brings him to the "open and well-known collaboration between the abductors and the government," which he offers as further proof of the court's incompetence.

"I again request that the witnesses Shim'oni and Tohar be questioned."

In this context, he adds that from a legal point of view the incident involving Israel and Argentina "is not closed."

This part of his presentation is heard in silence.

But the atmosphere in the courtroom changes when he says, "Today, progressive international law imposes obligations on the individual and subjects him to prosecution. By the same token, the right of an individual to complain of violations of international law should also be admitted."

In this case, the individual is Eichmann.

And Eichmann nods his head in agreement, as an "individual" who has been deprived of his "right to freedom and security" in an "extralegal manner."

And again, "[such individuals] cannot be declared by another state, retroactively, as subject to punishment. A state cannot be granted authority to enact retroactive legislation except with regard to its own citizens."

We come back to his earlier point: "The State of Israel did not even exist at the time the acts in question were committed."

And it is not by chance that the counsel for the defense now adds, "Similarly, it is only fitting that the doubts felt and expressed by part of Jewry concerning Israel's competence to exact punishment retroactively be taken into account."

What can you do? He is right. It is very hard for "part of Jewry" to make its peace with this.

The next point is one the defense counsel is very angry about. "The district court asserted its competence on the basis of the fact that there was no international tribunal to try [this case]. . . . But there is no need for such a tribunal, for a German judicial system exists, and the case can be taken to it."

The defense counsel hints threateningly that the defendant "may have to resort to paragraph 25 of the convention" and appeal, "as an individual, to the commission set up by the United Nations."

He then turns to the question of the responsibility of the individual for actions of the state, which, even if it is seen as a "gang of criminals," are still "acts of state" insofar as "his allegiance to the state" is concerned.

We have heard it all before.

Now he stirs up an old grievance that has been covered over with many layers of predictable arguments: "In the present case, we are dealing with judgments about historical events that affected the judges very deeply, not only as Jews but also, apparently, as surviving relatives of those who were persecuted."

He means the judges sitting on this court of appeals as well.

From this point on, he will turn from the procedural aspects of the appeal to the more substantive ones, to the "heart of the matter." And here I will stop.

The defense counsel is right: Winkelmann, Veesenmayer, von Thadden, Six, Becher, and the others were liars and cowards. When Servatius "sticks it" to them, Eichmann can smile a furtive smile of impotent revenge exacted from those who were fortunate enough not to have to face the gallows, as he does.

But we owe Servatius a debt of gratitude, at least for part of what he says: "The district court, in its verdict, declared that it was not important whether the defendant carried out the executions himself or issued orders that resulted in people being put to death. . . . Hence, those who had a hand in formulating the laws should be regarded as equally guilty. Depriving the Jews of their rights, their rights as citizens . . . all this was based on such laws."

He then throws a bombshell: "The man who was then the Director-General of the Reich Interior Ministry, Dr. Hans Globke, must have known that the Nuremberg Laws and the Reich Citizenship Law obligated the defendant and that he could not avoid [carrying out] those laws. . . . That was the point of departure of the persecutions." Raising his voice, he reads, "Let us not forget the flywheel [set in motion by] the ministries."

That is true. "I would like to hear the expert testimony of Hans Globke in this matter," Servatius says. "Those who drew up this legislation have not been brought to justice."

Auschwitz did begin at Nuremberg.

MARCH 23, 1962

THE BOOK AND THE APPEAL

"The court is well aware of worldwide opposition to the death penalty. Jean-Jacques Rousseau discussed it in his *Social Contract*, in the chapter dealing with the right to life and death. He says, 'There is no one so wicked that he cannot, to some extent, be brought back to virtue. No one has the right to take his life, not even for the sake of deterrence, if he can be kept alive without risk."

After a moment's pause, Servatius says, "The defendant does not pose any danger. He could even be helpful in preventing danger."

Eichmann looks up at the five judges as if trying to discern something in their faces. They do not perspire. There is no sign. There is silence in the auditorium.

I learn from the defense counsel that Eichmann has written a book, in which he set forth what he "felt and thought." "I believe," Servatius says, "that what the defendant has written shows honest repentance, an effort to bring even the unrepentant to repent."

It is a last-ditch effort to save him. For a moment, I am touched. There is some opposition to capital punishment in all of us. Every person sentenced to death arouses some pity and sadness.

What can you do? People commit crimes so weighty that they cannot bear the punishment. There is something indecent about his appeal for mercy. I am choking on it. This battle for Eichmann's life, waged according to due process of law, is more and more disturbing. If he did, in fact, write a book in which he said what he is supposed to have said, why is he fighting so hard for his life? Isn't there something about this that casts a strange light on his book?

What does this clinging to life mean? What is the significance of it?

If he did, in fact, write a book, why has the learned counsel for the defense dragged us back repeatedly to his foolish denials? Why does he want to hear what Dr. Wetzel of the Ministry for Eastern Affairs said about the gas vans? What importance do his relations with Winkelmann have now? Who cares about these things? What difference do they make?

Allow me to cite part of an interesting exchange that now ensues between the judges and the defense counsel.

Presiding judge: "I asked the question because the defendant's involvement in matters other than transportation is reflected in a variety of documents that he signed, and not just in Hungary."

Servatius: "It always had to do with disruptions that in the end affected the transports."

Presiding judge: "Does this also apply to his intervention, his letters to the Foreign Ministry, regarding Romania, where he conveys secret information that a thousand children are emigrating to the Land of Israel and tries to prevent it by all possible means? Did this, too, grow out of a transportation problem?"

Servatius: "No, but that was the content of the instructions given to him by the highest political echelon."

Presiding judge: "But what did that have to do with him?"

Servatius: "He was not authorized or obliged to intervene in such matters."

Yes, in the last part of his speech, before he quotes Montesquieu on the nobility of tyranny and Rousseau on the sanctity of life, the defense counsel is still trying to sell the Supreme Court his "transportation officer" idea, even after the district court has torn the "minor official" fiction to shreds.

In this exchange Servatius finally yields, drawing pitying smiles and nods from the audience. But it evokes the same nausea you feel when there is talk of the "penitent," "matters of transport," and "disruptions that affected the transports."

Presiding judge: "Mr. Hausner, would you begin now?"

Attorney general: "Yes, your honor."

The prosecutor begins with the presumed disqualification of the judges for belonging to the "injured nation." "They are disqualified on psychological grounds from trying crimes against their own people, and when it comes to crimes against other peoples, they are disqualified because it is none of their affair! . . . If there is a judge anywhere who claims to be objective and neutral about the crime of genocide and the strangling of infants, it is he who should be disqualified.

"The judges of Israel were not neutral about the crime, but they treated the defendant justly and fairly."

He goes on to castigate the defense bitterly for insisting that a German court was the proper venue for the trial. "He does not disqualify judges for belonging to the people of the murderers!" Invoking law and precedent, he insists that "it is precisely the victimized country that has jurisdiction." Poland, he reminds us, tried Hoess, Czechoslovakia Wisliceny, and Holland Sauter.

He then takes up the second argument, against retroactive jurisdiction. Speaking boldly and brilliantly, with many citations and references, he says, "It is not true that only an international tribunal is competent to try war criminals. The countries overrun by Hitler enacted their own laws for the prosecution of war criminals. . . . All of them"—he lists a number of examples—"did this as a result of the war or immediately after it, and all the laws were retroactive. They did not wait for an international tribunal to be set up, nor did they defer to German courts."

Now he gets to the main point, the combination of retroactivity and extraterritoriality. Judge Silberg interjects: "In other words, this can serve as proof that even when the two are combined, when a law is both retroactive and extraterritorial, it can still be valid?"

"Yes," the prosecutor replies.

The whole meaning of the Jerusalem trial is summed up in this set of circumstances.

"They tell us the appellant was merely a victim of evil laws. . . . But such laws are not real laws, just as illegal orders are not real orders." Now he raises his voice. "When I asked Dr. Servatius what law provided the basis for genocide, he said he had never seen such a law."

And then we hear him say, "The attempt, here in Jerusalem, to undermine the principle of individual responsibility, which is the common heritage of the entire civilized world, will not succeed."

Is Eichmann's "individual responsibility" any less important than the "sanctity of [his] life"?

MARCH 25, 1962

MAKING IT SHORT

There are many foreigners in the courtroom, as well as Israelis who come and go. Among them I see a number of men and women, our own people, who remain throughout. They came for the trial proper, and they are here again for the appeal.

Among them is Yitzhak Tabenkin,[60] sporting a white beard. He sits here for hours on end, his head propped up on his hand, listening and reflecting. From time to time he writes something in his notebook. He has not been absent once since the first day.

He thinks about what is being said, trying to derive some guidance from it as to what he should do, what he should believe. I sometimes think that what he is pondering so intently is the question of how and by what to live.

Another person who is always sitting here is the wife of Knesset Member Yohanan Bader.[61]

Sometimes Vera Weizmann[62] comes with one friend or another. They always sit in the front row and listen to the English translation.

The last few days I have seen Inspector Micky Goldman again. Now attached to Section 06, he was the boy who survived eighty lashes at the hands of the S.S. to be present on this miraculous

60. One of the leaders of the Israeli labor movement and the kibbutz movement.—Trans.

61. 1901–94. Journalist and member, from 1948–77, of the Knesset, representing the right-wing Herut Party and later its successor, the Likud Party.—Trans.

62. Widow of Israel's first president.—Trans.

occasion. Writer Leib Rochman, author of *By Your Blood Shall You Live*, sits here day in, day out. And Hayim Barlas, of the Jewish Agency.

There are many others in the audience whose faces are familiar to me, although I don't know their names.

But everything is different now. It is only occasionally that we once again get glimmerings of things as they really are.

It has been a long, tiring session, and the journalists are asking themselves what to write. Perhaps you, too, dear reader, have lost interest. The whole thing has been over for some time.

Only Eichmann shows no fatigue. "I shall appeal to the United Nations."

The prosecutor has answered every possible question.

And Eichmann alone remains, in the end, an unsolved riddle. Perhaps because things are simpler than we think.

MARCH 27, 1962

THE LAST ROUND

It is the scorched battlefield of the mind that is the subject of the last round. The courtroom is half empty.

What the prosecutor is saying now sounds like an echo of other things he has said, things shouted within these four walls, in this room that stands outside of time.

Dr. Wetzel and the "gas business," Sievers asking Eichmann for skeletons for his Patrimony Institute at the University of Strasbourg, the Gerstein report.

And we are back to Budapest, to the forced march in the snow, and we learn from one of the documents (Exhibit T/1113, page 126) that Hoess, who happened to be in Budapest with Juettner and Krumey, saw "bodies strewn along the sides of the roads and was shocked at the sight."

Hoess gave Eichmann a shock in return. As we recall, "[he] was shocked at the sight" of Auschwitz.

Hausner proves that Eichmann was responsible for the march as well.

What else?

A young Swedish diplomat named Raoul Wallenberg, "one of the righteous gentiles," tried to save as many condemned Jews as possible by giving them diplomatic protection; he provided them with foreign passports. Eichmann was so enraged that he threatened to kill him. "I'll shoot that Wallenberg, that lapdog of the Jews." (T/1243).

Alert and offended, Eichmann hastily scribbles a note of instruction to his attorney.

But Wallenberg was a Swede. You couldn't shoot Swedish diplomats just like that. The threat created a diplomatic incident.

After the Wallenberg affair, we learn all over again about gas from tank exhausts, gas from submarine-motor exhausts, cyanide gas, Zyklon-B.

What now? "Life for goods." Eichmann tells Sassen that "a million Jews should have been let go in exchange for those ten thousand trucks. . . . It would have proven that not all the Jews were used to stoke the ovens."

A few seconds' pause.

"I would like to draw the attention of the court to the comprehensiveness and cumulative weight of the evidence we have submitted," the prosecutor says.

During the "twilight of the gods," the Germans used the flames of the crematoria to destroy most of the memoranda, correspondence, and reports.

When you consider that the mountain of documents the prosecution has piled on the desk of the judges here in Jerusalem represents only a small part of the detailed German records, you can imagine what the destroyed Gestapo archive must have contained.

The final hour is approaching. "Instead of quoting Rousseau and Montesquieu," the prosecutor says, "I shall quote Adolf Eichmann's own words at session 96: 'I have already said there is no point in remorse, that that is something for little children. Remorse doesn't accomplish anything one way or another. It cannot bring back the dead.' Now we have been told there is a manuscript they would like to submit. . . ." The presiding judge interjects: "Mr. Hausner, you needn't deal with that."

Eichmann's book. "His struggle with the problem of guilt," as the counsel for the defense calls it.

And the prosecutor goes on. "He stayed at his post, as executor of the Final Solution, throughout the war." And he did what he did, "not only on orders but willingly, with open eyes, deliberately and 'joyfully,' to use his own words."

Eichmann is very pale, his face frozen by an unseen spasm.

"That is the true Eichmann, not the one who has wound up his journey of concealment, camouflage, and trickery here in Jerusalem."

As if anticipating a flicker of disbelief, he says loudly, "He was not always this way, the way he looks sitting before you. There was a time when his reach extended all across Europe, when his henchmen ran to and fro with orders to kill." For a moment, these words evoke for us the young Eichmann in his uniform and boots, with his revolver, his dagger, his cognac, his women, his black Mercedes and telephone. "It is in this light, honored judges, that I ask you to regard him and to sentence him."

The prosecutor's voice grows quiet. "This evil man plunged the Jews of Europe into a night of blood and terror." And like someone you can only hear off in the distance, he continues, "For the habitations of Israel that have fallen silent, for the diaspora communities that were destroyed, for the million children, the glory of our nation and its hope for the future"—here a tourist couple behind me, who had not made it to the trial proper, began weeping—"no man can exact adequate punishment.

"Whoever takes Eichmann's path of hate and murder . . . deserves to end up in ignominy and to be punished with death. . . . The penalty prescribed by law for the crimes Adolf Eichmann committed will be utterly meaningless if it is not applied in his case."

Eichmann stands at the boundary between sin and punishment. He does not move.

Why did he appeal?

We get the answer the following day, when Servatius rises to say his last words in reply to the prosecutor.

It is Thursday morning, March 29, 1962. The auditorium is filled to overflowing.

The counsel for the defense knows he cannot save his client.

And so, on his behalf, he addresses history, which will condemn him to what the prosecutor has called "a murderer's eternal disgrace." He makes one last attempt to clear him, to give him back his good name, before he is forced to part with it forever.

He tries, too, to do his client's behest and drag the murderer's comrades—his superiors, those he says used him as a scapegoat—down with him into the grave, into the shame and the fear. It is the final loneliness of one condemned to death taking vengeance against those who are to remain alive, happy and free.

One example: "Who gave the orders for the deportation from France? This has been proven overwhelmingly by the documents. The argument that the defendant should not have carried out this deportation is aimed at the wrong person. It should have been directed against the military governor, General Karl Heinrich von Stuelpnagel. . . . Yes, the ones who should be accused are Ambassador Abetz and his advisor Zeitschel, who asked Hitler for instructions in this matter. It should be Himmler, his chief of staff Oberg, and, finally, Dr. Knochen, head of the Security Police and the S.D."

And on and on, in great detail.

Eventually the defense counsel says, "The defendant directed the transports to the concentration camps and death camps, . . . but the fact that he was informed of the arrival of a transport does not mean that it was on his orders alone that the executions in the camps were carried out."

Not on his orders alone. It is the last line of defense.

We are coming to the end. He mentions the book of self-examination. The presiding judge interrupts him. "You may not speak about this. We have already ruled it out."

The defense counsel takes the place of the book. "The attorney general has highlighted the defendant's failure to show any sign of remorse, making it seem as if he had declared remorse to be pointless. By contrast, we must consider what he said when he was first interrogated here in Israel. He declared at that time that he deserved the death penalty, that he had no right to ask for mercy, . . . but to make the atonement more meaningful he was prepared to hang himself in public, as a warning to young people. . . . It is in this spirit that we must interpret what he said. . . . For there to be remorse there must be a feeling of guilt. The defendant has always denied being legally culpable. But he has acknowledged his moral culpability quite clearly."

Here we have the two points of Servatius's final ploy. No, he is not legally culpable. Yet he bears the burden of *their* crimes. "It is a sense of responsibility for the actions of others as well, those with whom we share collective involvement."

Eichmann the martyr.

To the very end, he has not confessed. Had he wanted to do so, he could have found some insignificant way of establishing his "legal" guilt. But no. His attorney continues his speech: "He was thrown as an individual into events of state. It was not his will that was decisive . . . He had sworn loyalty, . . . obedience."

The last chance has come and gone. The defense counsel has fulfilled his duty.

It is 10:55.

The presiding judge calls a recess, then we resume.

"It has been decided to reject the appellant's request to submit additional evidence, including documents, during the appeal phase," he announces. "There will now be a delay to consider the appeal. The parties will be given prior notice of the date when a ruling is to be handed down."

It is 11:35.

Signed but not sealed.

March 30, 1962

Afterword to the First Edition

These notes that became a book were published in the newspaper *Lamerhav* on the dates indicated. There is nothing in this book that was not written at that time, nothing that was added later on.

The book is not meant as a faithful record of the trial. There was valuable testimony that is not included, as well as incidents and dramatic moments. It is a case of man against the sea. What I have written is but a reflection of a reflection.

The book is a kind of diary, in which I allowed myself to append a journalist's notes to what I saw and heard.

The exact transcript, quoting everything that was said in the name of those who said it, will always remain the sole document worthy of being considered a record of the trial.

This book is merely a desperate attempt to capture something that cannot adequately be described.

Like everyone else present, I felt close, at this trial, to the line separating sanity from madness, but in my case it was for the first time. I felt I was beginning to comprehend the incomprehensible, however wide the gulf separating me from those who were "there" for even a single day.

Now it is all becoming more and more remote. It all seems as strange as it did the very first day.

The riveting enigma, the revulsion, the bewilderment—all end where they began. The desperate refusal to accept what happened is followed by resignation—but then returns. Yet if going back to this subject can teach us anything or contribute in any way to our salvation, we must go back to it, both to commemorate the dead and to come to grips with a disaster that will always threaten those who are weak and forsaken.

This is the feeling one has tracing the path of the destruction, seeing how things that seemed solid, certain, and secure proved to be mere illusions.

Every attempt to run away is futile: "Where can I flee from before Your presence?"[63]

Every attempt to come to terms with this subject can be painfully, shamefully presumptuous. Fortunate are the few who are able to approach these things in some other way.

After this trial, which was held in Jerusalem, I could at least begin to open certain books that, up to then, I had not dared touch. I say these things beyond fear or shame.

Sometimes the events are seen as a kind of mythology: a war between men and monsters, with God looking on.

If only one could believe that. As we know, it all took place *within* the human family.

That makes things simpler. Murderers, on their day of execution, deny us any feeling of pride. They have left the battlefield. The punishment catches up with them when they no longer deserve it. They profane it with their inability to withstand it.

Instead of a battle with the hordes of hell, we have the speeches of their defense attorneys, who ask us to judge them as human beings with weaknesses, with wives who are praying for them.

As they approach death, they become, as it were, different people. Their fight to stay alive takes them from the "steely-eyed world of the caesars" to the world of petty murderers, begging without letup for mercy. It is only with great difficulty that we can look upon these people, facing punishment, as the same ones who stood behind the crimes.

Still reeling from a terrible slap across the cheek, we are obliged to listen to "explanations" for the murder of the innocent, to hear the code words of death, to learn its specialized vocabulary.

The world will come back to this story and stop short in front of it. Humanity will retain the memory of the gas chambers. Without ever subduing it.

The 1940s will be seen as a watershed between eras.

Will the Jews be able to carry on with their dual existence? Can they ever forget that they are scattered among peoples who did

63. Psalm 139:7.—Trans.

not stand in the way of their annihilation, among countless individuals who lent a hand to the extermination or stood by, watching?

The death of the weak, denied escape or rescue, is not shameful, but there is dishonor in failing to exercise the right to live differently.

We must remember that what appears to belong to the realm of the unbelievable may belong, in fact, to the realm of the possible.

There remains, at last, the beautiful hope that untruth will not persist forever, that people will go on struggling for their right to respect and dignity, and that they will continue to believe in the rainbow that follows the flood.

Jerusalem
Nisan, 5722
April 1962

Afterword to the English Edition

Forty years have passed. On April 11, 1961, the trial of Ober-sturmbannfuehrer Adolf Eichmann opened in Jerusalem's Beit Ha'am auditorium. Eichmann, sitting at Reich Security headquarters, had headed Gestapo Section IV-B4, which dealt with the dispatch of millions of Jews from all over Europe to the "reception centers" of Maidanek, Treblinka, Auschwitz, Chelmno, Sobibor, and other extermination sites.

The news that Eichmann had been abducted to Israel by Mosad agents created a sensation throughout the world. Poet Nathan Alterman wrote: "The trial of Eichmann by a Jewish court in Israel will fill an eerie void that has been hidden somewhere in the soul of the Jewish people, in the history of its lives and deaths, ever since it went into exile."

I was present at the trial from beginning to end as a journalist. Many of those who took part in it—witnesses, investigators, judges, and journalists from Israel and around the world—are no longer with us. Thousands of Holocaust survivors have since passed on along with them. Biography yields to history. The Eichmann Trial itself, which once caused such a storm, has now been consigned to the archives, to tape recordings, photographs, and documentary films.

One generation follows another. The Eichmann Trial, too, belongs to the receding past and is now somewhat veiled. Those who lived through it remember it as a one-time event, pregnant with significance for the history of the young Jewish state. But the trial does not belong only to that generation or to those who experienced those dark years in the flesh. Among younger Israelis, there are those who see the destruction of European Jewry, the German industry of death, as an episode that impinges on them as well. They feel compelled to ask, again and again, What really happened? Why did it happen? It is to them, forty years later, that this new edition of my book is addressed.

More than once, the persistent question of whether the passage of time works in the murderers' favor has come back with cruel force. Is the evil bound to be forgotten? Or will the memory of this crime, unprecedented in human history, live on in generations to come, allowing them no rest? Even forty years later, it is hard to answer this question. We want to assume that culture means perpetual recollection and self-examination. But we cannot know how future generations will shape this memory or what they will do with it.

The Eichmann Trial took place in Jerusalem fifteen years after the Nuremberg Trials. It was concerned largely with the "Final Solution to the Jewish Question." It focused on a man whose work was the dispatch of the Jews to their deaths and who was involved in all the modes of killing to which those unfortunate people were subjected. But the trial did not concern itself with him alone. It is fair to assume that if other war criminals had been caught, they, too, would have been brought to trial in Jerusalem, under the Law for the Prosecution of Nazis and their Collaborators. But only Obersturmbannfuehrer Adolf Eichmann was captured and brought here, and it was his historic trial that, over the course of many months, dealt with three key questions: For what cause and to what end was an entire people, in Europe, in the heart of the twentieth century, sentenced to death? How was the annihilation carried out? What responsibility did individuals like Eichmann bear in the German industry of death?

It was a historic trial from the outset. Many documents dealing directly or indirectly with the mass murder were brought to light. One hundred and eleven witnesses who had survived their murdered communities testified before the court. Along with them appeared historians, jurists, experts, and scholars from all over the world who had devoted their lives, their talents, and their experience to the study of this dark chapter of history.

Israel, which was enjoying a period of respite between wars, lived this trial day and night. Many who had kept silent about what they had seen were prompted to speak out, while many native Israelis were exposed for the first time to the full scope and horror of the Final Solution. It was an open university, in which fundamentals of our national memory were being taught.

In the ensuing years, in the Soviet Union and Eastern Europe, archives and other sources of information that had been closed to Holocaust scholars have been opened. We know more today. But none of the additional evidence has contradicted in the slightest what was already known at the time of the Eichmann Trial; rather, it has only reinforced what was known and confirmed beyond any shadow of a doubt what the trial exposed as unquestionable historical truth.

Nevertheless, with the passage of time, I have come to realize that even the Eichmann Trial could not prevent the growth of the irrational phenomenon of Holocaust denial. Whereas the Nazis deprived the Jews of their lives, the deniers, it is said, continue to deprive them of their deaths. Not even this trial could counteract the words or deeds of this international movement, which enjoys broad financial support and makes consistent, sophisticated use of all media to spread its message. In trying to deny or minimize what was done, to reduce it to just another of World War II's tribulations, the movement takes full advantage of the human inability to grasp this enormous crime.

In 1974 I obtained a letter written by French university lecturer Robert Faurisson to Dr. Arye Kubovi, who was then head of the Institute for the Documentation of the Holocaust in Jerusalem. Faurisson, one of the world's leading Holocaust deniers, asks Kubovi to provide him, as a scholarly courtesy, with convincing proof of the existence of gas chambers in Poland during the war. Faurisson points out that all his research up to that point had shown that "this story is nothing more than a mythical fiction and not a historical truth."

I published the letter in the Tel Aviv daily *Yediot Aharonot*. The morning it appeared, I received a phone call at home from an Eliyahu Rosenberg, a survivor of Treblinka, who had served there as a Sonderkommando, one of those unfortunate Jews who were forced by the Nazis to work in the gas chambers and crematoria. His testimony at the trial (which appears in the chapter, "A Forest and a Small Railway Station") had been among the most terrible presented there. "How," he shouted over the phone, "can this Frenchman say there were no gas chambers? I was there! I was there!" I tried to calm him down, to tell him he had suffered enough in his life and did not need to take this calumny to heart. But the man was not to be placated. He asked me to get him Faurisson's address, saying, "I will go to Paris right now at my own expense and tell him. I was there!" Eliyahu continued to give testimony at war trials in Europe; he devoted his life to bearing witness. Eliyahu, a Jewish survivor of Treblinka—one of the few left.

The destruction of European Jewry should not be seen as overshadowing the terrible disasters and hair-raising crimes suffered by other peoples and groups in recent times, but it is unique in its character and scope. The Final Solution was the act of a state against an entire people, in the mid-twentieth century, in the heart of Europe. "Only an entire people can destroy an entire people," said Tzivia Lubetkin, one of the heroes of the Warsaw ghetto, in the course of the trial. A whole people was sacrificed "on the altar of race, the most voracious of all idols," in the words of the French writer François Mauriac, in his foreword to Elie Wiesel's first book, *Night*.

I was not in Europe at the time of the extermination. As a member of the Palmah, I went to Hungary, Czechoslovakia, and Austria after the Holocaust. There I encountered my hitherto unknown brother, the survivor. The encounter changed my life. I lived for about a year among these people, and slowly I came to grasp what had happened. Many of those Jews kept their stories to themselves. Some felt that their brethren who had remained outside the circle of destruction would be deaf to what they had to say. Yet it was not only our deafness, as it were, that set limits to what was said, but also the muteness of the survivors. The Eichmann Trial made it possible for many of them to tell their whole story, to unfurl part of the scroll of their personal torment.

Today, with the passage of time, it is clear that the trial caused a major upheaval, bringing with it many significant changes in the attitude of Israelis to the Holocaust and in their assessment of themselves. This reassessment is still going on. In the outside world, too, research is continually being published, bringing to light new aspects of the Holocaust story and calling the indifferent bystanders harshly to account. We know more today. We are convinced today that more Jews could have been saved from annihilation had the Allies behaved differently, had the Vatican said a few words on behalf of the Jewish people that was being slaughtered. The passage of time has not healed the wounds but reopened them.

Even forty years after the trial in Jerusalem, the Holocaust continues to be felt in Israeli life. It persists in the hearts of those who experienced it in the flesh and, as an ongoing legacy, in the hearts of their children and grandchildren. It persists in the scholarly literature as well as in fiction, poetry, drama, and film, both fictional and documentary, as well as in the innumerable memoirs and diaries that have been published since then. Young people born since the Holocaust and the Eichmann Trial devote themselves to the subject. Whole episodes that had been repressed have been reexamined and become the focus of stormy, painful debate. A new generation, having taken up the subject once again, is asking hard questions and seeking true answers.

In a program called the March of the Living, as well as tours coinciding with Holocaust Memorial Day and other days, Israeli youngsters visit the extermination camps in Poland. Besides affording an encounter with the places where masses of Jews lived and died, this is, for many, an initiation that aims to shape their very identity. To judge from their own words, they come back feeling more Jewish and more Israeli. They undergo the powerful experience of discovering their own roots, of questioning why things happened as they did, of pondering causes. But I have often asked myself whether this quest for Israeli identity has to depend on an encounter with the ovens. The Return to Zion began generations before the Holocaust, and the Jewish right to sovereignty in the Land of Israel does not derive from that ash heap; if it did, I would be reminded of the words of Rabbi Ula in the Midrash: "Let [the Messiah] come, but let me not [be here to] see him."

Journalists, writers, and academicians, too, hark back to those times. The tone becomes more critical, and the judgment changes. There is a growing tendency to blame the Jewish community in the Land of Israel for not contributing more to the rescue efforts, even though those who were sent from here to do such work report over and over again that little could be done. The issue arises repeatedly, each time as if it had never been raised before, as if a messenger bearing the evil tidings had only just arrived, his head covered with ashes.

In the wake of the trial, we here in Israel have seen a fascinating and growing tendency to reexamine the past. At one time we spoke here of "Holocaust and heroism," as if the two were distinct.

With the passage of time, Israelis have come to reject this distinction and embraced the thing as it was, in its wholeness.

This book was first published in 1962. I recount in it my daily impressions at the trial. After writing it, I was a different person. I asked myself, Now what? What to do next? I felt I had entered a prison from which there was no escape. After a break of ten years I went back to the trial and the testimony of the witnesses. We used excerpts from the tape recording of the Eichmann Trial, found in the state archive, in making the documentary film *The 81st Blow*. The film was made at the behest of Antek (Yitzhak Zuckerman), who had been among the commanders of the Jewish Fighting Organization in the Warsaw ghetto and among the founders of the Yitzhak Katznelson Museum of the Legacy of the Holocaust and the Revolt, at Kibbutz Lohamei Hageta'ot. I undertook this project together with my friends Jacquot Ehrlich and David Bergman. Two years later, in 1974, the film was given its first showing.

There is no narration in this film. The voices of the witnesses at the Jerusalem trial are heard over black-and-white newsreel and documentary footage of the rise of Nazism, the boycott, the persecution and humiliation, and, finally, the destruction, in all its manifestations. The film's name refers to the experience of a Jewish teenager Michael Goldman, who had received eighty lashes at the hands of the Nazi officer Schwamberger and miraculously survived. Arriving in the Land of Israel in 1945, he recounted the story of the lashing. His listeners found it hard to believe and assumed he was making it up. "And this was the eighty-first blow," Antek says. "Every one of us suffers it." The incredible! And this "incredible" continues to haunt us all. It haunts leaders and intellectuals, statesmen and historians, military analysts, poets, and writers. All have been victims of the incredible. They, too, stood watching as the barbarism of the Panzer divisions on the march passed them by and left them behind, representatives of an entire culture that was surprised to death. But it was the victims who suffered the most, who were deceived and misled right up to the very end. Our film, like the Eichmann Trial in Jerusalem, also deals with the problem of the incredible.

After *The Eighty-First Blow* we made two more films: *Flames in the Ashes*, which tells the story of Jewish resistance to the Nazis in occupied Europe, and *The Last Sea*, which deals with the flight of the surviving Jews from the mass graveyard that Europe had become and the illegal immigration to the Land of Israel for those who chose to come here, in defiance of the blockade imposed by the British navy. We labored for twelve years making these films.

In 1981 I visited Poland for the first time, accompanied by my wife and two fellow writers, Ben-Tzion Tomer and Gavriel Moked, both of them natives of Poland and survivors of the Holocaust. We spent some three weeks together there, visiting the desolate cities and towns and the death camps. On the way to Maidanek, in the ruins of the Jewish ghetto of Lublin, we saw a monument inscribed, in Polish and Yiddish, "In each handful of ash I seek my brethren." We reached the camp at Maidanek. It was a gray day, with pouring rain and all the flowers of Poland in bloom. And I remembered the lines: "In spite of yourself, you imbibe their alien fragrance, / The delight of spring in your heart—and you cannot help enjoying it."[64] We went from place to place until we reached a mound of ash under an enormous concrete dome, on which was inscribed in Polish: "Let our calamity be a warning to you." I turned and walked away. I stood next to elongated pits filled with time and ashes. "I stood dumbfounded, speechless, and my heart bled," in the words of Israeli poet Amir Gilboa. Had there been a special kind of weeping for such places, I would have wept it. My shoulders shook, and I became choked up. It was as if I had grasped the certainty of this catastrophe, its reality, among these barracks-turned-museum. We went on to other cities in the kingdom of death.

Poet Uri Tzvi Greenberg wrote about this in his book *Rehovot hanahar*: "And no trace of them remains on the face of the continent that has swallowed them up beyond recognition, / Like the sea that swallows what it swallows, leaving no trace on the surface of the water." In Krakow one of Poland's greatest writers told us, "The souls of these tortured Jews will hover over Poland forever."

Jerusalem
Tishrei, 5764
October 23, 2003

64. From Hayyim Nahman Bialik's Hebrew epic poem "In the City of Slaughter."—Trans.

Index

Index of Names

Index of Subjects